Cambridge studies in medieval life and thought

Edited by WALTER ULLMANN, LITT.D., F.B.A.
Professor of Medieval History in the
University of Cambridge

Third series, vol. 17

MORTMAIN LEGISLATION AND THE
ENGLISH CHURCH
1279-1500

CAMBRIDGE STUDIES IN
MEDIEVAL LIFE AND THOUGHT

THIRD SERIES

MORTMAIN LEGISLATION AND THE ENGLISH CHURCH 1279–1500

SANDRA RABAN

Fellow of Trinity Hall, Cambridge

CAMBRIDGE UNIVERSITY PRESS

CAMBRIDGE

LONDON   NEW YORK   NEW ROCHELLE

MELBOURNE   SYDNEY

Published by the Press Syndicate of the University of Cambridge
The Pitt Building, Trumpington Street, Cambridge CB2 1RP
32 East 57th Street, New York, NY 10022, USA
296 Beaconsfield Parade, Middle Park, Melbourne 3206, Australia

First published 1982

Printed in Great Britain by
Western Printing Services, Bristol

Library of Congress catalogue card number: 81–21685

British Library Cataloguing in Publication Data

Raban, Sandra
Mortmain legislation and the English church
1279–1500. – (Cambridge studies in medieval life
and thought. 3rd series; V.17)
1. England. Statute of Mortmain, 1279
2. Mortmain   3. England – Church history –
Medieval period, 1066–1485
I. Title
344.2064′362   HJ5529

ISBN 0 521 24233 9

For my parents

CONTENTS

GRAPHS AND TABLES

PREFACE

This book has been gestated for nearly a decade. Its origins lie in a study of the estates of the fenland abbeys of Thorney and Crowland. The effect of mortmain legislation on their endowments at a controversial period in the medieval economy proved more compelling than any other aspect of their chequered history of acquisition. Surprisingly, despite some invaluable pioneering works, it appeared that no one had written exhaustively upon the social significance of mortmain controls, although their operation had often been observed *en passant*. My first step towards a remedy for this omission was published in *Past and Present* in 1974. This preliminary article, 'Mortmain in Medieval England', served to show that the workings of mortmain law over a long period of time were both more complex and less predictable than had hitherto been assumed and that a full assessment would be of value to both political and economic historians.

The first chapter of the book deals with the enactment of the 1279 legislation and the circumstances which brought it into being. Such a survey must preface any investigation of the law in action, but since it is the aspect of mortmain legislation which has already received more attention than most, some of it very recent, my prime purpose here has been to coordinate the fruits of these researches and restrict my own contributions to the few remaining gaps. Succeeding chapters trace the evolution of practice with regard to licensing requirements and the way in which church and crown reacted to each other's activities, the one attempting to minimise the effects of the legislation and the other to ensure an acceptable standard of observance. Some of this territory has been charted before, but it has never been examined comprehensively enabling one to see the processes at work over a long time span and fully to appreciate the extent of change lying behind laws and methods of enforcement which apparently altered little over the centuries. In many ways, the heart of the book lies in its later chapters, where mortmain legislation is evaluated in the context of ecclesiastical endowment as a whole. Apart from the fact that this is the most neglected aspect of the subject, there are broader reasons for the prominence I have accorded it. It is increasingly recognised that evidence from the governed should rank as highly in the eyes of historians as that from the governors; to look at one without the other is to see one half of the picture only. It is therefore the special task of this study to present mortmain legislation from the point of view of the church. The moment is also ripe for combining the insights of economic, religious and administrative history and it is in this spirit that the volume as a whole is conceived.

Working for such a long time, I have accumulated many debts of friendship and help. First and foremost, I must thank Dr Marjorie Chibnall for her example of immaculate scholarship and for her unfailing advice and support from the time I set foot in Cambridge as an undergraduate. As my interests came to focus on mortmain tenure, I also gained immeasurably from the wisdom and guidance of fellow devotees. It gives me special pleasure to have done much of the research for this book while a Research Fellow at Lucy Cavendish College, Cambridge, where Dr K. L. Wood-Legh is Pro-President. It will be evident from both text and footnotes how much I owe to her. I deeply appreciated the generosity of Dr Tony Standen in offering me free use of his Ph.D. thesis on 'The Administration of the Statute of Mortmain'. Even though he is no longer engaged in academic work, I have felt reluctant to impose upon his kindness in undue measure. Consequently, I have included his findings where they have proved too important to omit, as was the case with his evidence for the introduction of new licensing procedures in 1299, but where we have covered much the same ground or have worked along similar lines but with different source material, I have been content to rely on my own researches. Dr Paul Brand is also due a large measure of thanks for succouring me in early years at the Public Record Office and for reading the first three chapters of the book with an Oxonian eye. He has done his best to invest a social and economic historian with instincts proper to the constitutionalist. The faults that remain are mine. Among the many others whom I would like to thank, I would single out Mrs Dorothy Owen for long years of encouragement and help. Dr Edmund King, Miss Barbara Harvey, Mrs Una Rees and Dr Mark Buck have all contributed ideas and references to material that I would not otherwise have discovered. Most of this book was written while I was lecturing at Homerton College, Cambridge, and a Fellow and Director of Studies in History at Trinity Hall. The stimulus and goodwill of colleagues and students alike have played their part in its final appearance. Financial support from the Calouste Gulbenkian Foundation at a critical early stage is also acknowledged with thanks. Like all historians, I would have found my task impossible but for the assistance of librarians and archivists. The staff of the Cambridge University Library have borne the heaviest burden with unfailing cooperativeness and good humour. I also recall with gratitude the services of the staff of the Students' Room at the British Library and at the Lincolnshire Archives Office and the Northamptonshire Record Office. Mrs Elaine Butt and Mrs Anne Ford have contributed at various stages to the emergent typescript and graphs with an enviable expertise. Most prefaces end with thanks to a long-suffering spouse, and this is no exception. Without the intrepid criticism of my husband, the following pages would be harder to read and without his support they might never have been finished.

SANDRA RABAN

Trinity Hall, 14 November 1980

ABBREVIATIONS

Am.H.R.	*American Historical Review*
Beds. Historical Rec. Soc.	Bedfordshire Historical Record Society
B.L.	British Library
Cal. Close	*Calendar of Close Rolls*
Cal. Fine	*Calendar of Fine Rolls*
Cal. Inq. Misc.	*Calendar of Inquisitions Miscellaneous*
Cal. Inq. Post Mortem	*Calendar of Inquisitions Post Mortem*
Cal. Pat.	*Calendar of Patent Rolls*
Camden Soc.	Camden Society
Cott.	Cotton Collection, British Library
C.U.L.	University Library, Cambridge
D.N.B.	*Dictionary of National Biography*
Ec.H.R.	*Economic History Review*
E.D.C.	Ely, dean and chapter
E.H.R.	*English Historical Review*
Jour. of Brit. Studies	*Journal of British Studies*
Lincoln Rec. Soc.	Lincoln Record Society
Lincs. Archives Off.	Lincolnshire Archives Office
L.Q.R.	*Law Quarterly Review*
Northants. Rec. Off.	Northamptonshire Record Office
Northants. Rec. Soc.	Northamptonshire Record Society
Oxf., Bodl.	Bodleian Library, Oxford
P.R.O.	Public Record Office
Proc. Brit. Acad.	*Proceedings of the British Academy*
Rec. Comm.	Record Commission
Rot. Hund.	*Rotuli Hundredorum*

Abbreviations

Rot. Parl.	*Rotuli Parliamentorum*
Selden Soc.	Selden Society
T.R.H.S.	*Transactions of the Royal Historical Society*
V.C.H.	*Victoria County History*
W.P.C.	Wrest Park Cartulary, Gentlemen's Society, Spalding

INTRODUCTION

On 14 November 1279 the Statute of Mortmain, sometimes known as *De viris religiosis*, was published and recorded in the form of a writ addressed to the justices of Common Pleas, ordering that in future:

no one at all, whether religious or anyone else, may presume to buy or sell any lands or tenements, or to receive them from anyone under the colour of gift or lease or any other title whatsoever, or to appropriate them to himself in any other way or by any device or subterfuge, so that they pass into mortmain in any way, under pain of their forfeiture.[1]

In these dramatic terms, the long tradition whereby church property grew through gift and purchase was called to an abrupt halt. So at least it appeared, but appearances were more than usually deceptive. That the law was not observed literally is common knowledge; the first of many licences permitting acquisitions, notwithstanding the statute, was granted in 1280.[2] The swift emergence of such licences does not necessarily imply that the statute was impotent, but it raises questions as to the precise nature of its intentions and effects. These need answering before the full complexity of mortmain regulation can be satisfactorily understood. Prominent among the queries are the extent to which contemporaries were determined in their wish to curb the temporal possessions of the church; whether, in the words of Plucknett, 'the flow of property to the church continued much as before, but from every gift the king took such toll as he could get';[3] whether indeed the strict implementation of restrictive

---

1 Translated from ed. F. M. Powicke, C. R. Cheney, *Councils and Synods*, 2 vols. (Oxford, 1964), vol. II, pt II, p. 865. For the full text of the statute, see below, pp. 193–4.
2 *Cal. Pat.*, 1272–81, p. 372.
3 T. F. T. Plucknett, *Legislation of Edward* I (Oxford, 1949, repr. 1962), pp. 99–100.

I

legislation was feasible given the administrative resources of the day. Finally, and most important of all, it is essential to know whether the church was engrossing land on a threatening scale by the mid-thirteenth century and whether mortmain legislation was of any significance in the ensuing pattern of accession.

So familiar is the existence of mortmain legislation in England that broad generalisations as to its workings have crept unchallenged into common use. Some are mutually exclusive; whereas one distinguished authority has considered the statute 'almost useless' as a curb on acquisition, another claimed that it exercised a profound impact on the land market.[4] Even where such judgements withstand closer examination, they miss the subtle evolution of practice over time. Economic and social conditions combined at different times to stimulate or depress ecclesiastical acquisition. It has been all too easy to forget this and to assume that the effects of the statute in the late thirteenth century were the same a century or more later, although the conditions within which it operated had changed. Moreover, the church itself was not a homogeneous body. The clergy comprised a diverse group of secular and religious differing widely in rôle and wealth. The statute of 1279 was directed indiscriminately at the richest black monk and the poorest mendicant or parish priest. Where needs and possessions varied so greatly, so inevitably did the impact of the new controls.

Although *De viris religiosis* is generally seen as a move to limit the wealth of the church, its target was not the church as such but the tenure by which its lands were held. Until the late fourteenth century, mortmain tenure was commonly understood as a synonym for ecclesiastical tenure, but technically it denoted tenure by any institution. In recognition of this, borough corporations and gilds were subject to the same restrictions as the church after 1391. A particular problem posed by mortmain tenure in the Middle Ages was that property once acquired by an institution was unlikely to return to the open market. This was emphasised in the case of the church by the stress laid by canon law on the

---

[4] K. L. Wood-Legh, *Studies in Church Life in England under Edward III* (Cambridge, 1934), p. 61; K. B. McFarlane, *The Nobility of Later Medieval England* (Oxford, 1973), p. 54.

preservation of ecclesiastical endowments as the property of God. Time and again church councils inveighed against the dissipation of ecclesiastical assets.[5] When the Canterbury province met at Oxford in 1222 to promulgate canons which became the basis of English church law for the rest of the Middle Ages, churchmen were enjoined not to alienate ecclesiastical property in any way to their relatives and friends or to anyone else.[6] Such reiteration suggests that observance was hard to secure, but a glance at any monastic cartulary will reveal the fierce tenacity with which the religious could fight to maintain their grasp on property they believed to be their own.

In any society, the persistent accumulation of landed wealth by certain groups without any prospect of its recirculation must eventually create social imbalance severe enough to provoke remedial measures. So far as the church was concerned this point was reached in much of Europe during the thirteenth century, but many factors might accelerate or retard its arrival. Examples can be adduced from more remote times and places. Tenth-century Byzantium, confronted by similar problems, had also attempted a legislative solution. In 964, the novel of the emperor Nicephorus Phocas, complaining that monasteries had 'turned all the attention of their souls to the care of acquiring daily thousands of measures of land, superb buildings, innumerable horses, oxen, camels and other cattle', forbade 'anyone to grant fields and estates of any kind to monasteries, houses for the poor and hostels, and to metropolitans and bishops, for such grants bring no benefit to them.'[7] At another chronological extreme, one of the first acts of the British when assuming the government of Malta in the early nineteenth century was to impose a mortmain law forcing the church to sell all bequests of land within a year.[8] It is also interesting to note that in modern India, a predominantly non-

[5] *Corpus Juris Canonici*, 2 vols. (Lipsiae, 1879–81), vol. II, bk III, tit. XIII, caps. I et seq.

[6] Powicke, Cheney, *Councils and Synods*, vol. II, pt I, pp. 100, 117, no. 36.

[7] P. Charanis, 'The Monastic Properties and the State in the Byzantine Empire', *Dumbarton Oaks Papers*, 4, 1948, pp. 56–7; R. Morris, 'The Powerful and the Poor in Tenth-Century Byzantium', *Past and Present*, 73, 1976, p. 13.

[8] J. Boissevain, *Saints and Fireworks* (London, 1965), p. 7.

Christian country, the constitution which provides for all religions to own and acquire property also provides that the state may make laws restricting this right in the public interest.[9] Thus, in enacting mortmain legislation in the thirteenth century, the English crown was taking steps which governments before and afterwards recognised as the most appropriate corrective to a widespread tenurial tendency.

Land accumulating in mortmain might not have provoked such opposition had its withdrawal from the market been the only disadvantage involved. This was not the case, however. The term 'dead hand' vividly described land dead to the community because, although individual members of an institution might die, the body itself lived on and tenure was vested in the corporation as a whole. Consequently, an overlord lost all the benefits which normally accrued on the death of a tenant. He could not exact a relief from his tenant's successor, nor exercise his right of escheat should the tenant die without heirs or be convicted as a felon. He also lost all chance of a wardship. This was doubly grievous since an under-age heir permitted the lord to enjoy the fruits of the child's estate and to arrange his or her marriage to his own personal advantage.[10] There can be no doubt that tenure in mortmain entailed a considerable material sacrifice on the part of the immediate lord. This was all the more marked by the early thirteenth century in that inflation had robbed him of a realistic return from regular obligations. Nor were these the only problems confronting the landlord when his tenant in mortmain was the church.

Ecclesiastical lands were commonly held in frankalmoin and, as one might infer from the word itself or its English equivalent of free alms, such tenure entailed spiritual duties rather than more mundane renders like cash or military service. Spiritual obligations might involve nothing more than an undefined duty to pray for the souls of the grantor and his family, although as time went on benefactors often demanded more specific services. These might

---

[9] J. Duncan, M. Derrett, 'The Reform of Hindu Religious Endowments', in ed. D. E. Smith, *South Asian Politics and Religion* (Princeton, 1966), p. 311.
[10] For a full account of feudal incidents in the context of alienation, see J. M. W. Bean, *The Decline of English Feudalism* (Manchester, 1968), p. 7 et seq.

range from simple obligations like the maintenance of lighted candles before certain altars to the establishment of perpetual chantries with elaborate provision for their upkeep.[11] Because tenure in frankalmoin so often went hand in hand with property held in mortmain, the problems arising from spiritual services came to play an important part in determining attitudes to mortmain itself.

In accepting gifts in frankalmoin, the church was catering for a deeply felt need in society, but at the same time it was raising intractable problems. The grantor of the property was able to calculate whether he and his successors could afford to forgo the secular income which it normally yielded and, if necessary, modify his plans. His overlord was in a more invidious position. True, the obligations to him were not in any way diminished in law unless he voluntarily surrendered them and they were also becoming less valuable in real terms with the passage of time. Nevertheless, he might find them withdrawn against his will if a tenant had miscalculated his ability to fulfil his outstanding obligations once part of the holding had ceased to render its usual returns. Overlords in this predicament might seek legal redress, but they ran the risk of provoking uncomfortable ecclesiastical sanctions. Thus, the situation could arise where the overlord's own tenant now lacked the resources to perform his services himself and the church, as subtenant, had no intention of doing so.

A further difficulty arose in boroughs, where holdings in frankalmoin tended to evade contributions to the *firma burgi* or other seignorial dues. Nor was there always an obligation to share in common undertakings such as defence or public works. Where a considerable proportion of the burgage tenements had fallen into ecclesiastical hands, the burden on the remaining burgesses might be disproportionately heavy. Bitterness about this is typified by the following extract from the laws of Dublin and Waterford *c.* 1300: 'For when religious houses enter upon property, they do nothing for the town, the heirs are reduced to

---

[11] Just over a third of the licences to alienate into mortmain granted to the nobility between 1307 and 1485 entailed a specific obligation on the part of the recipient. J. T. Rosenthal, *The Purchase of Paradise* (London, 1972), p. 141.

poverty, and the city is deprived of young men for its defence in time of war'.[12] A more specific objection to ecclesiastical tenure was cited by the citizens of London in 1312. They complained that the church controlled an estimated one-third of the rents in the city and that because it claimed exemption from murage, the burden of maintaining the walls fell unfairly on the remaining laymen.[13]

Grants to the church not only occasioned the material losses associated with mortmain and frankalmoin tenure; they also had important social and political concomitants. The conservatism of the church with regard to matters such as labour services from villein tenants is now well known and may have been appreciated at the time. Ramsey Abbey is but one example of a house which retained and even intensified them until a late date. Christchurch Cathedral Priory, Canterbury, continued to exact them on its Kentish estates long after they were generally commuted elsewhere. It is not just an accident of documentation which shows ecclesiastical estates as the prime target for peasant resentment of seignorial demands in the thirteenth and fourteenth centuries.[14] Another aspect of ecclesiastical tenure which certainly held great significance for contemporaries was the military danger of knightly families driven from the land. To some extent complaints about this can be dismissed as rhetoric, but their frequency commands some attention, as indeed does the prominence given to the issue in the statute itself. One of the reasons cited for its enactment was the fear that 'the services owed on such fees which were established originally for the defence of the realm are withdrawn unduly.'[15] Even where ecclesiastical purchasers left lay

---

[12] C. Gross, 'Mortmain in Medieval Boroughs', *Am.H.R.*, 12, 1907, pp. 733–4.

[13] H. M. Chew, 'Mortmain in Medieval London', *E.H.R.*, 60, 1945, p. 3.

[14] N. Neilson, *Economic Conditions on the Manors of Ramsey Abbey* (Philadelphia, 1899), pp. 26–7, 45 et seq.; R. A. L. Smith, *Canterbury Cathedral Priory* (Cambridge, 1943, repr. 1969), pp. 126–7; E. A. Kosminsky, 'Services and Money Rents in the Thirteenth Century', *Ec.H.R.*, 5, 1935, repr. in ed. E. M. Carus-Wilson, *Essays in Economic History*, 3 vols. (London, 1954–62), vol. II, p. 45 et seq.; R. H. Hilton, 'Peasant Movements in England before 1381', *Ec.H.R.*, 2nd ser., 2, 1949, repr. in *ibid.*, p. 78 et seq.

[15] Powicke, Cheney, *Councils and Synods*, vol. II, pt II, pp. 864–5: 'per quod servitia que ex huiusmodi feodis debentur et que ad defensionem regni ab initio provisa fuerunt indebite subtrahuntur'.

tenants in possession of the land, as must often have been the case, the potent forces of ecclesiastical lordship and the loyalties it might command should not be underestimated. The delineation of lay and spiritual spheres of influence was a perennial medieval issue and any substantial increase in the secular power of the church could only undermine the precarious *modus vivendi* which had been achieved.

The church might have been forgiven both its tenacity in retaining property and its eagerness to acquire more, notwithstanding the problems inherent in its tenure, had it not been so enormously wealthy. Just how wealthy is a question which has exercised numerous scholars with no very precise result. Calculations based on Domesday Book suggest that in 1086 the church held some twenty-six per cent of the land in England as tenant-in-chief of the king.[16] On the basis of the surviving 1279 Hundred Rolls, Kosminsky put forward a somewhat higher figure of one-third; an increase probably accounted for as much by the geographical distribution of the existing rolls as by continued acquisition, even allowing for the new foundations of the twelfth century.[17] At both periods far less land was actually held in demesne, because of extensive subinfeudation. No simple computation can account for the varied interests in land which the church came to hold, quite apart from its extra-territorial possessions.[18] If its aggregate wealth was something less than the figures based on holdings in chief would suggest, it was nevertheless sufficient to explain the frequent identification of the church with mortmain tenure and why initial curbs on alienation into mortmain were addressed to the church alone. Some anti-clerical sentiment doubtless contributed to the enactment of the 1279 statute, and it grew stronger with the passing years. Nevertheless to regard control over amortisation as a straightforward attack on the church is once more to oversimplify.

To raise further questions about mortmain legislation and its

[16] R. Lennard, *Rural England 1086–1135* (Oxford, 1959), p. 25.

[17] E. A. Kosminsky, *Studies in the Agrarian History of England in the Thirteenth Century* (Oxford, 1956), p. 109.

[18] A good account of their range is given in A. Savine, *English Monasteries on the Eve of the Dissolution* (Oxford Studies in Social and Legal History, 1, 1909), pp. 83–6.

workings is not to devalue earlier work of great distinction. Problems posed today would prove insoluble but for the existing foundation of knowledge. Indeed, they often arise because of it. Central to this heritage is the work of K. L. Wood-Legh, whose account of the law in action under Edward III is unsurpassed in its detail and lucidity.[19] Two further studies have been significant in placing the legislation in its social context: T. F. T. Plucknett's *Legislation of Edward I* and J. M. W. Bean's *The Decline of English Feudalism*.[20] A rich literature on more specialised aspects of the subject has also grown up.[21] Lawyers were the first to devote serious attention to mortmain legislation, tracing its evolution from medieval beginnings to their own day.[22] Since then it has steadily attracted some of the most notable medievalists working on English history, without, it must be admitted, ever provoking untoward controversy or excitement. Recently there has been a new flowering of mortmain scholarship. There is no evident explanation or focus for this apparently spontaneous revival of interest. It has embraced the circumstances surrounding the enactment of *De viris religiosis*, as well as the impact of the statute on different members of the church, and trends in ecclesiastical patronage.[23] Yet despite this industry, Plucknett's comment in

[19] *Studies in Church Life*, ch. 3.
[20] Bean, *Decline of English Feudalism*, p. 49 et seq.
[21] Gross, *Am.H.R.*, 1907, p. 733 et seq.; J. N. L. Myres, 'Notes on the History of Butley Priory, Suffolk', *Oxford Essays in Medieval History Presented to H. E. Salter* (Oxford, 1934), p. 190 et seq.; S. J. A. Evans, 'The Purchase and Mortification of Mepal by the Prior and Convent of Ely, 1361', *E.H.R.*, 51, 1936, p. 113 et seq.; Chew, *E.H.R.*, 1945, p. 1 et seq.; E. Miller, 'The State and Landed Interests in Thirteenth-Century France and England', *T.R.H.S.*, 5th ser., 2, 1952, pp. 123–6.
[22] E.g. W. F. Finlason, *An Essay on the History and Effects of the Laws of Mortmain* (London, 1853); T. Bourchier-Chilcott, *The Law of Mortmain* (London, 1905).
[23] P. A. Brand, 'The Control of Mortmain Alienation in England 1200–1300', in ed. J. H. Baker, *Legal Records and the Historian* (London, 1978), p. 29 et seq.; L. Desmond, 'The Statute *De Viris Religiosis* and the English Monks of the Cistercian Affiliation', *Cîteaux*, 25, 1974, p. 137 et seq.; E. D. Jones, 'The Crown, Three Benedictine Houses and the Statute of Mortmain, 1279–1348', *Jour. of Brit. Studies*, 14, 1975, p. 1 et seq.; Rosenthal, *Purchase of Paradise*. Other recent studies, not specifically devoted to mortmain, have incidentally added to our understanding, notably: K. L. Wood-Legh, *Perpetual Chantries in Britain* (Cambridge, 1965), p. 43 et seq.;

8

1949 that 'there has been little detailed study as yet upon the actual working of the statute' remains substantially true.[24] S. A. Standen went some way towards remedying this in his unpublished Ph.D. thesis, analysing particularly the development of procedure after 1279, but this is not generally available and further issues need to be explored.[25] In particular, there is no general survey of the response of the church to the legislation and to any impression it may have made on ecclesiastical acquisition, except for my own brief article.[26] The omission is all the more serious when understanding of the land market and the distribution of landed wealth is growing so fast in other directions and periods.[27] Professor Postan has suggested that the balance of landholding in the later thirteenth century was shifting in favour of larger landlords at the expense of older knightly families, a trend mitigated only by the purchases of career officials consolidating themselves in county society.[28] The transactions of churchmen are central to any exploration of this possibility, quite apart from their intrinsic interest. Thus it can be seen that mortmain studies as they stand at present are highly fragmented with some major points of current enquiry untouched. This study is designed to provide the synthesis and further investigation which are clearly needed.

A. Kreider, *English Chantries: The Road to Dissolution* (Harvard and London, 1979), p. 71 et seq.

[24] *Legislation of Edward I*, p. 100.

[25] 'The Administration of the Statute of Mortmain' (unpublished Ph.D. thesis, Washington University, 1973).

[26] S. Raban, 'Mortmain in Medieval England', *Past and Present*, 62, 1974, p. 3 et seq.

[27] For later periods, see H. J. Habakkuk, 'English Landownership, 1680–1740', *Ec.H.R.*, 10, 1939–40, p. 2 et seq.; *idem*, 'The Long-Term Rate of Interest and the Price of Land in the Seventeenth Century', *Ec.H.R.*, 2nd ser., 5, 1952, p. 26 et seq.; *idem*, 'The Market for Monastic Property, 1539–1603', *Ec.H.R.*, 2nd ser., 10, 1958, p. 362 et seq.; F. M. L. Thompson, *English Landed Society in the Nineteenth Century* (London, 1963); *idem*, 'The Social Distribution of Landed Property in England since the Sixteenth Century', *Ec.H.R.*, 2nd ser., 19, 1966, p. 505 et seq. and more specialised articles in recent numbers of *Ec.H.R.* For the medieval period, it is the peasant land market which has attracted most attention. See P. R. Hyams, 'Origins of a Peasant Land Market in England', *Ec.H.R.*, 2nd ser., 23, 1970, p. 18 et seq.

[28] M. M. Postan, *The Medieval Economy and Society* (London, 1972), pp. 161–3.

Information about alienations into mortmain comes from two main categories of material: the public records and those of the church itself. Central in importance to this study is the evidence drawn from the licences to alienate enrolled on the royal patent rolls, inquisitions *ad quod damnum*, escheators' accounts and entries on the close rolls. These together with associated records provide a profile of amortisation on a countrywide basis as well as much of the evidence for the evolution and efficacy of its regulation. Judicial proceedings, the year books and occasionally narrative sources also yield some useful supplementary information. Almost all these records, however, look at mortmain through the eyes of the crown and its agents. For the attitudes and response of the church one turns principally to its own records. The most rewarding of these are charters, usually in the form of cartulary copies. As a rule, monastic versions of licences have nothing to add to those recorded on the patent rolls, but copies of deeds belonging to transactions preceding the licence often cast a completely new light on what was taking place.[29] Other deeds, such as leases, can also illustrate the means by which the church sometimes by-passed the law altogether. In the privacy of their domestic records, churchmen were sometimes disarmingly frank about their motives and machinations. More than one plot is laid bare in an expansive rubric.

It is plain that the subject suffers from no shortage of source material. Indeed, a major difficulty has been to reduce the volume of evidence emanating from crown and church to manageable proportions. With this in mind, certain aspects of the study have assumed a pronounced regional bias. In order to minimise the disadvantages of this, the area comprising Lincolnshire and the old East Midland counties of Bedfordshire, Northamptonshire, Huntingdonshire and Cambridgeshire has been chosen with care. These counties offer a fair contrast of both geographical conditions and ecclesiastical foundations. In addition to a host of minor churchmen, both regular and secular, the institutions to be found there included two cathedral bodies, one secular and one monastic, several of the oldest and richest monasteries in the country and a

---

[29] Occasionally cartulary copies of licences can alert one to significant omissions in the calendaring. See below, p. 49.

high proportion of the priories belonging to the Gilbertine order. Since there is always an element of doubt about regional findings projected on to a wider scene, the general conclusions taken from the public records are designed to provide both a framework for and a check on local conclusions; while, in turn, local evidence should give substance to the outline drawn from government sources. To rely on either in isolation would be to miss an essential dimension in the understanding of mortmain tenure after 1279.

Chapter 1

THE STATUTE OF 1279 AND ITS
ANTECEDENTS

For many years historians have tried to find complete and satisfying explanations for the enactment of *De viris religiosis*, but without reaching incontrovertible conclusions. What is certain is that the motives were many and complicated. The statute did not burst upon late-thirteenth-century England without warning. It came as a climax to decades of anxiety expressed by vocal landlords. Yet although they were united in fearing the influence of the church and the erosion of their incomes as a result of its intrusion into their fees, they were a diverse group. Crown, magnates and lesser landlords each faced problems different in scale and nature and this divergence of interest is reflected both in the political skirmishing surrounding the mortmain issue and in the form which limitation took whenever action was achieved.

Lay agitation over the disadvantages of mortmain tenure becomes evident towards the end of the twelfth century. Emerging concepts of ownership at this time encouraged tenants to bestow their holdings as if they enjoyed full proprietorial rights, to the detriment of their overlords. As long as lords had retained genuine freedom to dispose of tenements, however hedged about by custom, it had been natural for alienees to seek their consent before making grants to the church. With weakening powers of lordship, this became less easy to enforce, although attempts were made.[1] Limiting clauses appear in conveyances. It was quite usual for private charters in the first half of the thirteenth century to contain a ban on grants to either church or Jews. An unusually detailed and restrictive example comes from Lincoln Cathedral

---

[1] Brand, 'Control of Mortmain Alienation in England', pp. 30–1; S. F. C. Milsom, *The Legal Framework of English Feudalism* (Cambridge, 1976), pp. 120–1.

archives. In 1243, Samson son of Nigel had to give an undertaking that he would not give, sell, pledge or lease his holding
for more than two years without a special licence from the dean.[2]
These devices were as popular with churchmen as with the laity.
Religious foundations were as vulnerable as any layman to the
loss of income consequent on the insinuation of other churchmen.
The dilemma was summed up in the charter granted by Burton
Abbey to the borough of Burton-on-Trent in 1273 conceding that
tenants 'may give sell assign and devise the said burgages with
all their appurtenances and with all their liberties to whomsoever
they will, except to all men of religion other than our house of
Burton.'[3] Restrictions concerning grants to the church appeared
early in borough charters, perhaps because of the greater weakness of seignorial control prevailing in urban centres. One of the
earlier examples is a Wells charter granted between 1174 and
1180. The holder of a burgage tenement there was free to mortgage, sell or give it 'according to the will of his own disposition,
except to religious houses'.[4] Provisions of this type had become
common by the mid-thirteenth century.[5] Salisbury's charter of
1227 substituted the licensing of alienations for complete
embargo:

it shall not be lawful for the citizens aforesaid to give or sell or mortgage their burgages and tenements which they have or shall have in
the said city to churches or to men of religion without the licence and
consent of the aforesaid bishop [of Salisbury] and his successors.[6]

There is some evidence that landlords received royal backing in
their efforts to control alienations into mortmain on their own
initiative. After 1247 the courts upheld landlords who prevented
ecclesiastical alienees from taking seisin, providing that the
holding was restored to its previous tenant. The crown was also

---

[2] Ed. C. W. Foster, K. Major, *Registrum Antiquissimum*, 10 vols. (Lincoln
Rec. Soc., 1931–73), vol. III, pp. 58–9, no. 696.
[3] Ed. A. Ballard, J. Tait, M. Weinbaum, *British Borough Charters*, 3 vols.
(Cambridge, 1913–43), vol. II, p. 87.
[4] *Ibid.*, vol. I, p. 65; Gross, *Am.H.R.*, 1907, pp. 736–7.
[5] Ballard, Tait, Weinbaum, *British Borough Charters*, vol. I, pp. 67–9; vol. II,
pp. 50–1, 87–9.
[6] *Ibid.*, vol. II, p. 88.

willing to prohibit entry into the fees of certain favoured individuals or bodies with some regularity after 1243. These prohibi-
tions too were enforceable at law.[7] Measures such as these were
clearly insufficient, however, since pressure for some sort of
legislative action to support landlords in their endeavours built up
steadily during the course of the thirteenth century.

The story of this growing determination has been told by
Plucknett, Bean, and most recently by Brand.[8] The first formal
protest was enacted in the 1217 reissue of Magna Carta which
contained two clauses relating to the subject. Clause 32 required
that no one should alienate so much land that the remainder was
unable to bear the burden of his services. Recent studies have
differed in their interpretation of this. Although apparently
directed as much at laymen as at ecclesiastics, it has been suggested that in practice the church was its target. Alternatively
and equally persuasively, it has been associated with a much wider
concern for the protection of inheritance.[9] Clause 36 forbade
collusive grants, whereby a church received land in mortmain
and then enfeoffed the grantor as its tenant.[10] This practice increased in attraction once the urge to make landed gifts to the
church had waned, since it enabled benefactors to keep up an
appearance of generosity without parting with much of real value.
All that was offered by this type of arrangement was the sacrifice
of an overlord's rights. The donor and his heirs continued to

[7] Brand, 'Control of Mortmain Alienation in England', pp. 33–4.
[8] *Legislation of Edward I*, p. 94 et seq.; *Decline of English Feudalism*, p. 49
et seq.; 'Control of Mortmain Alienation in England', p. 31 et seq. The
following account is heavily indebted to them and is intended as background to the working of the 1279 statute rather than a further contribution
to this aspect of mortmain studies.
[9] 'Nullus liber homo decetero det amplius alicui vel vendat de terra sua
quam ut de residuo terre sue possit sufficienter fieri domino feodi servicium
ei debitum quod pertinet ad feodum illud': J. C. Holt, *Magna Carta*
(Cambridge, 1965), p. 356. Also Milsom, *Legal Framework of English
Feudalism*, p. 119; E. Searle, 'Seigneurial Control of Women's Marriage:
The Antecedents and Function of Merchet in England', *Past and Present*,
82, 1979, p. 13.
[10] 'Non liceat alicui decetero dare terram suam alicui domui religiose, ita
quod eam resumat tenendam de eadem domo, nec liceat alicui domui
religiose terram alicujus sic accipere quod tradat illam ei a quo ipsam
recepit tenendam': Holt, *Magna Carta*, p. 356.

hold the land on the same terms as before, but because his gift had intruded the church into the tenurial hierarchy, it was the church and not his former lord who enjoyed the consequent incidents when he died.

The clauses inserted in the reissue of Magna Carta tackled only part of the problem. There is an otherwise unsupported suggestion in a writ of 1256 of the existence of legislation forbidding alienations into mortmain altogether unless made with the consent of the immediate lord.[11] Whether or not such a law existed, the desire for more effective protection of seignorial interests along these lines was expressed in Clause 10 of the Petition of the Barons in 1258.[12] A licensing procedure was duly incorporated in the Provisions of Westminster of the following year: 'Religious shall not be allowed to enter the fee of anyone without the permission of the chief lord, from whom that property is held.'[13] The subsequent history of this provision is mysterious. It was not included in reissues of the Provisions in 1263 and 1264, nor are there many signs that it was invoked while still in force.[14] The evidence as to whether, like other provisions, it was incorporated in the 1267 Statute of Marlborough is contradictory. The opening sentence of the 1279 Statute of Mortmain, which echoes the wording of the Provisions, implies that it may have been.[15] Certainly the abbot of Croxton was prosecuted in 1278 for neglecting to obtain his mesne lord's licence for the acquisition of two hundred acres of land and

---

[11] Brand, 'Control of Mortmain Alienation in England', pp. 33–4.

[12] 'Item petunt remedium quod religiosi non intrent in feodum comitum et baronum et aliorum sine uoluntate eorum, per quod amittunt imperpetuum custodias, maritagia, releuia et eschetas': ed. I. J. Sanders, *Documents of the Baronial Movement of Reform and Rebellion: 1258–67* (Oxford, 1973), pp. 80–1.

[13] 'Viris autem religiosis non liceat ingredi feodum alicuius sine licencia capitalis domini, de quo, scilicet, res ipsa immediate tenetur': *ibid.*, pp. 144–5. This clause does not feature in all the texts of the Provisions. The Burton Annals record a variant relating to purchases only. See below, p. 142.

[14] Brand, 'Control of Mortmain Alienation in England', pp. 34–5.

[15] 'Cum dudum provisum fuisset quod viri religiosi feoda aliquorum non ingrederentur sine licentia et voluntate capitalium dominorum de quibus feoda illa inmediate tenentur': Powicke, Cheney, *Councils and Synods*, vol. II, pt II, p. 864.

twenty acres of meadow in Bescaby (Lincs.) explicitly on the grounds that it contravened 'the provision of Merleberge that men of religion should not have power to enter the fee of another without the licence and will of the chief lord of that fee, to wit the lord of whom it is immediately held'.[16] Dr Brand has traced a number of cases which could imply support for its inclusion, but they also suggest that contemporaries were as unclear then about the statutory basis of licensing as their successors are today.[17] Thus, the position regarding control over alienation into mortmain on the eve of the 1279 statute was far from satisfactory even by the loose legislative standards of the day.

The greater the landlord the more likely he was to suffer from land alienated in mortmain by his tenants. The greatest lord of all was the king. It might be supposed therefore that he would have shared the concern of his landholding subjects and endorsed their attempts to regulate mortmain grants firmly. In practice, however, the crown had little direct interest in the problem since land held in chief was early subjected to special restrictions. In 1228, Henry III issued a writ giving comprehensive protection to crown lands. No one was to give or sell these to churchmen except by royal licence and inquests were to be held to determine the extent of the damage already done.[18] Dr Standen could find no trace of such enquiries and indeed questioned the whole efficacy of the writ, but there can be no doubt that some attempt was made to enforce it.[19] On several occasions, some admittedly

16 *Cal. Close*, 1272–9, pp. 500–1.
17 Brand, 'Control of Mortmain Alienation in England', pp. 35–6.
18 *Close Rolls*, 1227–31, p. 88. 'nullus, qui de nobis tenet in capite...aliquid de tenemento suo conferat vel vendat vel aliquo alio modo alienet alicui domui religiose vel aliquibus personis ecclesiasticis sine licentia nostra; firmiter etiam prohibeas quod nullus de nobis tenens in capite, sive miles, sive liber homo, sive alius, se transferat a terra quam de nobis tenet ad terram alicujus domus religiose vel persone ecclesiastice ad manendum super eam, per quod simus perdentes in serviciis, tallagiis, vel aliquibus aliis ad nos pertinentibus. Diligenter etiam inquiras per sacramentum proborum et legalium hominum comitatus tui qui de hominibus nostris de nobis tenentibus in capite in dominicis nostris, sicut predictum est, dederint vel vendiderint vel aliquo alio modo alienaverint aliquid de tenementis suis, et quibus viris religiosis vel ecclesiasticis personis ea alienata fuerint, et a quo tempore, et quantum singula illa tenementa valeant'.
19 Standen, 'Administration of the Statute of Mortmain', p. 23 et seq.

long after the event, the crown either confiscated land granted
without permission or, in one case, demanded its sale to a lay
tenant. In 1238, the monks of Coggeshall were compelled to
restore their purchases to lay hands, instead of receiving the
confirmation which they sought. The crown did not wish the
monks to make a loss and they were allowed to choose to whom
they would sell the holding, but the overriding concern was
patently the protection of military service owed to the king.[20]
There was a notable attack on alienations of this sort in the time
of Edward II. In 1314, the prior and convent of Elsham were
pardoned for acquiring property in Bonby (Humberside) in the
time of Henry III from John son of John de Mars, tenant-in-
chief.[21] Four years later the king restored another illegal alienation dating from the same period to the abbot and convent of
Bourne upon payment of a hundred-shilling fine.[22] The abbot
and convent of Kirkstead were particularly unlucky in 1324
when they were prosecuted for two illegal acquisitions which
appear to have preceded the royal ban, since they took place in
1222. Again one hundred shillings was the price of pardon.[23] The
prior of Montacute had the good fortune to be vindicated in his
acquisition of the same period, but the passage of a century was
no guarantee of immunity from royal retribution.[24]

Possibly the success of royal policy towards alienation in
mortmain influenced baronial thinking. The Provisions of Westminster suggest that overlords were looking for a licensing system
very similar to that of the king. On balance, however, it is more
likely that the barons had in mind the much more recent measure
of 1256 forbidding the alienation of land held in chief without
a licence to any recipient, lay or ecclesiastical.[25] Whatever the
motive behind their desire to institute control through licences,
the definitive mortmain legislation when it emerged in 1279,
was not conceived in this spirit. The statute *De viris religiosis* forbade the church to acquire any further lands or tenements

[20] *Close Rolls*, 1237–42, p. 34.
[21] *Cal. Pat.*, 1313–17, pp. 83–4.
[22] *Ibid.*, 1317–21, p. 193.
[23] *Ibid.*, 1321–4, p. 393; ed. W. Boyd, W. O. Massingberd, *Abstracts of Final
Concords* (London, 1896), pp. 162–3.
[24] *Cal. Close*, 1330–3, p. 514.   [25] *Close Rolls*, 1254–6, p. 429.

whatsoever. To all appearances, attempts to control ecclesiastical acquisitions had been abandoned in favour of total prohibition. No provision was made for acquisition under licence or in any other way.

The reasons for the enactment of this statute are as enigmatic as the form it took. The text itself draws attention to the military danger arising from ecclesiastical encroachment on knights' fees, and a much later royal grant of 1440 states explicitly that it was intended for the defence of the realm.[26] Such a suggestion is plausible if we are correct in thinking that knightly tenants were particularly vulnerable to ecclesiastical purchasers at this time, even if one might be sceptical about the extent of the military threat posed. The losses borne by overlords are also cited in the statute, and the provision that mesne lords might enter and recover illegally alienated holdings argues that amelioration of their position was intended. It is possible that this was merely designed as a method of enforcing the legislation, although there is nothing to suggest that the crown was either reluctant or unable to do this for itself. When it became clear that the statute was to be interpreted liberally, with grants to the church taking place under licence, the licence of the mesne lord was as essential as that of the king. This too suggests that the statute was intended to protect his interests. Chroniclers also illustrate the importance of mesne lords, although with hindsight they are often inaccurate about the wording of the statute. The Dunstable chronicler, who probably wrote within a few years of 1279, noted that 'in the same parliament of London, the king ordered that the religious might appropriate no further lands and tenements to themselves unless the rights and services of any mesne lords were safeguarded'.[27] His views were echoed a century later by the Meaux chronicler, who wrote that 'a statute was enacted against the religious forbidding them to acquire any more lands, possessions or rents without a licence from the king or the mesne lord from whom the property was directly held'.[28]

[26] *Cal. Pat.*, 1436–41, p. 480.
[27] Ed. H. R. Luard, *Annales Monastici*, 5 vols. (Rolls Series, London, 1864–9), vol. III, pp. xiv, 281–2.
[28] Ed. E. A. Bond, *Chronica Monasterii de Melsa*, 3 vols. (Rolls Series, London, 1866–8), vol. II, p. 178.

It was not only chroniclers who thought that the statute protected mesne lords. In 1323, Nicholas de St Mark could not endow a chantry at Thornhaugh (Cambs.) on Peterborough Abbey land 'without our [the abbey's] assent owing to the present impediment of the statute'.[29] Although mesne lord licences were not enrolled on the patent rolls and are consequently harder to trace, more than enough survive on a random basis to indicate their importance. In 1287, for example, four such licences were returned to the royal chancery in connection with the application of St John's Hospital, Northampton, for a royal licence.[30] Petitions in the 1290 parliament show these licences as a necessary part of the routine behind acquisition. The prior of Wareham was granted the royal licence he sought, having first produced his overlord's consent, but St Radegund's, Dover, found one of its proposed accessions rejected because the land was held of Dover Hospital and the prior's approval had not been given.[31] It is common to find notes on the dorse of inquisitions connected with the granting of royal licences either recording that the mesne lord's licence had been inspected, or postponing a decision about the issue of a licence until it was forthcoming. This is illustrated by two requests for licences dealt with in 1291. On inquisitions relating to the first, there is an endorsement showing that the mesne lords' consent to Thomas de Bray's grant of a messuage, land and rent in Silsoe (Beds.) to a chaplain in the church there had been examined. In the second case, endorsements show that action was postponed because the mesne lord licences which would approve Ralph Paynel's grant of land to a chaplain in St James's church, Barton, had not yet been produced.[32]

Two administrative memoranda, amongst others issued by the king in the 1292 parliament, have a bearing on this issue. One required royal officials to refrain from granting a licence until written evidence of the overlord's consent was brought forward and the second forbade a licence where the grantor was left with no other holding.[33] This was no innovation, since evidence shows

29 Ed. W. T. Mellows, *Henry of Pytchley's Book of Fees* (Northants. Rec. Soc., 2, 1927), pp. 24–5.
30 P.R.O., C143/11/9.   31 *Rot. Parl.*, vol. 1, p. 54, no. 103; p. 62, no. 204.
32 P.R.O., C143/15/10; C143/15/13.
33 *Rot. Parl.*, vol. 1, p. 83, no. 13.

that both restrictions were already in effect.[34] In preceding years, neither St Radegund's, Dover, nor the chaplain at Barton had been able to obtain licences without mesne lord consent. Bruern Abbey was also refused a licence in 1291 because the grantor would have been left without any means of sustaining his outstanding obligations.[35] The 1292 measures therefore indicate the crown's willingness to incorporate formally such safeguards into the regulations governing licence procedure. They may also betoken a continuing anxiety on the part of the baronage that its interests were inadequately protected. Nothing in the royal archives would bear this fear out, however. A high proportion of licences were refused for the benefit of the mesne lords alone. The absence of further baronial protest after the end of the thirteenth century implies some acceptance of this. Mesne lords had good reason to be satisfied with the arrangements which had been made. Even so, by invoking royal authority in support of their efforts to curb alienation, they had forfeited almost more than they had gained. The initial right to license alienation was theirs, but final control was vested in the crown. Royal power was now exercised in an entirely new field. What Henry III had established in connection with land held in chief had been extended to all holdings.[36]

Protection of military service and concern for baronial grievances are not the only possible explanations for the appearance of the 1279 statute. Tighter control over ecclesiastical acquisition was consonant with the general policies of Edward I. One suggestion views the statute as yet another piece of legislation arising out of the problems laid bare in the Hundred Roll enquiries.[37] Another argues that legislation was made desirable by the challenge of the Master of the Templars in a case heard in the Trinity Term 1279 during the Yorkshire Eyre. Questioning the statutory basis for the writ brought against him for entering lay fee without consent, he made a direct appeal to royal judgement.[38] The confusion shown by contemporaries over whether

[34] See below, pp. 40–1.
[35] P.R.O., C143/15/8.
[36] Bean, *Decline of English Feudalism*, pp. 65–6.
[37] Standen, 'Administration of the Statute of Mortmain', p. 49.
[38] Brand, 'Control of Mortmain Alienation in England', pp. 35–6, 40.

there was or was not a law about licensing, and the timing of the Templar protest, convincingly account for royal intervention.

The 1279 legislation was also in line with developments abroad. In France, where royal assumption of the initiative in limiting ecclesiastical accessions has also been identified with the growing power of the crown,[39] the definitive legislation was contained in the 1275 *constitutio ecclesiarum utilitati*. Like the Statute of Mortmain in England, this was the climax of a long series of unsatisfactory *ad hoc* measures. Since the twelfth century, private charters had had clauses analogous to those found in England precluding grants to clerks, monks, Hospitallers or Templars.[40] When arrangements of this type failed to suffice, the crown ordered that alienations against an overlord's will were to be restored to lay hands. In 1233-4, Louis IX issued a mandate in favour of Raymond count of Toulouse directing that all such gains inside his fee should be surrendered within a year and that all future alienations were to be subject to royal and comital approval.[41] France was a much larger and less centralised country than England, with a correspondingly more intricate social network. Not only was there a far wider range of local custom relating to mortmain, but also the tenurial ladder often had far more rungs than its English counterpart, which created problems when a system of mesne lord licensing became accepted. With each lord wanting to protect his own interests, a chaotic situation soon emerged whereby innumerable payments and licences were required before an acquisition might be legally secure. It was not uncommon to buy out the objections of four or five intermediate lords.[42] Unlike the English statute, the 1275 *constitutio* was designed by Philip III to assist the church. Royal officials were ordered not to harass ecclesiastics over gains made in the territory of magnates who had the right to control amortisation for themselves. Even more important, they were ordered to desist from

---

[39] This account is indebted to Miller, *T.R.H.S.*, 1952, p. 123 et seq.; A. Luchaire, *Manuel des Institutions Françaises* (Paris, 1892), p. 177.

[40] Luchaire, *Manuel des Institutions Françaises*, p. 176.

[41] Ed. M. A. Teulet, *Layettes du Trésor des Chartes*, 3 vols. (Paris, 1866), vol. II, p. 262, no. 2276.

[42] E. Chénon, *Histoire Générale du Droit Français Public et Privé*, 2 vols. (Paris, 1926-9), vol. I, p. 789.

intervention whenever the consent of three lords above the grantor had been secured. Where property had been alienated without permission either in royal demesne or in subtenancies, more than twenty-nine years before, a fine was fixed at two years' income. More recent acquisitions need not necessarily be surrendered, but were also subject to fines varying from one to three years' income depending upon the terms on which they were held. In an associated document, the crown finally limited the right to authorise amortisation to itself, the twelve peers of France and the five great counts.[43] The measures of the *constitutio* were retrospective and confined to royal officials and the royal demesne, but they established the idea of a scale of charges which could subsequently be revised and imposed order where it was badly needed.

Broadly similar forms of mortmain control were widespread in Europe at this period, but details varied and not all arrangements were reflected in English practice. There is no sign that the custom prevalent in certain French regions of allowing the church to hold land in the name of a layman was sanctioned. The advantage of this arrangement was that it enabled the overlord to reap the benefits he would normally enjoy when a layman died, but also permitted the church to continue its acquisitions.[44] The nearest equivalent in England was the unusual provision found in grants made by Edmund earl of Cornwall to Dorchester Abbey and Thremhall Priory reserving to himself, amongst other dues, payment of a relief on the death of the head of house.[45] A second continental practice found in many areas was the provision whereby the church was compelled to dispose of accessions within a given time. Bequests in particular were difficult to avoid, whatever the law said. In France such gains had to be relinquished within a year, and in Sicily within a year, a week and a day.[46]

---

[43] Ed. M. de Laurière et al., *Ordonnances des Roys de France de la Troisième Race*, 21 vols. (Paris, 1723–1849, repr. 1967), vol. i, p. 303 et seq.

[44] A. Esmein, *Cours Elémentaire d'Histoire du Droit Français*, 2nd edn (Paris, 1895), p. 277; Chénon, *Histoire Générale du Droit Français*, vol i, p. 788.

[45] Ed. L. M. Midgley, *Ministers' Accounts of the Earldom of Cornwall 1296–7*, 2 vols. (Camden Soc., 3rd ser., 66 and 68, 1942–5), vol. i, p. xv.

[46] A. Pertile, *Storia del Diritto Italiano*, 2nd edn, 6 vols. (Turin, 1892–1903), vol. iv, p. 392.

Agreements specifying similar periods were drawn up with individual religious orders in Douai.[47] In fourteenth-century Venice there were even restrictions on the length of leases to the church, at first ten years, but later two, after which the lease had to be sold and the proceeds devoted to pious uses. This legislation was copied at both Padua and Treviso.[48] Such an approach was not wholly untried in England, as is shown by Henry III's move in 1238 forcing the monks of Coggeshall to sell their illicit gains instead of allowing them to retain them after paying a fine. There are no signs, however, that a formal waiting period within which territorial accessions might be converted into a more acceptable form was ever operative. Some bequests, like the messuage in London which Roger of Evesham left to the abbey of Malmesbury, were regularised under licence.[49] Others were doubtless sold unofficially before they came to the notice of the authorities. Most common of all, once the licensing system was well established, must have been the type of arrangement made by Thomas Martyn in 1461 in his bequest to Ely Cathedral Priory. The priory was to receive property in Cambridge if a licence could be obtained, but if any difficulty transpired, the holdings were to be sold and the proceeds given instead.[50]

The Statute of Mortmain can thus be regarded as part of a widespread response by secular government to unrestrained acquisition by the church. Whether, as in France, there was a revenue element involved is more debatable. In the later Middle Ages fines were regularly charged on royal licences to alienate, but none feature on the patent rolls before April 1299, nor can a significant number be traced by any other means in these first two decades.

The few fines which were demonstrably charged on licences to alienate into mortmain before 1299 may either have been incurred for other reasons or relate to accessions made later than might otherwise appear. The most conspicuous example, and that most difficult to explain satisfactorily, concerns the twenty-

---

[47] G. Espinas, *Les Finances de la Commune de Douai* (Paris, 1902), pp. 353–4.
[48] Pertile, *Storia del Diritto Italiano*, vol. IV, p. 391.
[49] *Cal. Pat.*, 1281–92, p. 470.
[50] Oxf., Bodl., Ashmole 801, ff93v–4v.

pound fine demanded in 1290 for a licence permitting the abbey of Shap to acquire the advowson of Warcop (Cumbria). Payment was delayed and ultimately pardoned because the grantor died before the transfer could be effected. In the meantime, the sum figured on the pipe rolls as an unpaid debt. The abbey had begun negotiations by 1288 at the latest and met with small encouragement. An inquisition held in March of the following year pointed out that the alienation would not be in the king's interest because the advowson was held in chief. Its endorsement further notes that 'the king did not grant it because it was to his damage'. It is likely therefore that the fine compensated the king for agreeing to the alienation of property held in chief, notwithstanding the earlier decision. The fine was specifically associated with mortmain legislation in 1293 and 1300, occasions when the crown was considering its relaxation, but it may nevertheless be a more accurate reflection of the treatment of land held in chief than land passing into mortmain. Under the arrangements of 1256, a licence and possibly a fine would have been required for the alienation of the Warcop advowson even if the church had not been involved.[51]

Several inquisitions *ad quod damnum* held before 1299 are endorsed with a record of a fine. Such for example are those for Bayham, Forde and Newstead-by-Stamford, all held in 1293-4.[52] However, in almost every case, the licence for which the fine was paid proves to have been granted after a long interval, after 1299.[53] Another inquisition, of the regnal year 1284-5, concerning an accession to St Mary's, Winchester, is endorsed 'let it be done for God'.[54] This may imply that a fine had been excused, but could equally well refer to relief from the fee for sealing. There remain, however, one or two references to fines for which no satisfactory explanation comes to mind. Such is the case for the endorsement 'let it be done for fifteen shillings' on an inquisition

---

[51] *Cal. Pat.*, 1281–92, p. 388; P.R.O., E372/136, m7d and subsequent rolls; *Cal. Close*, 1288–96, pp. 289–90; 1296–1302, p. 367; P.R.O., C143/11/18.

[52] P.R.O., C143/21/13, 17, 29.

[53] In the case of the foregoing inquisitions, between 1299 and 1301. *Cal. Pat.*, 1292–1301, pp. 403, 494, 570.

[54] P.R.O., C143/9/32.

relating to a licence to grant a messuage and two bovates of land in Horncastle (Lincs.) to Kirkstead Abbey conceded in 1285.[55] There is also a problematical entry on the pipe roll for 1298–9 referring to a fine demanded of St John's Hospital, Northampton, for a licence to enter lay fee in the previous year, although it is just possible that it may represent a fine for illicit alienation to the hospital.[56] These exceptions apart, a systematic examination of the surviving sources reveals no evidence of fines for licences.

Prima facie it seems unlikely that the crown was prepared to allow licences to be issued without any payment other than administrative fees; we are conditioned to expect government to exact payment on the slightest pretext. Yet nothing suggests that this occurred in the first twenty years after the enactment of *De viris religiosis*. Moreover, there are indirect suggestions that 1299 was a year when changes in fining procedure took place.[57] Certainly the crown came in time to show a closer interest in the financial possibilities of mortmain controls, but although there were odd fines charged before 1299 for which no obvious explanation emerges, there seem slight grounds for regarding the 1279 statute as a deliberate attempt by Edward I to augment his income.

Foreign example and social and political pressures at home encouraged the king to take steps to curb the church's territorial expansion, but the strongly negative line of the statute can be attributed to neither. Instead, it can be explained perhaps in terms of Edward's hostile relationship with his archbishop. Pecham had been received as the new primate earlier in 1279 in an atmosphere of extreme cordiality.[58] This soon degenerated in the face of the prelate's struggle to maintain ecclesiastical jurisdiction and to eradicate the long-standing pluralism resulting from the crown's use of church offices to reward its officials. In particular, the archbishop's order to post up copies of Magna Carta was provocative if not unprecedented. The parliament of November 1279, which produced the Statute of Mortmain, had also witnessed the

[55] P.R.O., C143/9/6; *Cal. Pat.*, 1281–92, p. 176.
[56] P.R.O., E372/144, m4d; *Cal. Close*, 1296–1302, p. 267.
[57] See below, p. 55 et seq.
[58] D. L. Douie, *Archbishop Pecham* (Oxford, 1952), p. 51.

confrontation of king and archbishop which culminated in Pecham's public withdrawal of some of his more challenging acts.[59] In such an atmosphere, the savage terms of the statute fall into perspective, although it has been pointed out that the archbishop's retraction had occurred by 11 November at the latest, three days before the appearance of the statute.[60]

To look for such an explanation may in any case be unnecessarily subtle. There was already a strong tradition of negative regulations concerning mortmain, just as there were already precedents for the licences which succeeded the statute.[61] Even the provision for mesne lords to enter and recover illegally alienated holdings was not unprecedented.[62] Whether or not those who drew up the statute or the earlier charters ever envisaged their literal implementation is a moot point. Dr Standen would argue that a licensing system was an integral part of crown policy concealed by the form in which the statute has come down to us.[63] Certainly thirteenth-century attitudes to legislation differed so much from our own that it is difficult to know how much weight to attach to the form in which the statute stands. Contemporaries did not regard their texts as sacrosanct. Judges were frequently inaccurate in quoting them and exercised great freedom in their interpretation.[64] Even in the more sophisticated legal atmosphere of the present day, normative legislation is not unknown. According to a newspaper report, recent Swedish legislation forbidding parental violence provided no sanctions against offenders. In explanation, a spokesman for the Justice Department argued that 'the law is more a way for society to point out to parents that it doesn't agree with physical punishment or [*sic*]

---

[59] *Ibid.*, pp. 118–19.
[60] Brand, 'Control of Mortmain Alienation in England', p. 39.
[61] See above, pp. 12–15, 16.
[62] The 1268 charter of Bridgetown Pomeroy laid down that where lands and burgages were granted 'to any religious house or any religious men, it shall be lawful for me, my heirs or assigns to enter the aforesaid lands and the aforesaid burgages and expel the aforesaid burgesses' who proposed the alienation. Ballard, Tait, Weinbaum, *British Borough Charters*, vol II, pp. 88–9.
[63] Standen, 'Administration of the Statute of Mortmain', p. 55 et seq.
[64] T. F. T. Plucknett, *Statutes and Their Interpretation in the First Half of the Fourteenth Century* (Cambridge, 1922), chs. 3–5, 8.

children'.[65] The complete ban on ecclesiastical acquisition laid down so unequivocally in *De viris religiosis* can plausibly be regarded in the same light: more an expression of the deep concern felt by contemporary society about land held in mortmain than a serious attempt to prevent further accessions of any sort in the future. The appearance of licences permitting acquisition, notwithstanding the statute, so soon after its enactment must add weight to such an interpretation.

The Statute of Mortmain can thus be seen as fulfilling a variety of needs. In part it was a result of an unremitting campaign on the part of English magnates to protect their feudal rights effectively, a campaign which achieved its last expression in the memoranda of 1292. Quite apart from any political capital to be gained from increased control over alienation, the king himself also had an interest in curbing indiscriminate acquisitions by the church, notwithstanding the 1228 legislation. Any diminution in the wealth of his tenants-in-chief was reflected in the value of the feudal incidents falling to the crown. This interdependence of crown and magnates was summed up by one of Edward II's justices in asserting that the statute was 'to restrain the purchases of Holy Church because through their purchase disadvantage accrued to the chief lords because they lost wardships, marriages and other [profits] attached to seignory to the distress of the crown'.[66] The timing of the enactment and the precise form it took present problems, but the inadequacy of earlier legislation and frayed tempers at court may explain why the dislike of mortmain tenure which had simmered over so many decades suddenly manifested itself in such an acute form.

Yet, however intricate the circumstances giving rise to the 1279 statute, they should not blind one to the fact that the laity had made important gains at the expense of the church. The original aim of the crown and articulate landlords had been to control land passing into ecclesiastical hands. Even if the crown had gained more than its tenants did in the process, this aim was achieved. By the end of the thirteenth century, the church de-

---

[65] *Guardian*, 30 June 1979.
[66] Ed. M. D. Legge, Sir W. Holdsworth, *Year Books of Edward II*, vol. xx, 10 Ed. II, (Selden Soc., 52, 1934), p. 129.

pended upon lay consent at royal and overlord level before any acquisitions could be made. In the following centuries such permission often involved additional expenditure which might render the acquisition unattainable. Even though the church may not have sought worldly property on the same scale as formerly, such restrictions inevitably came as a harsh blow.

Chapter 2

THE WORKING OF THE STATUTE

On 14 November 1279 the justices of the bench and probably all shire officials were ordered to see that the Statute of Mortmain was read out and observed in England and Wales, although the position in Ireland was more ambiguous.[1] Thereafter, churchmen were theoretically powerless to extend their possessions, but in practice the situation was not so clear-cut. In the first place, it was by no means certain that the crown would not relent and repeal or amend the law, or at least allow certain exemptions. The church lobbied hard with this in view. Between April and July 1280, Hugh de Brisingham, a friar at Salisbury, tried to mobilise Robert Burnell, the royal chancellor, in the interest of the Franciscans. He wrote, unsuccessfully, asking Burnell to obtain a letter which would exempt the friars of the whole province from the statute.[2] In the November parliament of 1280, six proposals to modify the statute were put forward by the church as part of a series of *gravamina*. The most important of these *articuli cleri* asked that bishops, the secular clergy and mendicant orders should be exempt from the statute. There was some hope also that inadequately endowed religious houses might be made an exception

---

[1] *Cal. Pat.*, 1272–81, p. 335; Brand, 'Control of Mortmain Alienation in England', p. 36. A letter from the chancellor in Ireland in 1296 asserted that the statute had not yet been published there, but an Irish applicant had been granted a mortmain licence in 1290. The 1301 Eyre of Louth shows that it was strictly enforced in Ireland by that date. The Irish chancery did not normally have authority to issue licences in mortmain in the early fourteenth century, but John Darcy, justiciar of Ireland, was allowed to grant licences under special circumstances for three years in 1328. By the late fifteenth century, the right to license alienations in mortmain was one of the powers conferred on lieutenants of Ireland. G. J. Hand, *English Law in Ireland 1290–1324* (Cambridge, 1967), pp. 4–5, 164–6; *Cal. Pat.*, 1327–30, p. 315; for an example, see *Cal. Pat.*, 1467–77, p. 243.

[2] A. G. Little, 'The Franciscans and the Statute of Mortmain', *E.H.R.*, 49, 1934, pp. 673–6.

to the ban on acquisition. In addition, a more favourable version of two phrases in the statute, 'any lands' and gains made 'in any way', was sought. The first precluded recovery of existing property which had been granted out, while the second prevented property reverting through escheat. The king reserved his decision.[3] That nothing was achieved may be inferred from a further campaign, mounted by the clergy in the Easter parliament of 1285, to modify the statute. This time they pleaded relaxation on the grounds of hospitality, chantries, the building of new religious houses and parochial needs. Again the crown was adamant; acquisitions were already allowed under licence and would continue to be licensed where need was shown. No further concessions were to be considered. In face of this intransigence, the clergy were powerless to do more than complain that their ancient rights were being eroded.[4] They did not give up all hope, however. In 1294, the bishop of Lincoln attempted to bribe the crown into a more amenable attitude by offering a tax of a fifth of clerical temporalities in exchange for repeal of the statute.[5] This failed, but further plans for the mitigation of the statute were put forward in 1300, 1301 and 1309. On these occasions, the clergy asked that the crown might permit transfers of land already held in mortmain to other ecclesiastical bodies and that recoveries might be made from ecclesiastical tenants.[6]

All these efforts were in vain; the church never achieved statutory change. The force of its arguments was recognised, but the crown claimed that provision for deserving cases was already available through the licensing system. Accommodation of grievances was not denied. It was, however, to be at the discretion of the secular power and not as of right.

[3] Douie, *Archbishop Pecham*, p. 121 et seq.; Powicke, Cheney, *Councils and Synods*, vol. II, pt II, pp. 885–6, no. 20.

[4] *Ibid.*, p. 958, no. 12; p. 961. The crown's reply interestingly suggests a legislative basis for licensing, although it may be nothing more than an early example of the confusion of practice with the terms of the statute: 'Quod religiosi et clerici possint adquirere possessiones, quia rex statuit quod nichil fiat sine licentia sua; nichil de novo statuet, set rex dabit licentiam ut opus fuerit et videbitur expedire.'

[5] Ed. H. Rothwell, *The Chronicle of Walter of Guisborough* (Camden Soc., 3rd ser., 89, 1957), p. 250.

[6] Powicke, Cheney, *Councils and Synods*, vol. II, pt II, pp. 1205–6, 1217, 1269.

In common with all legislation of the period, the Statute of Mortmain was not framed with great precision. The informal nature of late-thirteenth-century law echoes in the classic order of Justice Hengham on a conflict between the Statutes of Marlborough and Westminster II: 'Do not gloss the statute, we understand it better than you do, for we made it, and one often sees that one statute defeats another.'[7] It was not therefore unrealistic of the church to expect flexibility in the application of the statute and to seek a generous interpretation of its terms in practice. Just how generous the authorities were prepared to be emerged gradually in individual cases in the decades after 1279.

The *articuli cleri* had already seized upon two of the most crucial phrases of the statute. Yet, clerical pressure notwithstanding, it quickly became clear that the church was not to be allowed to recover holdings granted to tenants in perpetuity. A most telling indication of this emerges as the result of a petition by the whole Cistercian order in England for a licence 'to enable them to recover their own fee, lest it fall into the hands of others, to their serious disadvantage'. Far from pointing out that they could already do so, the crown turned down the petition because it asked too much.[8] Many houses were demonstrably forced to recover their own fee under licence and some had licences which actually restricted them to doing so.[9]

The right of ecclesiastical lords to resume villein tenements was not in principle queried. Because a villein had no estate in the land, ownership remained with the lord, so resumption of villein land did not technically constitute acquisition. Nevertheless mistakes arose and confiscations occurred because nice distinctions of tenure and personal status escaped the blunt perceptions of officialdom. In 1321, the abbess of Wherwell secured the return of a messuage and a virgate of land in 'Assheshe' (Isle of Wight) seized by the authorities as an illegal acquisition in fee. She successfully established that it was a villein holding abandoned by

---

[7] Plucknett, *Statutes and Their Interpretation in the First Half of the Fourteenth Century*, p. 95.

[8] *Rot. Parl.*, vol. 1, p. 51, no. 69.

[9] T. A. M. Bishop, 'Monastic Demesnes and the Statute of Mortmain', *E.H.R.*, 49, 1934, p. 304.

its tenant.[10] On two occasions the abbot of Osney was accused of fraudulent acquisition through a villein tenant, although it transpired that the tenants in question were acquiring in their own right as freemen and that it was only by chance that they also held villein land of the abbey.[11] Judgements in favour of the abbot of Abingdon were unequivocal about the lord's position. In 1329, he was upheld when he entered a villein tenement 'as was lawful for him to do'. In a second brush with the law in the same year, when he sought the return of a villein holding which he had entered because it had been illicitly alienated by its tenant, it was stated that he, 'wishing to provide against the damage to him and the peril of disinheritance of his church arising from such alienation, entered the land as he was entitled to do'.[12]

Although the question of resuming villein tenements was quite straightforward in principle, problems arose where villeins became involved in the free land market. This was conceived by the crown as a possible means by which ecclesiastical lords might evade licensing requirements by seizing as villein tenements lands which had been purchased, possibly collusively, from lay fee. An undated copy of *Articles of the Office of Escheator* enjoins escheators to seek out fraudulent alienations of this sort.[13] In 1318, the prior of Spalding was accused of making unlicensed gains from lay fee in Weston, Moulton and Pinchbeck (Lincs.) through his villeins. Restitution was achieved on payment of a fifty-mark fine.[14] In 1324, he was more circumspect and amortised his gains voluntarily.[15] It is doubtful whether such activities represented a serious attempt to undermine mortmain legislation; there were safer and more efficient ways of evading the law than piecemeal collusion with the twenty different villeins involved in 1318. The central concern of landlords in acquisitions such as these was the integrity of their villein land and rights of lordship,

---

[10] *Cal. Close*, 1318–23, p. 289.

[11] *Ibid.*, 1323–7, p. 23; 1327–30, pp. 349–50.

[12] *Ibid.*, 1327–30, pp. 496–7.

[13] *Statutes of the Realm*, 9 vols. (Rec. Comm., 1810–22), vol. I, p. 240.

[14] B.L., Add. MS 35296, ff147v–8; *Cal. Pat.*, 1317–21, p. 211.

[15] B.L., Add. MS 35296, ff150–v; Jones, *Jour. of Brit. Studies*, 1975, pp. 9–11. Accounts of the sub-escheator for Lincolnshire for 1328–9 suggest that the prior may have been pursued once again for similar dealings at that date. P.R.O., E136/2/10–11.

threatened by the confusion of tenures resulting from villein dealings in free land. Comparable concern at Peterborough Abbey resulted in the *Carte Nativorum* recording charters held by villeins surrendered to the abbey when their free tenure was converted to tenure at will. Forfeiture was presented as the alternative to cooperation and it was this step which appeared to conflict with the mortmain regulations.[16] A recent study of two incidents at Ramsey Abbey, one in the mid-fourteenth century and the other early in the fifteenth, shows how mortmain legislation might even be manipulated against ecclesiastical landlords by contestants in the wider struggle for peasant freedom. In the later case, it has been suggested that official intervention was invoked by the villeins in the hope that they might be given custody of the land while it was in royal hands, since a local farmer had been appointed after the earlier confiscation.[17] Considerations of this nature made the practical application of mortmain law in respect of villein holdings difficult, no matter how clear-cut the position in theory.

The recovery of escheated holdings was also subject to some confusion in practice, although again it seems likely that the statute was not intended to diminish the church's normal rights of lordship. Royal officials were compelled to restore holdings which they had confiscated, because inquisitions declared them escheats, and by implication lawful. Such was the ruling which gave back property to the Hospitallers in 1320 and to Selby Abbey in 1323.[18] Other normal legal arrangements should also have fallen outside the jurisdiction of the mortmain law. Land leased out either for a term of years or at will could revert without a licence, although the abbot of Louth Park appears to have acquired one after enquiry by the escheator in 1291, when his life tenant quitclaimed a holding because he could no longer perform the services.[19] In 1320, the parson of Beddington (London) recovered six acres there when it was shown that his

[16] E. King, *Peterborough Abbey 1086–1310* (Cambridge, 1973), pp. 99–104.
[17] A. Jones, 'A Dispute Between the Abbey of Ramsey and its Tenants', *E.H.R.*, 91, 1976, pp. 341–3.
[18] *Cal. Close*, 1318–23, pp. 264, 622.
[19] *Cal. Pat.*, 1281–92, p. 464; *Cal. Inq. Misc.*, 1219–1307, p. 437, no. 1548.

predecessors had let them at will.[20] In 1323, St Osyth's also recovered land demised for life in the same way.[21] Shortly before this, the abbot of Beaulieu was permitted to enter tenements which had been abandoned because of arrears of services. He was specifically stated to be acting as chief lord and not in contravention of the statute.[22]

In addition to these issues, there was some question as to whether the church was forbidden to receive property under a lease, although the terms of the statute implied that restrictions only applied if property was thereby effectively amortised. During a 1306 lawsuit, involving a sixteen-mark rent held for six years, one of the lawyers pleaded that such leases were illegal under the statute. He was not upheld, however, and there is no evidence to suggest that property temporarily granted to the church was ever subject to confiscation without remedy.[23] Indeed, in 1288, the abbot of Buckland secured the return of holdings in Devon which the escheator had seized as acquisitions in defiance of the statute precisely on the grounds that they were leased to him for a sixteen-year term.[24] The common practice of preceding acquisition by a lease offered some scope for collusion to evade the law and perhaps for this reason attracted government attention to leasehold. Furness Abbey found its licensed acquisition of some Irish estates challenged because of an earlier twenty-year lease, but many other institutions enjoyed such arrangements without query.[25]

Exchanges of property were another area of possible ambiguity. Forty-four licences for that purpose were granted under Edward I and a further seventy-nine under his son, so there can be little doubt that they fell within the purview of the statute. The same conclusion must be drawn from the prosecution of those who had neglected to obtain a licence. In 1309, the prior and convent of Newstead in Sherwood received a pardon for exchanging part of an acre in Walkeringham (Notts.) on which they had built a mill,[26] while in 1318 one of the Pipewell cartularies records that

---

[20] *Cal. Close*, 1318–23, p. 248. [21] *Ibid.*, pp. 624–5.
[22] *Ibid.*, pp. 299–300, 612.
[23] Ed. A. J. Horwood, *Year Books XXXIV and XXXV Edward I* (Rolls Series, London, 1879), pp. 148–50.
[24] *Cal. Close*, 1279–88, pp. 517–18.
[25] *Cal. Pat.*, 1334–8, p. 224. [26] *Ibid.*, 1307–13, p. 159.

an unlicensed exchange between the abbey and Thomas de Latimer in Braybrooke (Northants.) was annulled by the itinerant justices.[27] Numerous private charters nevertheless suggest that transactions of this type took place without royal consent. An example from the Daventry cartulary shows half an acre of land and a penny rent in Staverton (Northants.) surrendered in exchange for another half-acre of land belonging to the nuns of Catesby, probably in 1298.[28] Perhaps the absence of a licence was justified on the grounds that no property was passing into mortmain anew. However, the year book for 1342 records a case which established the illegality of exchanges even where the property held by both parties was already amortised.[29] At Godstow nunnery a licence was duly obtained in 1358 to authorise an exchange with the canons of St Frideswide's, but it is interesting to note that it was something of an afterthought.[30] The legal obligation to seek a licence was clear, but it was not easy to enforce in practice, more especially as the amounts of property involved were usually extremely small.

The freedom of the church to dispose of its property as well as acquire was also a question of some note. The Statute of Mortmain stated that selling, either by ecclesiastics or by laymen, was forbidden when it was designed to lead to further amortisation, but almost certainly the crown was principally concerned with lay vendors. Control over the church's losses as well as its gains was undoubtedly exercised, but not on the basis of the 1279 statute. Many religious houses were under royal patronage and it was on the grounds that the king might lose his spiritual benefits that freedom of alienation by the church was initially curtailed. As early as the twelfth century, 'Glanvill' recorded that 'it should be noted that neither a bishop nor an abbot can alienate in perpetuity any part of his demesne without the lord king's consent and confirmation, because their baronies are a

---

[27] B.L., Add. MS 37022; Stowe 937, f72–v.

[28] B.L., Cott. Claud. D xii, f82, no. 65. There was another instance in 1287. *Ibid.*, f10v, no. 33.

[29] Ed. L. O. Pike, *Year Books XVI Edward III* (Rolls Series, London, 1896), Pt 1, p. 160.

[30] Ed. A. Clark, *The English Register of Godstow Nunnery near Oxford* (Early English Text Soc., London, 1911), p. 380, no. 510.

charitable endowment from the lord king and his ancestors'.[31] In addition, the royal measure of 1256, which forbade the acquisition of lands held in chief without a licence, applied equally to laymen and ecclesiastics.[32] Eventually it appears that all lay patrons came to enjoy some right to control alienations from churches with which they were associated, just as they might license alienations from their fee. Bracton had suggested that chapters could not proceed with alienation 'without the royal consent, or that of him who is patron, for the consent of all those whom the matter touches will be necessary and requisite'.[33] In some cases this consent is recorded.[34] The position was further defined in 1285 when the second Statute of Westminster laid down that:

Our lord the king hath ordained, that if abbots, priors, keepers of hospitals, and other religious houses founded by him or by his progenitors, do from henceforth aliene the lands given to their houses by him or his progenitors; the land shall be taken into the king's hands, and holden at his will, and the purchaser shall lose his recovery as well of the land, as of the money that he paid. And if the house were founded by an earl, baron or other persons, for the land so aliened, he [from] whom, or [from] whose ancestor, the land so aliened was given, shall have a writ to recover the same land in demesne.

Provision was also made for instances where endowments were preserved intact, but the spiritual obligations incurred by their acceptance were neglected.[35] This measure was invoked from time to time. In Edward II's reign the escheator seized the manor of Standish (Gloucs.) held by St Peter's Abbey, Gloucester, on the grounds that the house had withdrawn alms of a quarter of corn per week over a ten-year period.[36] Similar confiscations

---

[31] Ed. G. D. G. Hall, *The Treatise on the Laws and Customs of the Realm of England commonly called Glanvill* (London, 1965), p. 74.

[32] *Close Rolls*, 1254–6, p. 429.

[33] Ed. G. E. Woodbine, *Bracton on the Laws and Customs of England*, 4 vols. (Harvard, 1968–77), vol. II, p. 52.

[34] S. Wood, *English Monasteries and Their Patrons in the Thirteenth Century* (Oxford, 1955), p. 155.

[35] *Statutes of the Realm*, vol. I, p. 91.

[36] The abbey recovered the land because no obligation could be proved. *Cal Close*, 1323–7, p. 64.

punctuate the escheators' accounts for Lincolnshire in the following reign.[37]

The thinking behind this legislation was similar to that behind the 1279 Statute of Mortmain in that the interests of landlords, albeit spiritual, would be harmed by uncontrolled alienation. However, given the economic climate of the thirteenth century, which was favourable to landlords and therefore unlikely to coerce them into sales, and given the natural tenacity of the church underpinned by canon law strictures, alienation of this type was not likely to become a serious source of concern. It was not until the fourteenth century, when conditions became more difficult, that the restrictions can be seen to bite. A writ was sought against Tickford Priory in the early 1320s because the prior had alienated a virgate of land and the advowson of Sherington (Bucks.) given by the petitioners' ancestors.[38] A more significant index of deteriorating conditions than isolated cases was the commons petition of 1376 that the relevant part of Westminster II should be implemented with renewed vigour.[39] Alienation was a last resort, however, and where possible the most common expedient favoured by houses suffering financial hardship was to lease their estates rather than to sell them. This too fell under royal ban when it was clearly a device to raise capital. In 1321, St Peter's Abbey, Gloucester, received a pardon for granting out property either for life or for fixed terms without licence. The offence covered both land held in chief and that held of others.[40] Two cases in 1329 make it clear that leases were permitted providing that the annual render represented the fair market rate. In October, Simon de Bereford, escheator south of the Trent, was ordered to leave ten acres in Maidstone and eighty acres in Bishopsbourne (Kent) in peace because, although they had been leased by the archbishop of Canterbury from his demesne, the rents exceeded the annual value of the land. The crown's attitude was made even more explicit in dealings with the crutched friars of Ospringe earlier in the year. The master complained that his lands had been confiscated although demised 'at their true value,

[37] P.R.O., E136/11/2a; E136/11/12, m1; E136/117/5, m2.
[38] *Rot. Parl.*, vol. I, p. 399.   [39] *Ibid.*, vol. II, p. 333.
[40] *Cal. Pat.*, 1317–21, p. 577.

37

so that the demise was not to the damage of the king or any other, or to the diminution of the estate of the house'. The argument sufficed and restitution was achieved.[41] Many houses may have faced the problem of securing a high enough rent to satisfy royal officials, when their financial vulnerability left them in a weak bargaining position *vis-à-vis* prospective lessees. Yet even in this period of economic embarrassment, alienations from the church, whether temporary or permanent, never attained the proportions or significance of its accessions. Thus, although the grounds on which alienations away from the church were limited were much the same as those used to justify control over its accessions, the chronology and legal basis for the restrictions were different.

Although there were many aspects of the 1279 statute which required clarification, the most significant way in which it was modified by interpretation was in the substitution of a licensing policy for the complete embargo which its terms laid down. The first licence permitting the church to make acquisitions, notwithstanding the statute, was granted in 1280. It enabled the warden of the chapel of St Catherine at Wanborough (Wilts.) to buy lands and possessions to the value of ten pounds per annum in order to fulfil the founder's will.[42] In that year eleven licences were granted and thereafter the practice became established. Although there were long-standing precedents for using licences as a means of controlling undesirable transfers of land, it was some decades before a fixed common form was achieved. This slow evolution towards the settled procedures of the fourteenth century is the most informative period in the history of English amortisation.

Unlike the licence to Wanborough, most early licences specified exactly which holding was to pass into mortmain. A more typical licence of 1280 enabled Thomas le Barbur to sell his house in the parish of St Nicholas-in-the-Shambles in London to John of Colchester, formerly almoner to Henry III, so that it could be devoted to the use of the friars minor.[43] By the end of 1280, churchmen had already appreciated the convenience of a single licence which covered several gains. Thus, the hospital of St

---

[41] *Cal. Close*, 1327–30, pp. 510, 480.
[42] *Cal. Pat.*, 1272–81, p. 372. [43] *Ibid.*, p. 381.

Mary-without-Bishopgate received a licence enabling the canons to buy a messuage in the suburbs and to accept two bequests.[44] Royal acquiescence to this practice enabled it to become widespread, with corresponding benefit to the church.

Methods of dealing with licences developed *pari passu* with their contents. Procedure remained fluid into the early fourteenth century, but even after this date new practices were introduced from time to time. The stages in these procedural developments are not always fully explicable, since most of the evidence has to be inferred from actual transactions. Only rarely is there an explicit statement about how licences could be obtained or why modifications in procedure were introduced. Nevertheless, in broad terms the picture is clear enough.

Sometimes it was the recipient who sought the licence and sometimes the grantor, depending on the nature of the grant. Chantry endowments were usually organised by the donor, but where the initiative for an acquisition had come from the church itself, the recipient normally shouldered the responsibility. According to the memoranda of 1292, the first step towards a licence was to present a petition in parliament.[45] By this means, or perhaps sometimes more informally, the governmental machinery was set in motion. From this point onwards, there was much to recommend a powerful patron who would steer the petition through all hazards until it reached fulfilment in a licence. It is quite common to find licences granted at the request of a member of the royal family, the baronage or royal officials. In 1320, for example, Leeds Priory received a licence at the request of Bartholomew de Badlesmere.[46] The letter of Hugh de Brisingham in 1280 to chancellor Burnell, which also and with greater efficacy asked for his help in securing a licence for the Salisbury friars to extend their premises, shows how this sort of favour might be procured.[47]

Successful petitions resulted in a writ issued in chancery addressed to the escheator or local sheriff ordering him to hold an inquisition *ad quod damnum* to find out whose interests would be damaged by the alienation. Such inquisitions were established

[44] *Ibid.*, p. 418.
[45] *Rot. Parl.*, vol. I, p. 54 et seq.; p. 78, no. 4.
[46] *Cal. Pat.*, 1317–21, p. 433.   [47] Little, *E.H.R.*, 1934, p. 674.

as essential by 1284 at the latest, and possibly as early as 1281.[48]
Until 1290, inquisitions were chiefly expected to clarify whether
or not the alienation would harm the king or anyone else, and if
so whom, how much and in what way; who the immediate overlord was, how much service was owed to him, and the net annual
value of the holding. However, certain petitions presented in that
year met with instructions to hold inquisitions 'according to the
new form' or even 'new inquisitions according to the new form'.[49]
This was yet another manifestation of the concern, dating from
the 1217 reissue of Magna Carta, about an alienee's continuing
ability to perform the unaltered obligations to his lord. Increasingly from March 1290, an additional enquiry had been inserted
about the holdings remaining to a grantor and whether or not
they could sustain his services to an overlord and his public duties
should he already be liable to serve on sworn assizes or recogni-
tions.[50] Inquisitions of the same period which had been held
without taking account of this matter were deemed insufficient
for action; hence the new or supplementary proceedings. Such,
for example, befell the archbishop of York in his proposed acquisitions. As a result, further inquisitions were held, although some
of the original jurors were no longer available either through
infirmity or through absence in London on the king's business,
and four verdicts were returned concerned solely with the new
demand.[51] The importance of the innovation can be gauged from
its inclusion among the ordinances of the crown recorded in the
1292 memoranda. No royal licence to alienate in mortmain was
to be granted unless the writ authorising the inquisition *ad quod
damnum* mentioned 'all the articles, according to the new form,
laid down by the king', nor could the grant proceed if the inquisition showed that the grantor was left without other holdings.
An additional safeguard required that the writ should be returned
along with the inquisition and this was observed. As is shown

---

[48] Brand, 'Control of Mortmain Alienation in England', p. 37.
[49] *Rot. Parl.*, vol. I, pp. 63–4; P.R.O., C143/13/30; C143/14/21.
[50] The first writ to include this article is dated 12 March 1290. P.R.O.,
C143/13/26. A note on the dorse of an inquisition of the previous year
directs enquiries of a similar nature. C143/12/17.
[51] P.R.O., C143/14/16. Similar evidence for a second inquisition comes from
Bridlington Priory. C143/13/16.

by a note on the dorse of an inquisition held on 6 February 1293, these were not empty formalities. The bishop of London was refused permission to grant a messuage in Cambridge to the Carmelite friars there because 'the writ did not make mention of all the articles'.[52]

The arrangements embodied in the 1292 memoranda set a final seal on procedural developments. Although all the preliminary measures relating to licences mentioned there were already operative, the new regulations nevertheless marked their firm recognition. The form for an inquisition *ad quod damnum* was established and no further action could be taken towards a royal licence unless that form was observed.

Once an inquisition had been completed and returned to the chancery, the final decision had to be taken as to whether or not a licence should be granted. Even if all the conditions of the 1292 memoranda, including the consent of mesne lords, had been met, favourable decisions were by no means automatic. Notes are to be found on the dorse of writs or inquisitions recording that the king would take counsel before proceeding further and it is sometimes stated that the parties were summoned to parliament or the court to hear the result.[53] As a consequence of this practice, grants of licences tend to be concentrated around sessions of the great council or parliament.[54] When it was finally decided that a licence might be given, the chancellor issued it in the form of letters patent under the great seal, although very occasionally it might take the form of a charter.[55] The licence was then enrolled on the patent rolls, where the source of the authority on which the great seal had been appended was sometimes recorded. In the 1290s this was often 'by inquisition returned from the council' or some such formula, but action on the authority of the king or by writ of privy seal increasingly became the norm.[56]

Once the procedure for securing a licence had been established, the next major development was the widespread use of a type of

[52] *Rot. Parl.*, vol. I, p. 83, no. 13; P.R.O., C143/19/11.

[53] E.g. P.R.O., C143/24/14; C143/25/6.

[54] Brand, 'Control of Mortmain Alienation in England', p. 37.

[55] P.R.O., Lists and Indexes, *List of Inquisitions ad Quod Damnum*, 2 vols. (H.M.S.O., 1892–1912, repr. 1963), vol. I, p. iii.

[56] E.g. *Cal. Pat.*, 1292–1301, p. 26.

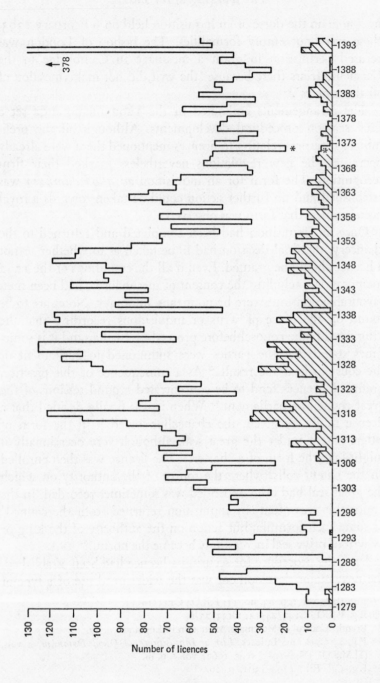

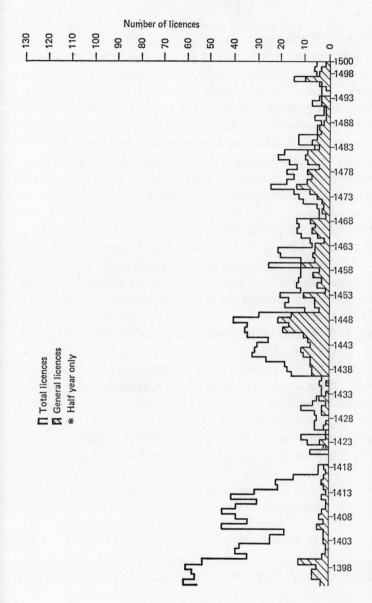

Graph 1 General licences as a proportion of all licences in mortmain granted in England and Wales and recorded on the patent rolls

43

licence designed to give general authorisation to alienations rather than to concede a particular piece of property already selected. The licence granted to the warden of the chapel of St Catherine at Wanborough in 1280 had been of this sort, but although it was the first licence to be enrolled permitting alienation into mortmain, this type of licence acquired a standard form less quickly than the more specific variety. Early variations can be seen from two granted in 1282. That issued to Waverley Abbey permitted recoveries from abbey fee to the value of a hundred shillings per annum, while the licence granted to Alan de Freston, archdeacon of Norfolk, took a fixed amount of land as its basis. He was licensed to acquire six acres of land in Corston (Salop) to augment the endowment of his church there.[57] Among the most notable of the early general licences, and one which was not enrolled on the patent rolls after it was granted by the king in parliament at Lincoln in 1301, was that obtained by St Mary's, York. This entitled the monks to make gains to the value of two hundred pounds per annum. Their petition claimed that the house was stricken through the double disaster of a ten-thousand-mark debt to the earl of Lincoln, resulting from an unsuccessful lawsuit, and the loss of two hundred pounds' annual income.[58] Clearly it was something of a special case because reference was often made to the circumstances of the grant in subsequent dealings, and a confirmation of the outstanding value of the licence was secured in 1309.[59] The high value of the permitted acquisitions, although not entirely without parallel, also put it into a class of its own and made it possible for this abbey to receive property much more freely than most other houses in the ensuing years.

General licences first appear in consistent form and appreciable numbers in 1309. In that year seven were granted and thereafter, as Graph 1 shows, they almost invariably featured somewhere in the annual total. Broadly, their numbers rose and fell in line with those for all licences, specific as well as general. During the fourteenth century, they constituted a small but significant pro-

---

[57] *Ibid.*, 1281–92, pp. 16, 20.
[58] *Cal. Close*, 1307–13, pp. 134–5.
[59] *Cal. Pat.*, 1307–13, pp. 108, 236, 324–5, etc.

portion of the whole. In the fifteenth century, they often assumed a more dominant position, but it is noticeable that these licences were much less frequently invoked.[60] The conventions governing the use of general licences, and in particular the way in which these conventions were modified during the fourteenth and fifteenth centuries, make them one of the most useful guides over a long period to the changing attitudes of crown and society to amortisation.

Fully developed general licences normally empowered their recipients to acquire lands, rents and sometimes advowsons to a fixed annual value. In the later Middle Ages, annuities and reversions also featured as an option. A few early licences authorised generous acquisitions; the abbey of St Alban's was allowed to acquire property worth one hundred pounds per annum under a licence of 1311, as was Winchester Cathedral Priory in 1316.[61] As Graph 2 shows, however, smaller sums were much more common; ten pounds or twenty pounds per annum was the most

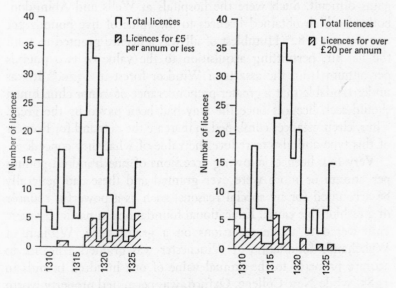

Graph 2 Values specified in general licences granted under Edward II

<hr />

[60] See also below, Table 1, p. 47; pp. 50–1.
[61] *Cal. Pat.*, 1307–13, p. 346; 1313–17, p. 532.

usual figure throughout Edward II's reign. A trend towards less generous licences becomes discernible as the reign progressed. Licences for acquisitions valued at less than five pounds per annum, which were not granted at all before 1312, accounted for over a third of the total in 1326. Licences permitting acquisitions to an annual value of twenty pounds or less remained by far the most numerous for the rest of the Middle Ages (See Table 1). What had probably started out as an extraordinary privilege was becoming a common grant. In consequence, the crown could not make extravagant concessions without prejudicing some of its control over amortisation. By minimising the value of what could be acquired, the crown was able to keep the situation in check. The reduction in scale was also mirrored in the status of the recipients. Those who carried off the licences with the largest face value were the most powerful ecclesiastics: prelates or wealthy black monk houses like St Alban's or St Augustine's, Canterbury. Those who contented themselves with minimal grants were generally the least influential, whose resources made extensive gains difficult. Such were the hospitals at Wells and Abingdon, both of which obtained licences to the value of five pounds per annum in 1318.[62] Humblest of all was a licence granted to John the hermit, permitting acquisition to the value of two pounds per annum from the assarts of Windsor forest in 1320.[63] It was understandable that a greater preponderance of minor churchmen should seek licences once the way had been paved by the great. Thus, circumstances combined to increase the demand for licences of this type and also to reduce the value of what they conceded.

Very few licences allowing accessions of one hundred pounds per annum or more were ever granted and these can generally be accounted for by special reasons, such as a powerful sponsor or a fashionable cause. Educational foundations in particular were empowered to make accessions on a grand scale. William of Wykeham's foundation at Winchester was granted a licence to acquire property to the annual value of one hundred pounds in 1385, while New College, Oxford, was permitted property worth three hundred pounds per annum in 1384 and a further two hundred and fifty marks' worth of property, temporal or spiritual,

[62] *Cal. Pat.*, 1317–21, pp. 119, 147.   [63] *Ibid.*, p. 451.

Table 1. *General licences 1309–1500*

	No. of licences granted	% paying fines on original grant	% granted to a value of £20 p.a. or less	% granted to a value of £100 p.a. or more	% exhausted by 1500	% not taken up by 1500
Edward II	226	5	85	3	15	19
Edward III	557	6	87	2	17	30
Richard II	109	35	72	6	23	37
Henry IV	36	53	67	11	19	42
Henry V	11	27	45	27	0	82
Henry VI	246	46	69	8	4	67
Edward IV	140	63	76	8	6	76
Edward V	—	—	—	—	—	—
Richard III	13	54	85	15	0	100
Henry VII	40	48	88	0	10	83

A small number of general licences not enrolled on the patent rolls, but inferred from a later specific licence, are included in these figures.

47

in 1390.[64] Newly founded colleges at Oxford and Cambridge fared well as a whole. In 1347, Pembroke College, Cambridge, was granted a licence to acquire advowsons to the value of one hundred pounds per annum; in 1438, All Souls' was licensed for accessions to three hundred pounds per annum; and in 1441, King's College, Cambridge, received a licence to acquire lands and advowsons to two hundred pounds per annum.[65] Houses high in royal favour also benefited. The Dominican nuns at Dartford, established by Edward III in the 1340s, received a licence to acquire tenements worth three hundred pounds and advowsons worth another three hundred pounds in 1356.[66] This quite unprecedented grant was not the limit of crown generosity. As in other such cases, there were rather more tangible gifts. In 1367, one thousand marks were forthcoming to make the purchase of an endowment possible. There had also been earlier grants, chiefly of pensions, pending the acquisition of a regular endowment, but also of useful sums such as two hundred marks towards the cost of the church and one hundred marks for lead for the roofs given in 1358. Creature comforts were also remembered in the gift of four casks of wine per annum.[67] St Stephen's, Westminster, was another royal foundation to be succoured. Set up as a college by Edward III in 1348, it received a licence for property worth one hundred pounds per annum in 1369.[68] Chantry foundations such as Fotheringhay or Barnard Castle Colleges, backed by the aristocracy or other influential men, and the Carthusians, who attracted most of the residual interest in enclosed orders, also held licences granting substantial accessions.[69]

The crown sought to protect itself, and other vulnerable interests, not merely by keeping the value of most authorised alienations within bounds, but also by placing restrictions on their nature. In its fully developed form, this was achieved in two ways. The more common forbade licensees to acquire any

[64] *Ibid.*, 1381–5, p. 444; 1385–9, p. 3; 1388–92, p. 265.
[65] *Ibid.*, 1345–8, p. 444; 1436–41, pp. 173, 522.
[66] *Ibid.*, 1354–8, p. 486.
[67] Ed. W. Page, *V.C.H. Kent*, 3 vols. (1908–32), vol. II, pp. 182–3.
[68] *Cal. Pat.*, 1367–70, p. 340. It received a further licence for accessions to £100 per annum in 1479. *Ibid.*, 1476–85, p. 172.
[69] *Ibid.*, 1446–52, p. 113; 1476–85, p. 67; 1370–4, pp. 386–7.

property held directly of the king. A very high proportion of the general licences granted after the beginning of Edward III's reign contained a clause to this effect. During the fifteenth century a slightly less restrictive variant allowed recipients to acquire property held of the crown in socage or burgage. The licence granted to the abbey of St James-by-Northampton in 1440 is unusually explicit in confining the canons to lands and rents held in socage or burgage and specifically excluding property held by knights' fee or grand serjeanty.[70] A highly restrictive provision found among the earliest general licences confined licensees to gains from their own tenants. Though harsh in its implications, it does not seem to have been common. Indeed, there is only one instance recorded on the calendared patent rolls after 1400. However, this may be misleading, since there were certainly more limitations of this type than appear in the calendars for the early fourteenth century. The licence which Thorney Abbey received in 1314 permitting acquisitions to the annual value of twenty pounds shows no limitation in the calendar, although the monks were clearly confined to their own fee in both the copy on the manuscript patent roll and that in the abbey's own cartulary.[71] Similarly, Ramsey Abbey's licence of 1309 and Spalding Priory's licence of 1312 are each shown as confining them to existing fee in their cartularies in spite of appearing unlimited in the calendar.[72] Had this type of restriction come into general currency, the impact on the church would have been considerable. As it was, the limitation frequently seems to have been directed at the older, richer establishments whose already extensive properties gave cause for concern and whose case for additional holdings was weak. The more frequent exclusion of land held in chief as a possible acquisition, while doubtless inconvenient in certain instances, did not preclude the extension of endowments beyond their pre-1279 size.

[70] *Ibid.*, 1436–41, p. 407. This does not explicitly refer to land held in chief although it is implied.

[71] *Ibid.*, 1313–17, p. 183; P.R.O., C66/142, m18; C.U.L., Add. MSS 3020–1, f33, iiii.

[72] *Cal. Pat.*, 1307–13, pp. 190, 485; ed. W. H. Hart, P. A. Lyons, *Cartularium Monasterii de Rameseia*, 3 vols. (Rolls Series, London, 1884–93), vol. II, p. 121; B.L., Add. MS 35296, f148v.

Quite apart from the disadvantages arising from restrictions about what type of acquisitions could be made, a general licence did not smooth away all the problems attendant on taking property into mortmain, since in itself it was insufficient to complete the process. Except in a few specific instances of late date,[73] the possession of such a licence did not absolve its holder from going through all the normal procedures of amortisation, including the application for a specific licence and the holding of an inquisition *ad quod damnum*, whenever an accession under the general licence was planned. Any attempt to treat the general licence as a short cut or sufficient authorisation in itself was prosecuted. In 1327, the two Lincolnshire Gilbertine houses of St Katherine's-without-Lincoln and Sixhills both received pardons for unduly precipitate seisin of holdings which they were seeking under general licence. Neither had waited for the inquisition *ad quod damnum* to be returned to chancery and the issue of the requisite licences.[74] The patent rolls of Edward III's early years are studded with other such examples, although there are reasons for believing that royal zeal declined during the later fourteenth and fifteenth centuries.[75]

One or two hazards common to all types of licence were particularly likely to arise with general licences because of the long interval which could take place between the grant and the completion of acquisitions. A delay of several years or even decades before a licence was invoked was common. Woburn Abbey was granted a licence to acquire land, tenements and rents to the value of twenty pounds per annum in 1385, but took no further action for eleven years.[76] Bourne Abbey waited forty-five years before taking up its licence of 1327.[77] Welbeck Abbey took twenty years longer still.[78] About 40% of the general licences granted by Edward III had not been used at all within twenty years of their issue and some were abandoned altogether. Although some licences were fully executed within a short time, accessions to the full value of a general licence could

---

[73] See below, pp. 93–4. [74] *Cal. Pat.*, 1327–30, pp. 130–1, 137.
[75] See below, p. 90 et seq. [76] *Cal. Pat.*, 1385–9, p. 75; 1391–6, p. 702.
[77] *Ibid.*, 1327–30, p. 12; 1370–4, p. 184.
[78] *Ibid.*, 1327–30, p. 107; 1391–6, p. 154.

take the best part of a century or even longer. Spalding Priory, which was considered to have achieved the goal of twenty pounds per annum set by its licence of 1312 only in 1391, is a typical fourteenth-century example.[79] Lesnes Abbey finally exhausted its licence of 1309 as late as 1500.[80] With delays such as these, circumstances could imperil the full implementation of the original grant. Where a licence had been granted to the grantor rather than the grantee, for example, his death rendered the licence void. In 1333, Nicholas de Hugate secured permission to acquire land and rent to the value of twenty pounds per annum as endowment for a six-chaplain chantry, but died before this could be carried out. In consequence, his executors were obliged to procure a second licence to bring the project to fruition. Yet a third licence was required in 1354, when death in turn claimed all but three of the executors, leaving the matter still uncompleted. This time, the outstanding value of the licence was made over to the hospital of St Nicholas, Beverley, whose corporate nature precluded the embarrassments of further mortality.[81] Much of the delay in this case had arisen from plans too ambitious for the available resources, but the purchase of suitable endowments, unless planned well beforehand, could rarely be accomplished quickly, and over-optimism about their cost was a common enough phenomenon. Thus, lay licensees who wished to found chantries were amongst the most frequent victims of the need to renew licences. Failure to observe it could lead to confiscation. The prior and convent of Montacute received a pardon in 1331 for accepting ten shillings' rent from Jean daughter of Edward Coker when the licence only authorised a grant from her father.[82] More serious because more widely applicable was the ruling expressed late in Richard II's reign that the death of the sovereign negated all outstanding licences. This emerged when Shouldham Priory was granted a pardon in 1397 for the appropriation of Caister church (Norfolk). A licence for this had been obtained

---

[79] *Ibid.*, 1307–13, p. 485; 1391–6, p. 17. In the fifteenth century it was more typical for a licence never to be invoked. See above, Table 1; and below, p. 67.

[80] *Cal. Pat.*, 1307–13, p. 158; 1494–1509, p. 225.

[81] *Ibid.*, 1338–40, pp. 171–2; 1354–8, p. 48.

[82] *Ibid.*, 1330–4, p. 36.

from Edward III, but the delays attendant on securing a parallel licence from the papacy and waiting for a vacancy in the living meant that the priory was unable to proceed with the matter until 1390–1. The canons had then acted without further application to the king 'understanding that the late king's said licence would be sufficient without the king's licence or confirmation', a misjudgement which resulted in forfeiture.[83] The number of re-grants and confirmations of concessions of all types whenever succeeding monarchs mounted the throne suggests that their necessity was taken seriously, although there is little evidence to show that it was enforced.

Given all these disadvantages, it is pertinent to enquire into the popularity of general licences. What, in particular, made so many religious houses go to the trouble of acquiring them, when often they had no immediate plans for putting them into effect and quite frequently never invoked them at all? One explanation is that possession of a general licence was some guarantee that a petition for a future specific licence would not be turned down. This made it feasible to plan accessions over a long period of time incurring necessary expense without fear of last-minute obstruction from the crown. The efficacy of this argument hinges on the strength of the evidence that licences were ever seriously stinted. Some idea about this can be formed by correlating inquisitions *ad quod damnum* with licences entered on the patent rolls. The result suggests that the crown was not unduly hard on the church. Both the contents and the endorsements of the inquisitions show that the criteria for refusing a licence were usually based on the evidence that someone's interest would be damaged rather than on any royal caprice. Thus, in 1283, Thornholme Priory's proposed acquisition of a messuage in Lincoln was rejected when it was learnt that the interests of both crown and the earl of Lincoln would be harmed.[84] Likewise, in 1293, the nuns of Hinchinbrooke were not allowed to keep two acres in Huntingdon which they had been given because the inquisition showed that the land was held in chief and that the king would suffer.[85] The proportion of petitions which terminated at the inquisition stage

---

[83] *Ibid.*, 1396–9, p. 253.
[84] P.R.O., C143/6/18.   [85] P.R.O., C143/19/21.

varied from year to year. As Graph 3 shows, in the regnal year 1294–5, only 38% of inquisitions were ultimately reflected in licences, but by the last decade of Edward I's reign a far more generous proportion was achieved. A success rate of 90% or

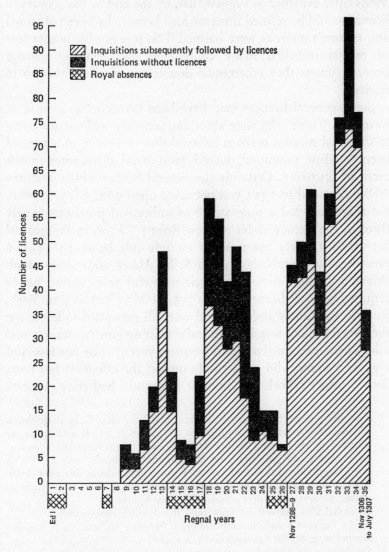

Graph 3 Inquisitions *ad quod damnum* and dependent licences in mortmain temp. Edward I

more can be found in four of the ten regnal years and the average was 84%. There are certain problems associated with these figures, notably concerning the availability of inquisitions and the validity of percentages based on such small numbers.[86] Nevertheless, there seems little evidence to suggest that, by the end of the century, a licence would be refused if mesne lord licences had been obtained and no one's interests were harmed.[87] So it is not likely that fear of refusal impelled many churchmen into securing general licences, unless they entertained doubts out of all proportion to reality.

Some general licences may have been taken out as a form of insurance. Those who were absorbing property without attending to the legal niceties perhaps believed that possession of a general licence, albeit unutilised, would avert royal displeasure in the event of discovery. Certainly the general licence which Thorney Abbey obtained in 1314 was not acted upon until 1327. Instead, the abbot directed a programme of unlicensed purchases chiefly through the agency of his nephew Robert.[88] Faith in the general licence as a safety net was not entirely misplaced. In 1312, a precedent was established when Selby Abbey and Guisborough Priory were allowed to offset their unlawful gains against newly acquired general licences.[89] In 1315, St Mary's Abbey in York, Bury St Edmund's and Stratford were all permitted to legitimise their surreptitious acquisitions under existing general licences and others benefited similarly in subsequent years.[90] The possession of a general licence did not entirely protect the offender, however; both St Mary's York and Bury St Edmund's had their property

---

86 The statistics are based on inquisitions in P.R.O., class C143 (inquisitions *ad quod damnum*). Some inquisitions are no longer extant and others are scattered in classes such as ancient petitions or inquisitions miscellaneous. Some licences do not have a matching inquisition in the early years after 1279, suggesting that inquisitions were not always held at this time. Thus, because the inquisitions are incomplete, they must be matched individually against licences rather than correlated as gross figures.

87 Rosenthal also received the impression that licences were readily obtainable in the fourteenth and fifteenth centuries. *Purchase of Paradise*, p. 135. See also below, p. 69, for a random check in 1391–2.

88 See above, p. 49, and below, pp. 96–7.

89 *Cal. Pat.*, 1307–13, pp. 432, 435.

90 *Ibid.*, 1313–17, pp. 215, 305, 374.

confiscated until a royal pardon was forthcoming. At best such licences were a palliative for royal wrath rather than protection against it. Thus, caution is also not wholly convincing as an explanation for the eagerness with which they were sought.

Another possible motive behind the demand for general licences was the church's ingrained tradition of extending endowments in every possible way. It was yet another privilege to be grasped by a group avid for privileges so that the glory of God be made further manifest. An upsurge in licences granted to local houses which is sometimes discernible when the king was in progress suggests that some were the result of opportunism and royal largesse. The Gilbertine houses of Sixhills, St Katherine's-without-Lincoln and probably North Ormsby and Louth Park all gained general licences while Edward II was at Lincoln in February 1316.[91] Similarly, late in 1327, his son granted general licences to Henwood, Coventry Cathedral Priory and St John's Hospital, Coventry, while staying in Coventry.[92]

Most potent of all among the likely incentives to acquire licences, at least in the early fourteenth century, was financial saving. Acquisition under a general licence was cheap since it quickly became customary for both the initial licence and subsequent licences based on it to be granted without payment of a fine. This assumed great importance once the crown decided that fines might be charged on ordinary mortmain licences.

The whole issue of fines for amortisation is a vexing one and this is reflected in the complex arrangements which developed in relation to general licences. Even the fines for ordinary licences to alienate into mortmain are by no means straightforward. The position varied markedly over the years and the criteria used to assess them defy a simple explanation.

No fines can be proved as a regular charge before 1299, but in that year they were charged on nineteen out of the total of forty-four licences granted. Their regular, though far from invariable, incidence thereafter (see Graph 4) presages either a significant change in crown policy or more simply a change in procedure.

Dr Standen has pointed out that the fine roll for the year

[91] *Ibid.*, pp. 385, 400.   [92] *Ibid.*, 1327–30, pp. 193–4.

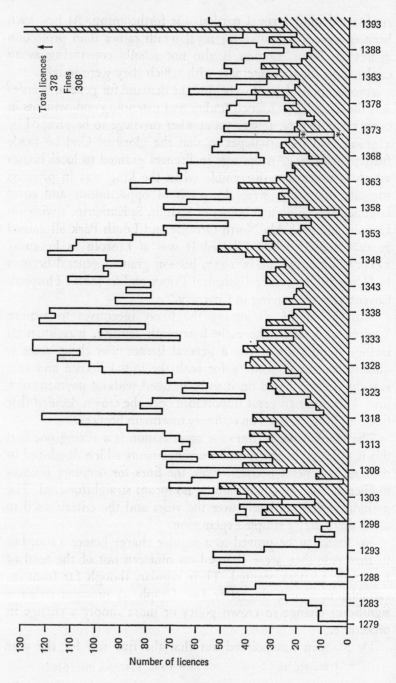

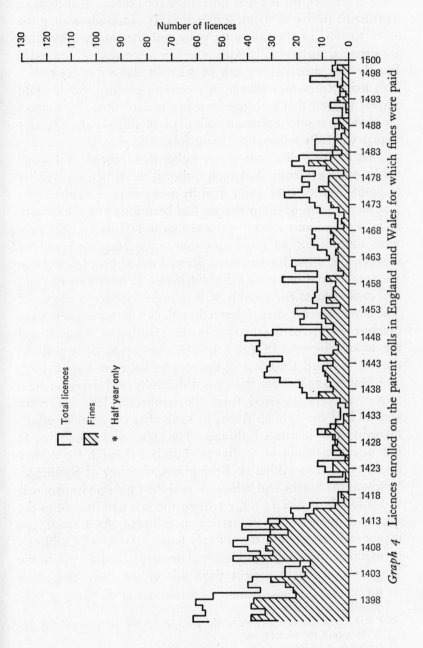

Number of licences

Graph 4 Licences enrolled on the patent rolls in England and Wales for which fines were paid

☐ Total licences

▨ Fines

* Half year only

57

1298–9 records, for the first time, fines for licences to alienate in mortmain: twelve of them, scattered fairly randomly among the other entries. In the following year, and thereafter, these fines are grouped methodically with others in a schedule to the roll.[93] Exactly the same pattern can be seen on the originalia rolls.[94] This may represent a change in recording practice, but it could equally suggest that a change in policy towards fines for licences for alienations into mortmain took place in 1298–9 and that this change was fully systematised in the following year.

That it was a change in policy rather than procedure is borne out by other evidence. As Graph 3 shows, the crown was readier to grant licences after 1299 than in previous years. This argues that some means of compensation had been found by the government for occasions when royal interests were affected. Not only were inquisitions *ad quod damnum* more often followed by licences, but more licences were granted altogether: from ten in 1297 and seven in 1298, the number rose to forty-four in 1299 and continued to rise steadily well into the fourteenth century.[95] The latter evidence may be less telling than it appears. There were marked short-term fluctuations in the granting of licences, and the sudden increase in 1299 may be due to mundane political reasons. Edward I was out of the country between August 1297 and March 1298. That this caused difficulty and delay for petitioners may be inferred from the temporary letter of entry secured by Peterborough Abbey in 1288 after considerable effort, involving two journeys to France. The abbey was attempting to purchase the manor of Southorpe (Cambs.) through the agency of the royal justice Elias de Bekingham. Geoffrey of Southorpe, to whom the manor had belonged until the final impoverishment of his family in the 1270s, resenting the sale and in debt to the queen, denounced the transaction as collusive. As a result, the manor was taken into the queen's hands. Aware of Geoffrey's accusations, the monks had meanwhile despatched a clerk to the king in Gascony to present their side of the case. This clerk

---

[93] P.R.O., C60/97 et seq.; Standen, 'Administration of the Statute of Mortmain', p. 124 et seq.

[94] P.R.O., E371/60 et seq. Five of the fines in 1298–9 are grouped together at the top of the membrane.

[95] See below, Graph 6, p. 155.

brought back the writ for an inquisition and another returned with the jurors' verdict to Gascony. Hence the king's letter of entry pending his return.[96] Thornton Abbey, less hampered by malice, quietly ignored licensing requirements and, when detected, pleaded the royal absence by way of justification.[97] Other houses in the same predicament may have been more law-abiding and awaited the king's return, thus accounting for the rise in licences granted in 1299. Certainly, as Graph 3 shows, there was a similar rise after an earlier royal absence between May 1286 and August 1289. Nevertheless, absence alone cannot account for the underlying trend upwards from 1299 after nearly a decade of stability.[98] Bean argued that by 1299 caution in the use of the procedures recorded in the 1292 memoranda had worn off, but the length of time involved seems to carry caution too far, especially since the arrangements set out in 1292 were already operating from 1290.[99] For whatever reason, as Bean points out, by 1299 all hesitations had disappeared.[100] What better calculated to banish them, at least for the crown, than the introduction of fines?

Mounting evidence that the crown may have changed its policy in favour of fining for licences in 1299 is supported by the political difficulties faced by Edward I at this date. After the crisis of 1297, he had limited means of raising money. Dr Maddicott has shown that this was a period when military expenses continued to be very high, while 1299 marked the end of five years of exceptionally heavy taxation. Nor were Italian bankers in a position to bridge the gap between the crown's needs and its resources.[101] The appeal of fines from mortmain licensees in these

---

96 Mellows, *Henry of Pytchley's Book of Fees*, pp. 62–7; *Cal. Fine*, 1272–1307, p. 285; King, *Peterborough Abbey*, pp. 41–4.

97 P.R.O., C143/16/8.

98 See below, Graph 6, p. 155.

99 Bean, *Decline of English Feudalism*, pp. 55–7. Bean's figures differ slightly from my own, partly because I have calculated pardons for illicit acquisition separately where he has not. For the problems of arriving at statistics, see below, p. 153.

100 Bean, *Decline of English Feudalism*, p. 57.

101 E. Miller, 'War, Taxation and the English Economy in the Late Thirteenth and Early Fourteenth Centuries', in ed. J. M. Winter, *War and Economic Development* (Cambridge, 1975), p. 20; J. R. Maddicott, 'The English Peasantry and the Demands of the Crown 1294–1341', *Past and Present*,

circumstances is obvious. It is only surprising that the expedient had not been adopted earlier.

Accepting the likelihood that fines for licences for alienations into mortmain were introduced for the first time in 1299, one might go further and try to establish the exact date at which the decision was made. On 1 April of that year, a royal ordinance arranged that fines for a range of privileges, including alienations into mortmain, should be assessed by the exchequer if interests worth more than twenty shillings per annum were concerned, but otherwise by the chancellor at his discretion.[102] Thus, there can be no doubt that fines for licences to alienate into mortmain were envisaged by that date, although the first to appear on the patent rolls was dated 10 April.[103] March and April of that year were the busiest months in terms of licences granted,[104] and since no fine was paid on those granted in March, the presumption is that the new policy was formulated at much the same time as the general ordinance and may perhaps have been associated with it.

Much effort has gone into discovering a consistent rationale behind the assessment of fines with proportionately meagre results. Their imposition appears quite haphazard, with the amount charged dependent upon royal vagary and upon the price each recipient was prepared to pay. Nevertheless, some valid generalisation is possible. Royal policy towards fines is best seen as progressive. Before 1299, it seems as if there was little thought of making a charge for the privilege. Once the decision to introduce fines had been taken, there ensued a period when the criteria used for assessment, although somewhat obscure, are susceptible to limited analysis. So far all attempts to correlate the sums charged with the value of the property to be acquired have proved abortive.[105]

---

supp. 1, 1975, pp. 1, 6; M. Prestwich, *War, Politics and Finance under Edward I* (London, 1972), pp. 215, 270; T. F. Tout, *Chapters in the Administrative History of Medieval England*, 6 vols. (Manchester, 1920–33), vol. II, p. 99.

[102] *Cal. Close*, 1296–1302, p. 304; P.R.O., E368/70, m34d.

[103] *Cal. Pat.*, 1292–1301, p. 417. A licence concerning an illicit alienation dated 7 April has been discounted; *ibid.*, p. 405.

[104] Jan., 0; Feb., 0; Mar., 9; Apr., 8; May, 4; June, 7; Jul., 3; Aug., 2; Sept., 3; Oct., 1; Nov., 7; Dec., 0.

[105] Wood-Legh, *Studies in Church Life*, p. 62; P.R.O., *List of Inquisitions ad Quod Damnum*, vol. I, p. iii.

Values were not ignored, however. They could determine procedure, as the 1299 ordinance showed. In August 1299, a licence for the friars preachers of Sudbury was said to have been granted by the council because the value of the proposed acquisition did not exceed fourpence.[106] Had it been worth more, it would doubtless have gone through the designated channels. Yet although financial yardsticks were in operation, and probably influenced the decision as to the size of the fine, they clearly formed only one aspect of an assessment. Others might include the degree of influence exercised by sponsors. Licences granted at the request of members of the royal family or powerful magnates were usually free of charge. The issue might also be affected by the need for compensation where the property to be alienated was held in chief or within a royal borough. Political crises, as in 1299, might also be a determining factor. Edward II was undoubtedly exploiting mortmain licences for cash in 1311–12, when his struggle to protect Piers Gaveston was at its height. Not only were more licences subject to fines (fifty-five out of seventy-four in 1311 and forty-two out of sixty-six in 1312), but some were granted against his debts for provisioning. On 17 March 1312, for example, Bolton Priory received a licence to acquire land and rents worth twenty marks per annum in return for a twenty-mark fine and the acquittance of the king's sixteen-pound debt for corn and victuals which the canons had provided for his use.[107] An equally marked drop in fines between 1319 and 1320 probably reflects Edward's attempt to win over as many potential supporters as possible by limiting his exactions. The incidence of fines was governed not only by the nature of the alienation, but also by the identity of the recipient. Until 1350, the mendicant orders, whose modest gains were usually for the enlargement of their premises, were normally exempt from fines. By contrast, those wishing to found or augment the endowments of chantries frequently paid for the privilege. In 1319, when only ten out of the seventy-four licences granted were subject to fines, five of the unfortunates concerned chantries. Some consideration was given to the existing wealth of the petitioner and to how badly an additional source of income was needed. A nominal

[106] *Cal. Pat.*, 1292–1301, p. 434.   [107] *Cal. Pat.*, 1307–13, pp. 440, 442.

hundred masses was the price of a licence for the Carmelite friars of Maldon, enabling them to extend their premises in 1314.[108] This attitude persisted and a century later Bisham Priory received a licence without payment, but 'for God, because they are poor'.[109] A free licence might also be the reward for loyal service, as in 1320 when the brother and heir of John de Munden, a secular clerk, was given permission to alienate a messuage in order to found a chantry in St Paul's Cathedral in return for John's diligence in collecting the papal tenth.[110] No universal rule for the imposition and assessment of fines on mortmain licences can be adduced. Rather it seems as if a diversity of considerations resulted in widely differing charges. So complex could the matter become that in 1336 the dean and chapter of Lincoln lost heart and surrendered a licence because the fine had not yet been settled.[111] The advantage of such flexibility outweighed the disadvantages, however, making it possible for the crown to combine a genuine concern for the needs and resources of the church with a concern for its own interests and those of its vassals.

Just as there is evidence that the crown had become aware of the revenue potential of mortmain licences by 1299, so there are signs that during the course of the fourteenth century the desire to profit from them intensified. The regular incidence of fines for acquisitions by mendicants after 1350 is just one indication of this, although it may also be associated with the enquiries of 1349 and 1350 into their property. For some reason, possibly connected with the anti-mendicant campaign led by Richard Fitzralph, the crown ordered inquisitions into all mendicant holdings to discover whether they had made accessions 'with which they do not enlarge their dwellings but rather erect buildings thereon and lease them out to laymen'. Surviving returns suggest that the suspicions were unfounded, and indeed the fines charged on licences to mendicants in the following years would probably have been larger if they were guilty on any scale.[112] At perhaps half a mark, the fines retained a charitable connotation, but they

108 *Ibid.*, 1313–17, p. 203. 109 *Ibid.*, 1413–16, p. 339.
110 *Ibid.*, 1317–21, p. 442. 111 *Ibid.*, 1334–8, p. 250.
112 A. G. Little, *Franciscan Papers, Lists and Documents* (Manchester, 1943), p. 144 et seq.

nonetheless represented a change of policy. Graph 5 shows that the proportion of specific licences as a whole for which fines were paid also showed an upward trend as the century progressed. The clearest indication of the government's attitude is to be found in 1392. In the previous year, a statute had ordered that all property which the church was able to enjoy by a legal device which avoided amortisation was to be acquired under licence by the following Michaelmas under pain of forfeiture.[113] Under such coercion, it is significant that of the resulting 378 licences, both general and specific, 81% incurred fines. Moreover, on Dr Standen's calculation, more than £4,000 was raised from this source in the regnal year 1392–3, far in excess of the sums achieved in the sixteen years earlier in the century for which he gives figures.[114]

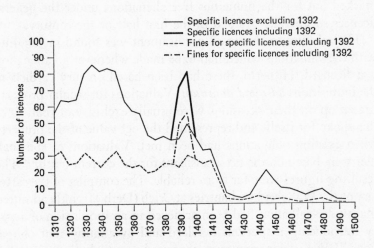

Graph 5 Running averages of fines for specific licences to alienate into mortmain in England and Wales from the patent rolls

Against this background, the practice of allowing acquisitions under general licence free of charge assumed new significance. For most of the fourteenth century, the tradition of immunity was observed. Only 33 out of the 781 general licences granted

[113] *Statutes of the Realm*, vol. ii, pp. 79–80; see below, pp. 127–8.
[114] They had never previously exceeded eight hundred pounds. Standen, 'Administration of the Statute of Mortmain', Table v, p. 188.

between 1309, when they first appeared regularly, and 1377 were subject to fines. Equally, few fines were imposed on individual alienations under the general licences. They occurred chiefly when the last transaction was deemed to exceed the permitted value under the licence. Such was the case in 1361, when St Osyth's paid a two-pound fine for its last acquisition under a general licence of 1333. Only £7 6s 8d worth of income was still outstanding, while the projected gain was assessed at £7 14s 2d.[115] The chief problem from the crown's point of view was the length of time it took to bring this loss of revenue to a halt without doing violence to custom. In effect, each general licence granted had mortgaged the crown's future freedom to charge a fine. The increase in the proportion of fines for specific licences charged after the mid-fourteenth century might well have been yet more marked but for the numerous free alienations under the general licences so liberally granted in the first half of the century.

The solution to this royal predicament was found in juggling with the valuations which had to be made whenever an alienation was licensed. Hitherto, these had been based on jury verdicts at the inquisitions *ad quod damnum*. Valuations for secular property drawn up on these occasions were usually exclusive of rent, since this spoke for itself, and represented the net value of the property when existing obligations had been met. Valuations of spiritualities were based on the tax assessment for the current tenth.[116] The resulting figures were far from reliable. The compiler of the cartulary of the Wakebridge chantries at Crich (Derb.) frankly admitted that under-valuation had been achieved in an inquisition of 1350 by introducing a spurious overlord and overstating rent obligations.[117] Few stratagems were confessed so openly, but given the notorious inclination of its subjects towards under-assessment, and the concern expressed in 1343 and again in 1385 that churchmen acquired more than their entitlement under general licences, the crown was perhaps justified when it began to accelerate the

---

[115] *Cal. Pat.*, 1330–4, p. 490; 1340–3, p. 565; 1343–5, p. 139; 1361–4, p. 48.
[116] E.g. *ibid.*, 1317–21, p. 243; 1321–4, p. 121.
[117] Ed. A. Saltman, *The Cartulary of the Wakebridge Chantries at Crich* (Derbyshire Archaeological Soc. Record Ser., 6, 1971), pp. 10–14; pp. 36–8, no. 2; pp. 43–4, no. 7. Dr Wood-Legh very kindly drew my attention to this reference.

Table 2. *Accessions under general licence by Crowland Abbey*

Date	Valuation of inquisition *ad quod damnum*			Valuation against general licence		
	£	s	d	£	s	d
1334	2	8	5	2	10	5
1336		14	0	1	0	0
1377		13	4	3	6	8
1398	3	13	4	13	2	11
Total	£7	9	1	£20	0	0

exhaustion of such licences artificially by drawing a distinction between the valuation provided by the inquisition *ad quod damnum* and that for which it was to count against the general licence.[118] This practice, which is first recorded in 1323, could mean that as little as a third of the face value of the licence was ultimately achieved. This is illustrated by the acquisitions under a general licence granted to Crowland Abbey in 1327. According to its terms, the monks were allowed to acquire land and rent worth twenty pounds per annum.[119] Table 2 shows how this worked out in practice. Butley Priory was more fortunate in securing property worth £5 18s 9¼d under a 1321 licence for acquisitions to the value of ten pounds per annum and a further £13 15s 5¾d worth under a 1365 licence permitting alienations to the value of twenty pounds per annum: in both cases nearer to two-thirds of the face value of the licence.[120]

Thomas Burton, sometime abbot of Meaux, writing in the early years of the fifteenth century at the latest, made the interesting suggestion that increased valuations may have been proffered as an alternative to fines. He described how, when making an acquisition licensed in 1392 under a general licence allowing gains worth thirty pounds per annum, the monks were given the choice of either paying an outright fine of ten marks or accepting an assessment of nine marks to set against the general licence.

[118] R. Graham, *English Ecclesiastical Studies* (London, 1929), p. 285 et seq.; *Rot. Parl.*, vol. II, p. 137; vol. III, p. 213.
[119] *Cal. Pat.*, 1327–30, p. 181.
[120] Myres, 'Notes on the History of Butley Priory', pp. 195–7.

Since the inquisition *ad quod damnum* had valued the tenement at half a mark, he felt bitterly aggrieved. In the event, the monks settled for the devaluation of their privilege rather than part with hard cash, but were in no doubt that a deliberate attempt had been made to diminish their rights: 'Thus do the present ministers of the king try to nullify the grants and licences made by the king's progenitors to their subjects'.[121] Burton's evidence appears to be without parallel, either in narrative sources or in archives, but he was writing of events concerning his own house in his own lifetime and it is difficult to see what he had to gain by inventing the incident. It is quite plausible that the crown threatened to charge fines in order to induce churchmen to accept increased valuations without fuss.

The government's attitude towards general licences hardened in other ways as the fourteenth century wore on. Fewer new general licences were conceded in the later fourteenth and early fifteenth centuries and more of them were subject to fines.[122] The figures for 1392, when the crown held the whip hand, are illuminating. While 69 general licences were judged fully satisfied, only 13 new ones were granted in their place, and all but one of these were the subject of a fine.[123] The contrast with earlier practice is marked: general licences were to be issued with restraint and, like any others, were to yield revenue at the discretion of the crown.

The imposition of fines for alienations under general licence continued to exercise the crown, and the fifteenth century saw further experiments. Beginning under Henry V, charges were often made on the occasion of each acquisition rather than for the general licence itself. In 1417, the borough of Coventry was given a licence to acquire property worth forty pounds per annum. A fine of forty pounds was then paid in the following year upon accessions worth £9 7s 4d per annum, while another five pounds in 1423 secured more property worth 13s 4d per annum.[124] The

---

[121] Bond, *Chronica Monasterii de Melsa*, vol. I, pp. xliv, li, lxi; vol. III, p. 176; *Cal. Pat.*, 1391–6, p. 103.

[122] See above, Graph 1, pp. 42–3; Table 1, p. 47.

[123] Since six of the new licences also comprehended the foundation of a gild, they are perhaps not truly representative so far as fines are concerned.

[124] *Cal. Pat.*, 1416–22, pp. 105, 167; 1422–9, p. 138.

new policy was more straightforward to operate and less of a gamble than dealings under the earlier system. It also enabled the crown, if it so chose, to make charges on acquisitions under older general licences granted before fines were generally imposed. This happened to Glastonbury Abbey in 1426, 1428 and 1439, when it took up its general licence of 1383. Fines were then paid, although none had been charged either for the general licence itself or for the first accession dependent on it.[125] A very few alienees paid for both their general licences and specific acquisitions, even when no great interval of time had elapsed.[126] Yet, although the advantages of charging on the occasion of an accession were manifest, they did not win universal acceptance. There were problems from the crown's point of view. Relatively few late medieval general licences were ever invoked. So, unless a fine was charged on the initial grant, the chance was lost forever. Perhaps for this reason, Henry VI's reign witnessed a substantial return to charges at this early stage.[127] Typical in this respect was the general licence secured by the executor of Richard Whittington for a chantry in the chapel of St Mary over the charnel house in St Paul's Cathedral churchyard in 1430, for which a fine of twenty shillings was paid.[128] Whichever option was exercised, however, the privileges associated with general licences under Edward II and Edward III had been completely overridden. It had become accepted that the crown could exact a fine for either general or specific licences regardless of any prior concession or payment, even if this opportunity was not always taken. Thus, by the second decade of the fifteenth century, the crown had succeeded in bringing the fiscal shortcomings of earlier custom under tight control. As Graphs 1 and 6 show, the crown became more liberal in its grant of general licences after Henry VI was admitted to government in the late 1430s. This was undoubtedly a reflection of royal piety and patronage, but it was also generosity made more practicable by the reforms of his immediate predecessors.

Ordinary mortmain licences demonstrate similar changes in

[125] *Ibid.*, 1381–5, p. 334; 1396–9, p. 471; 1422–9, pp. 331, 477; 1436–41, p. 292.
[126] *Ibid.*, 1405–8, p. 472; 1413–16, p. 257; 1485–94, p. 465; 1494–1509, p. 41.
[127] See above, Table 1, p. 47. [128] *Cal. Pat.*, 1429–36, pp. 56–7.

policy. As Graph 5 shows, a trend towards intensified charges for specific licences is evident from the mid-fourteenth century, when the incidence of fines declined much less sharply than the number of licences granted. There are also suggestions that, from the later fourteenth century, assessment of fines may have been based on a scale of charges relating to the value of the property to be alienated.

Once again it is Thomas Burton who is most informative. In describing an acquisition licensed in 1383, when the crown doubled the valuation of a messuage in York given in the inquisition *ad quod damnum*, he was moved to launch into an exposition of the principles governing assessment. He started as far back as the thirteenth century with the introduction of the inquisition *ad quod damnum* into mortmain procedure. He explained that in time the chancellor came to double the jurors' valuations so that the church scarcely received half the face value of a general licence. He then asserted that a statute was introduced, requiring either payment of a fine of five times the annual value of an acquisition, or deduction of an equal sum from the value of a general licence. For Burton, the harshest blow was struck by Thomas Arundel, prince of the church, but chancellor first and foremost. On his order, the assessment was increased to twenty times the inquisition valuation.[129]

As Desmond, who first drew attention to this account, observed, these claims are not easily verified.[130] There is no trace of the statute requiring fines or valuations against general licences of five times the inquisition valuation. On the other hand, the parliament rolls do reflect considerable public anger from the mid-1370s over the flouting of mortmain legislation. Much of this evasion centred on enfeoffments to use, but particular concern about the abuse of general licences was expressed in 1385.[131] Thus, Arundel, who was chancellor from 1386 to 1389 and again in 1399, took office for the first time at a moment when reassessment of licence procedure might have seemed appropriate.

---

[129] Bond, *Chronica Monasterii de Melsa*, vol. III, pp. 215–19; *Cal. Pat.*, 1381–5, pp. 291–2.

[130] Desmond, *Cîteaux*, 1974, pp. 146–7.

[131] *Rot. Parl.*, vol. II, pp. 356, 368; vol. III, pp. 19, 117, 213, 291, 319.

The major problem in accepting Burton's account is its failure to correspond to evidence from licences granted to bodies other than Meaux. Crowland Abbey certainly had its acquisition worth one mark per annum according to the inquisition *ad quod damnum* assessed at five marks in 1377, but Dunstable Priory, for example, escaped in 1395 with an assessment of only a hundred shillings on property valued at fifty-eight shillings.[132] Any invariable practice of multiplying the valuations provided by inquisitions *ad quod damnum* so that they could be offset against general licences must therefore be doubted. Nor does a more systematic picture emerge if fines are considered. A random sample of twenty-five consecutive inquisitions taken during the regnal year 1391–2, a date when Arundel's changes might be evident if Burton's story is true, yields the following result: of the twenty-five, only one inquisition does not appear to be reflected in a licence. Thirteen of the remaining twenty-four can be matched against licences for which fines were charged. The rest were granted free under general licences. None of these thirteen fines amounted to the twentyfold increase on the inquisition valuation described by Burton. In three instances they represented an exact fivefold levy and in a further four the figure was somewhere between four and six. Only one fine was more than ten times greater than the inquisition valuation and only one less than four times greater. In five out of the thirteen cases, the fine bore an exact arithmetical relationship to the valuation of the inquisition.[133] While offering no support to the claim of twentyfold multiplication of inquisition valuations, this does suggest that fines approximating to five times the inquisition valuation were common. A letter written *c.* 1456 by Henry Fillongley to his uncle Sir John Fastolf about the latter's proposed foundation of a college at Caister (Norfolk) suggests that a fine of five times the value of an alienation remained likely in the mid-fifteenth century: 'Sir, hit ys to gret a good that ys axed of yow for youre lycens; for they ax for every C. marc that ye wold amortyse D. marcz, and woll gefe hit noo better chepe.'[134] By

---

[132] *Cal. Pat.*, 1377–81, p. 36; 1391–6, p. 600.   [133] P.R.O., C143/413/1–25.
[134] Ed. J. Gairdner, *The Paston Letters*, new edn, 3 vols. (London, 1896), vol. 1, 397, no. 290.

the sixteenth century, a ratio of three to one was considered normal, if Sir Robert Brooke's abridgement of the year books of Henry VIII can be accepted.[135] A recent study of fines for chantry foundations would endorse a figure of three to five times the annual value of an alienation in the 1470s, while suggesting that it was on the high side for this type of alienee in the mid-fifteenth century. By the early sixteenth century, however, concern over chantry endowment, possibly tinged with greed, led to growing reluctance to grant licences and prohibitive fines of seven and a half to ten times the annual value of the alienation where this reluctance was overcome.[136]

Some arithmetical basis for assessment of fines cannot be rejected out of hand when it is claimed by more than one contemporary at more than one date, but it was clearly not applied rigidly. Fines were frequently tailored to individual circumstances and made up to the nearest round figure. Negotiations were still in order and a letter from Sir John Fastolf to John Paston late in 1456 shows how they were conducted. Fastolf believed that he had a good case for obtaining a licence cheaply, based on his as yet unrewarded loyal service to the crown. To strengthen his case still further he planned to incorporate a royal chantry into his college, a not uncommon device among hopeful chantry founders. He asked Paston to urge the archbishop of Canterbury and bishop of Winchester to speed the licence forward and also to make acquaintance with someone close to the archbishop and chancellor who would keep the matter before them and report back on their views.[137]

The difficulties attaching to Burton's account can best be explained by the fact that he knew some rough method of calculation was in use and deduced its form from the experience of his own house. Thus, the alienation licensed in 1383, which was valued by the inquisition at forty shillings and against the general licence at four pounds, suggested a doubling of the valuation, while the ten-mark fine asked for half a mark's worth of property in 1392

---

[135] *La Graunde Abridgement*, 3rd edn (London, 1586), p. 31.
[136] Kreider, *English Chantries*, pp. 80–3. The majority of mid-fifteenth-century fines were between one and three times the annual value of the alienation.
[137] Gairdner, *Paston Letters*, vol. I, p. 411, no. 301.

suggested a twentyfold increase on the inquisition valuation. Significantly enough, although he wrote of a fivefold multiplier, he cited no example from Meaux. Perhaps he drew for this information on more representative general knowledge. He may, however, have been correct in claiming that exactions reached an unprecedented level late in Richard II's reign. The year in which Meaux was asked to consider a very high fine was that in which houses were scrambling to regularise previous evasions under threat of forfeiture.[138] The Evesham chronicler also complained of the very high cost of amortisation at that time.[139] Excessively large fines may therefore have been temporary and punitive, not to be repeated even when anxieties about certain sorts of alienation into mortmain were revived in the early sixteenth century. Fillongley's letter suggests that a fivefold assessment was, if anything, considered to be on the high side of normal again by the mid-fifteenth century.

The later fourteenth and fifteenth centuries saw the culmination of the licensing system introduced in 1280. The form of licences and the procedure by which they were granted had been established by the early fourteenth century. Thereafter, the crown sought increasingly to turn them into a source of revenue and, as a concomitant, to modify the effects of the numerous general licences which were customarily free of charge. By the fifteenth century, this had been largely achieved. Thus, what had begun as a feudal rearguard action to protect the crown and magnates from ecclesiastical rapacity had finally developed into a fiscal device with the church as its victim.

---

138 See below, p. 128.
139 Ed. W. D. Macray, *Chronicon Abbatiae de Evesham* (Rolls Series, London, 1863), p. 306. His reference can only apply to the licence taken out in September 1392; *Cal. Pat.*, 1391–6, pp. 171–2.

Chapter 3

ENFORCEMENT OF THE STATUTE

Measures for the enforcement of mortmain legislation were laid down in some detail in the 1279 statute, although, as with so many aspects of the text, these too present problems. The statute appears to provide for two separate and potentially conflicting lines of action. In the event of illegal acquisition, the crown and other immediate lords, as appropriate, were to enter and take seisin within one year. Should the immediate lord not enter within this time, his right devolved on the next lord over him for the following six months. If he too neglected the opportunity, the right passed to each successive overlord up to the king. Thus far the procedure seems straightforward. However, the statute also provided that if all mesne lords had not entered within a year, the crown might enter and take the land into royal keeping pending the enfeoffment of a suitable military tenant. It is difficult to see how the rights of any mesne lord other than the immediate overlord as given in the first procedure could be reconciled with the second, nor is there much evidence as to how this apparent conflict worked out in practice.[1]

Mesne lord intervention was evidently not a dead letter. In the time of Edward I, William Tochet entered and took possession of property in Appleby (Humberside) belonging to Thornholme Priory. His grievance was that his tenants, under cover of a lease, had alienated the holding in perpetuity to the priory without first seeking a licence. As a remedial measure, his entry was abortive. The priory retaliated by ejecting him and he was forced to resort to a writ of novel disseisin. When the justices found that a charter of enfeoffment had indeed been made, it was the escheator who acted, presumably because of the lapse of time. He took the tenement into royal keeping and there it remained

[1] Brand, 'Control of Mortmain Alienation in England', pp. 36–7.

72

until well into the following century.[2] A more successful instance of mesne lord intervention, but with no less ironic a conclusion, occurred in the mid-fourteenth century. Queen Isabella made good her recovery of two shops on Bristol bridge which had been alienated without her consent, only to fall victim in her turn to the crown, because she too then attempted illegal alienation.[3] An appeal to Edward II brings to light an occasion where a lord further up the feudal hierarchy took action. Guy de Beauchamp, earl of Warwick, recovered property in Kibworth Harcourt (Leics.) which two men holding of one of his tenants had granted to the warden and scholars of Merton Hall, Oxford, arguing that they had no right to make such a grant without his licence.[4] Known cases of mesne lord action tend to concern affairs which had been brought to royal attention. Many more instances may have occurred without leaving any trace, particularly as mesne lords were often better placed than royal officials to notice illicit activity.

Far more is known about the crown's efforts to enforce mortmain legislation, although here too records are less full than might be expected. Sometimes infringements of the law were detected by itinerant justices who were instructed to seek them out under the *capitula itineris* of their eyres, but the officials within whose province the enforcement usually fell were the escheators.[5] They or their deputies, the sub-escheators, were expected to seek out and confiscate all acquisitions made without licence inside their jurisdiction. They acted either on a royal writ or more commonly on their own initiative when they discovered a breach of the law for themselves. As local agents, they were far more likely to learn of illicit dealings than the remote court and were in a better position to assess the likely truth of tale-bearing and accusation.

Once property had been seized, the escheator was supposed to hold an inquisition to find out what it was worth and then to collect this sum annually until he was ordered to surrender the holding into other hands.[6] This procedure applied not only to

2 *Cal. Close*, 1323–7, p. 110.   3 *Cal. Pat.*, 1358–61, p. 446.
4 *Cal. Close*, 1323–7, pp. 484–5.   5 E.g. P.R.O., C143/21/19.
6 Ed. J. F. Willard, W. A. Morris, W. H. Dunham, J. R. Strayer, *The English Government at Work 1327–36*, 3 vols. (Cambridge, Mass., 1940–50), vol. II, pp. 120–1.

unlicensed alienations into mortmain but also to those made by tenants-in-chief to other laymen. The pursuit of these two offences absorbed a great part of the escheator's time, although the resulting revenue was disproportionately small. E. R. Stevenson shows that in 1327, the escheator south of the Trent was administering 293 items of old escheats, of which over half (154) concerned unlicensed alienations of either type. The revenue from this source, however, was only £20 17s 2½d out of a total of £294 8s 1¼d. Wardships, of which there were seventy-five, and the five vacancies in religious houses under royal patronage were more lucrative.[7]

Former holders of property which had been impounded were faced with several alternatives. The crown was sometimes willing to allow them to recover their holdings pending judgement. In 1281, the manor of Maple Derham (Hants.) was restored to St Swithun's, Winchester, so that the prior might 'till and sow the land until the next parliament, in order that there may then be done what the king shall cause to be ordained by his council'.[8] Similar arrangements were made ten years later for both Thornton Abbey and Alvingham Priory, although, as was customary, each had to provide security for the revenue which would fall to the crown if the confiscation was upheld.[9] More often, especially as time went on, the property remained in the king's hands, administered either directly by his officials or through a farmer. In 1313, for example, Roger de Gretford, a yeoman of the chamber, was granted the keeping of another confiscated accession of St Swithun's, Winchester, during the king's pleasure.[10] Permanent restitution to the previous holders depended upon their proving that the confiscation had been unjustified or admitting to illegal acquisition and persuading the crown to grant a pardon and the return of the holding.

The escheators' powers were a godsend to those with grievances against churchmen. One particular instance concerns a mid-fifteenth-century dispute over jurisdiction between the cathedral

[7] *Ibid.*, vol. II, p. 145.
[8] *Cal. Close*, 1279–88, p. 78.
[9] P.R.O., C143/16/8; C/143/16/12; C/143/16/15.
[10] *Cal. Fine*, 1307–19, p. 169. Many examples of renders from such farms can be found in the escheators' accounts. P.R.O., E136, passim.

74

authorities and the mayor and escheator of Norwich which led
to false accusations that the prior and convent had made a number
of illicit acquisitions. Exercising his disputed powers, the escheator
confiscated the holdings until, in 1444, the cathedral won back
both tenements and jurisdiction.[11] A more common inducement
to unjust accusation was defeat in a land dispute. This is illustrated
by the experience of Crowland Abbey over its manor of Dowdyke
with Sutterton (Lincs.). Sometime early in the thirteenth century,
the monks had granted a mortgage to a local landlord, Ketelbern
of Keal. When he had proved unable to repay their loan, they
foreclosed on a carucate of land in Sutterton, an action hotly but
unsuccessfully contested by both Ketelbern and his successors. It
was a continuation of this dispute which led to problems in the
early fourteenth century. The first occasion perhaps arose from
genuine confusion, since it was the belated recognition by Ralph
of Keal that he had no further right in the property which led
the escheator to suspect an infringement of the 1279 statute.
He threatened to take the manor of Dowdyke and advowson of
Sutterton into royal keeping, until in 1315 the monks secured a
writ ordering their peaceful possession after an inquisition had
shown that their tenure long antedated 1279. The writ was
invoked again in 1321 because the escheator still threatened
sequestration on the same grounds. Actual confiscation of 5s 8d
rent, held of the Keal family, on the pretext that it had been
relaxed to the abbey by the earl of Richmond without a licence
after the statute, seems to have rested on nothing more than
malicious accusation.[12] There is little doubt that the monks were
in the right, as an inquisition held in 1328 recognised. Holdings
in Dowdyke and Sutterton were amongst their most ancient
possessions: a Dowdyke manor features in Domesday Book and
the Sutterton advowson can be found in twelfth-century deeds.[13]
That such venerable tenure could be imperilled by ill will argues

---

[11] *Cal. Pat.*, 1441–6, pp. 232–3.
[12] W.P.C., f124v et seq., P.R.O., E136/1/30, m5; *Cal. Inq. Misc.*, vol. II,
p. 42, no. 176; p. 258, no. 1036; *Cal. Close*, 1313–18, p. 143; 1318–23,
p. 306; 1327–30, p. 435. Restoration of the rent was ordered in 1329.
[13] Ed. C. W. Foster, T. Longley, *The Lincolnshire Domesday and the Lindsey
Survey* (Lincoln Rec. Soc., 19, 1924, repr. 1976), p. 60, no. 5; W.P.C., ff50–1,
123; *Cal. Inq. Misc.*, vol. II, p. 258, no. 1036.

that the church ran a considerable risk of confiscation based on false information.

Reaching the truth on these occasions was a difficult task for royal officials. The inquisitions on which they often had to rely for information were not well equipped to give definitive rulings in cases fraught with claim and counter-claim over several generations. Even where there was no conflict of interest, jurors could not necessarily possess the precise knowledge of tenures needed to obviate injustice. Certainly they were unlikely to have a sufficiently exact sense of chronology to state categorically whether or not later-thirteenth-century acquisitions had occurred before 1279. If they were lucky some notable event could help to pinpoint the alienation in their minds. An inquisition ordered in 1290 knew that an alienation to Thornton-on-Humber had taken place twenty-two years earlier because the grantor 'was taken in the war' and the property came into the hands of the abbey immediately after the war.[14] More often there was nothing special on which the jurors could focus. Some measure of the chronological problems can be gained from confusion even as to the date of the statute. The author of the Waverley Annals, writing almost contemporaneously, entered it under 1280.[15] Vagueness of this sort was compounded by the prevalence of undated charters in the later thirteenth century. Events at Alvingham Priory show just how muddled the situation might become. The statute caught the canons in the process of acquiring the advowson of Yarburgh and other property in Yarburgh, Alvingham itself and Grainthorpe (Lincs.). Confusion as to the exact date of transfer emerged at inquisitions in 1289–90, 1291 and 1309. The escheator was almost certainly right in suspecting that some unlicensed alienations to the priory had taken place, but the advowson of Yarburgh, queried in 1309, had been granted as early as 1275. A final compromise was achieved in 1327, when most of the disputed grants were confirmed in return for a twenty-shilling fine.[16] Even with less complex transactions, mistakes were

[14] *Cal. Inq. Misc.*, vol. I, p. 426, no. 1504.
[15] Luard, *Annales Monastici*, vol. II, pp. 392–3.
[16] Oxf., Bodl., Laud Misc. 642, ff114v (parchment sewn in), 118v, 119v–20, 121–v; P.R.O., C143/16/12; *Cal. Close*, 1307–13, p. 113; *Cal. Pat.*, 1327–30, p. 167.

often made. In 1321, for example, the hospital of St John the Baptist at Lynn recovered an adjacent plot of land, with houses on it, which had been lawfully acquired five years before the statute, and in the following year the chaplain of the Spagard chantry in St Helen's, Worcester, secured the return of a rent on the same grounds. In both cases, the property had been confiscated because the escheator believed that the statute had been contravened.[17]

Quite apart from mistakes arising from misinformation or ignorance, there was a risk of victimisation from corrupt officials. The frequent modifications in the escheator's office between its establishment under Henry III and its final form in the mid-fourteenth century is some index of the general dissatisfaction with the way in which the duties were carried out. By 1283 there were two escheators, one operating on either side of the River Trent. These in turn were replaced by eight escheators in 1322. In the following decades, experiment and political exigency led to the two arrangements working in rotation: Edward III at first reverted to two escheatries but had returned to eight by 1332, two were again in operation in 1335, but parliament forced him back to eight in 1340. Finally, in 1341, the escheatries were reorganised to coincide with the shrievalties, although the offices were not necessarily combined. This became a permanent solution. Agitation in the parliaments of the fourteenth and fifteenth centuries for the escheators to be appointed annually, and to be substantial landowners in the area where they worked, reflected fear of the havoc which might be wrought by a career official free of local commitments and out to line his pocket, and the converse desire for the appointment of a local man sensitive to pressure from his neighbours. The choice of sub-escheators might be more crucial than that of the escheators themselves in this respect. Exposure of illicit dealings must often have depended on sub-escheators' local knowledge. Hence it is of some interest to learn that they too were usually men of some standing in the neighbourhood. The only effective protection which the church had against the escheators' misuse of their power was their

17 *Cal. Close*, 1318–23, pp. 386, 613–14.

personal responsibility in the event of a proven error.[18] This must have been small comfort, however, if property was time and again confiscated on inadequate grounds.

Whether the frequency of unjustified confiscation, threatened or actual, amounted to harassment of the church must be considered. If Crowland Abbey was typical, there could be a case for believing that such harassment did exist and for thinking that *De viris religiosis* was unintentionally punitive as well as restrictive. Apart from the monks' unfortunate experience at Dowdyke with Sutterton, they suffered confiscations of their property elsewhere. In 1299, the abbey had obtained a licence to receive three rods of land forming the glebe and the advowson of Wigtoft church (Lincs.) from Richard son of Peter de Hoddil. In spite of this, an inquisition accused the monks of illegal acquisition and the three rods were in the escheator's hands well before the end of Edward II's reign. There they remained until at least July 1329.[19] Further entries on the close rolls and in the escheators' accounts show that a messuage and bovate of land in Kirkby-la-Thorpe (Lincs.) had been taken into royal hands following an inquisition which had been given incorrect information. The tenement had been surrendered by a tenant holding either at will or on a short-term lease and not in perpetuity. Thus, on Edward III's accession, Crowland was in the unfortunate position of having three separate properties in the escheator's hands, all of which had been mistakenly confiscated.[20] This was not the abbey's last brush with the escheators, although it was the worst. A final ill-based confiscation, in Oakington (Cambs.), was restored to the monks in the early 1360s after a second inquisition had upheld their claim that it had escheated to the abbey when its tenant died without heirs.[21] On an intervening

[18] Willard, Morris, Dunham, Strayer, *English Government at Work*, vol. II, pp. 115–20, 128.

[19] *Cal. Pat.*, 1292–1301, p. 481; *Cal. Close*, 1327–30, pp. 173–4, 480–1; W.P.C., ff135v–7; P.R.O., E136/1/30, m28. Wigtoft first appears in the escheator's account for 1322–3, but since the immediately preceding accounts are missing, it is impossible to tell exactly when it was seized.

[20] *Cal. Close*, 1327–30, p. 482; *Cal. Inq. Misc.*, vol. II, p. 251, no. 1012; P.R.O., E136/1/38; E136/2/1, mm23, 46.

[21] Probably 1361. *Cal. Close*, 1360–4, pp. 218–19.

occasion, they had also managed to convince the authorities that confiscation should not have taken place, but in this instance it would be hard to argue injustice. In 1333, the escheator seized a messuage and five or six acres of arable in Langtoft (Lincs.) on the grounds that the abbot had acquired them without licence from Isabella the widow of Robert Waryn. An inquisition held the following year declared this incorrect; the property had been acquired by Richard Benewyk and the abbot 'never had any state in those tenements'. Considerable doubt must attach to this verdict. Deeds conveying the tenement directly from Isabella and her family to the abbey are recorded in the abbey cartulary, and Richard was clearly acting as nominee.[22] Possibly recent experience had taught the monks to pack a jury. Similar practices may also have secured the recovery of an almost identical holding in Holbeach (Lincs.) which, according to the escheator, had been given to the abbey by the parents of one of its inmates and was accordingly confiscated in 1420. As it appears only briefly in the escheator's accounts, there is nothing to show its fate.[23]

Some religious houses showed great unease about the severity with which the mortmain laws might be enforced. In 1314, Eynsham Abbey made a particularly telling move in obtaining a licence to retain two virgates of land and the advowson of Wheatfield church (Oxon.), which had been acquired long before the statute. The monks explicitly stated that this was 'for greater security' in view of the lapse of time and general ignorance about the origins of the holding. It is also significant that they rated the insurance worth a ten-pound fine.[24] Mistrustful caution was again the keynote in 1349 when the abbot and convent of Winchcombe sought a new licence enabling them to keep their appropriated church at Enstone (Oxon.). The inquisition *ad quod damnum* on which their earlier licence of 1309 had been based had mentioned that the advowson and manor of Enstone were held directly of the crown, but this fact had not been included

---

[22] P.R.O., E136/2/43 dorse; W.P.C., ff152v–3; *Cal. Close*, 1333–7, p. 231; *Cal. Inq. Misc.*, vol. II, p. 348, no. 1424. There are minor discrepancies over names, but there can be little question that the same tenement is involved in each case.

[23] P.R.O., E136/119/2, m5.

[24] *Cal. Pat.*, 1313–17, p. 92.

in the licence itself. The monks feared that this oversight might 'by the subtlety of some' form the grounds for a prosecution. Although the king recognised that the blame for the omission probably lay with a careless chancery clerk, a hundred-shilling fine was still necessary to secure its rectification. To be doubly sure, in 1350, the abbey expended a further twenty pounds on a royal confirmation.[25]

Experience justified such wariness. In 1316, Ellerton Priory was obliged to pay a forty-shilling fine in pardon for acquisitions under a licence of 1304 because the royal 'charter then granted to them was conceived in an insufficient form'. This was in addition to the fine charged on the original, inadequate licence.[26] There was also the unusual case of St Faith's, Horsham, which in 1326 secured the return of ten acres of marsh and a fishery belonging to Horsham mill. At the time when the monks had made a legitimate acquisition under licence, it had been an exceptionally parched season and the marsh had dried out sufficiently to be used as meadow. As a consequence, no mention had been made of marsh or fisheries in the licence and the escheator had later seized them. Recovery was only made on payment of a twenty-shilling fine.[27] St Mary's Abbey, Dublin, was even more ruthlessly treated in 1329. Its right was challenged to property in Balycur belonging to its own fee, which the abbey claimed that it had recovered in the royal court in 1290–1 'in good faith and not in fraud of the statute of mortmain, before the statute was published in Ireland'. The harshness of the crown's attitude lay not so much in the original confiscation as in its direction to the chancellor of Ireland that even if he found the abbey's contention to be true, which it may have been, he was only to issue a pardon in return for 'a reasonable fine'.[28] Even where all due care had been taken to observe the letter of the law and where mistakes had been made inadvertently by royal officials, responsibility still rested with the church. The chances of an ecclesiastical body finding itself in the position of paying to protect property

[25] *Ibid.*, 1307–13, p. 152; 1348–50, pp. 264, 512.
[26] *Ibid.*, 1301–7, p. 302; 1313–17, p. 540.
[27] *Ibid.*, 1324–7, p. 295.
[28] *Cal. Close*, 1327–30, p. 444; see above, p. 29, n. 1.

the right to which should never have been called into question were not perhaps great, but they were real.

Some of the strongest evidence that the church was suffering hardship as a result of mortmain legislation appeared in 1344. In that year, a royal ordinance required that:

If prelates, clerks beneficed or religious people which have purchased lands, and the same have put to mortmain, be impeached upon the same before our Justices, and they shew our charter of liberties, and process thereupon made by an Inquest of *ad quod damnum*, or of our Grace, or by fine, they shall be freely let in peace, without being further impeached for the same purchase. And in case they cannot sufficiently shew, that they have entered by due process after licence to them granted in general or in special, that they shall be well received to make a convenient fine for the same.[29]

This concession followed the form of a petition presented by the clergy in parliament and, significantly, coincided with commissions to enquire into illicit alienations or acquisitions above the value of licences. Like the laity, who similarly won concessions, the clergy had seized the opportunity to persuade the crown to moderate its pursuit of illegalities in return for cooperation over taxation.[30] The parallel treatment of clergy and laity suggests that the church had not been singled out for special attention. However, the fact that it was not alone in its vicissitudes did not make them any the less burdensome.

Much of the foregoing argument has been founded upon individual examples. Yet, although particular houses had unfortunate experiences, sometimes more than once, government records do not suggest widespread abuse. There are usually only a handful of such cases recorded on the patent and close rolls in any one year. Three was the highest annual total under Edward I, while the higher figure for Edward II's reign (a peak of ten in 1321) reflects more intensive pursuit of illegal alienations and should be set against more frequent confiscation on adequate grounds.[31] The patent and close rolls do not tell the whole story,

---

[29] *Statutes of the Realm*, vol. I, pp. 302–3.

[30] *Ibid.*, pp. 300–3; *Rot. Parl.*, vol. II, pp. 151–2; *Cal. Pat.*, 1343–5, pp. 97, 281–2, 399.

[31] See below, p. 89.

however. Barlings Abbey's recovery of one bovate of land and seven acres of meadow in South Carlton (Lincs.) in 1316, as shown in the abbey cartulary, is not recorded on the close rolls, although the inquisition which had established the correctness of its behaviour has survived. The escheator had seized the property because he believed it had been acquired without a licence, whereas in fact it was a dower holding which had reverted to the abbey under a licence of 1291.[32] A number of other inquisitions survive, a high proportion bearing witness to ecclesiastical virtue. Of the four held under writs dated 1314, for example, all showed that the acquisitions in question had taken place before the publication of the statute.[33] Unless the escheators' accounts survive, it is not always clear whether officials had seized the disputed holdings or had merely threatened to do so. If, as in the case of the earlier challenge to Crowland's Dowdyke and Sutterton property, no confiscation had occurred, then it is arguable that royal enforcement of mortmain legislation caused little hardship. By good fortune, at Kirkby-la-Thorpe, the abbey was subject to confiscation after the harvest, leaving nothing for the escheator to collect in that year.[34] So there too hardship was diminished. Moreover, in cases where wrongful seizure did result in loss, the escheator was ordered to restore not only the holding but also the issues from it while it had been in his keeping. Superficially just, these arrangements nevertheless imposed otherwise unnecessary expense on churchmen. The costs of obtaining an inquisition as required and paying the customary *douceurs* to all concerned before innocence could be proved, as well as the inconvenience arising from confiscation should it occur, were a gratuitous extra burden. The impression remains that the church had some cause for concern about the enforcement of mortmain legislation. There were major administrative difficulties which, with the utmost goodwill on the part of officialdom, could lead to inequitable treatment. Even if injured innocence spoke in notably strident tones, the evident fear of houses like Eynsham, coupled with the

---

[32] B. L., Cott. Faust. B i, ff162v–4; *Cal. Pat.*, 1281–92, p. 429; *Cal. Inq. Misc.*, vol. II, p. 55, no. 227.
[33] *Cal. Inq. Misc.*, vol. II, pp. 40, 46–8, nos. 169, 193, 201, 204.
[34] P.R.O., E136/1/36.

refusal of the crown to offer a sympathetic hearing where its servants had been incompetent, tip the balance in favour of oppression, albeit of a limited nature.

As well as providing for those who were prosecuted without cause, the ordinance of 1344 catered for others who were guilty of unlicensed acquisition. Leniency was ordered, allowing them to regularise their position by means of a fine. In practice, houses detected in illicit acquisition were often accommodated in this way. The treatment of Selby Abbey in the early fourteenth century serves to illustrate the point. In August 1300, the sheriff of Lincoln was ordered to seize extensive holdings in Amcotts and Eastoft (Humberside) which had been obtained contrary to the Statute of Mortmain.[35] The correct procedure for the abbey in such circumstances was to petition the crown for a pardon and restitution. That this was not always a formality can be seen from the fact that it was not until November 1304 that the abbey was allowed to fine for a pardon for these and sundry other illegal acquisitions.[36] Even after a delay, a happy outcome could not be guaranteed. Sometimes confiscated holdings were lost for good. In 1290, the prior of 'Westmerl' (West Mersea?) met with refusal 'because he had entered without a licence in contempt of the king'.[37]

The Lincolnshire escheators' accounts for Edward II's reign show several holdings seized because their acquisition had contravened the statute.[38] None was large, but few were recovered speedily if at all. A toft in Torksey (Lincs.) yielding five shillings per annum, forfeited by the prioress of Fosse and in the king's hand before the end of Edward I's reign, was still rendering its annual farm to the escheator under Henry V although it ceased to do so by the following reign.[39] Four more holdings taken into royal keeping at this period still featured in the account of 1457–8,

---

[35] *Cal. Fine*, 1272–1307, p. 432.
[36] *Cal. Pat.*, 1301–7, p. 302.
[37] *Rot. Parl.*, vol. 1, p. 57. no. 147.
[38] For most of the reign these accounts form part of the accounts rendered by the escheator south of the Trent. From November 1323 separate accounts were rendered by the escheator for Lincolnshire, Northamptonshire and Rutland.
[39] P.R.O., E136/1/21, m3; E136/118/3, m1, E136/119/1.

the last to survive for the medieval period.[40] Not all shared this
extreme fate, but many confiscations were lost for a generation
or more. A toft and one acre of arable in Belvoir (Leics.) and
Woolsthorpe (Lincs.) acquired by the prior of Belvoir and in
royal keeping in 1304–5 remained there until 1324. Eight acres
of arable in Tallington (Lincs.) belonging to the same house and
confiscated between 1315 and 1322 were still in royal hands in
1335, although they had not in fact been acquired illegally.[41]
Another tenement in Belvoir was almost certainly lost for a longer
period than appears from its isolated entry in the account for
1322–3.[42] Confiscations made in succeeding reigns received
equally varied treatment, some remaining in royal hands over a
long period and others appearing only fleetingly in the accounts.
The number of long-term confiscations never became very large,
however. As late as the 1450s only ten properties had been in
royal custody for more than half a century, a surprisingly modest
total for a county the size of Lincolnshire.[43]

In certain cases confiscations did not feature in the escheators'
accounts, and recovery was impossible because the crown had
already granted the holdings to other tenants. This happened to
Thornholme Priory in 1308, when illegally acquired holdings in
Appleby (Humberside) were granted to Philip de Redmar on a
twenty-year lease. Deprived of legitimate means of recovery and
doubtless incensed by the return of the property to the family
from whom it had once been bought, the canons took matters
into their own hands. They assaulted de Redmar and his servants
while they were digging peat at Appleby, overturned their wagons

[40] Four acres of arable in Blyborough (Lincs.) acquired by the prior of
Durham; one acre of arable in Firsby (Lincs.) acquired by the abbot of
Bardney; one rod of arable in Welton-le-Marsh (Lincs.) acquired by the
abbot of Thornton; one acre of arable in Irby (Irby-in-the-Marsh, Lincs., or
Irby-upon-Humber, Humberside) acquired by the local rector. P.R.O.,
E136/1/28, m8; E136/1/30, mm3–4; E136/119/8, m1.

[41] P.R.O., E136/1/21; E136/1/28; E136/1/30–31; E136/2/45; *Cal. Inq. Misc.*,
vol. II, pp. 357–8, no. 1468.

[42] P.R.O., E136/1/30, m3.

[43] They were in Blyborough, Firsby, Welton-le-Marsh, Irby, Wyton (Humberside), Bonby (Humberside), Little Carlton (Lincs.), Heydour (Lincs.),
Cadney (Humberside) and Swineshead (Lincs.). Poor legibility makes it
necessary to use earlier rolls to check their presence. P.R.O., E136/117/8;
E136/117/14 et seq.; E136/119/7–8.

and stole two horses. The prior further asserted his claims by making dykes and planting hedges on de Redmar's lands.[44] A more unfortunate instance, because confiscation had been misconceived, occurred in Leicestershire. The escheator took possession of a messuage and eight bovates of land in Melton Mowbray which he believed to be a post-1279 acquisition of Lewes Priory. The king then granted the tenements for life to Eleanor, the wife of Hugh le Despenser the younger, on 29 May 1325. Once more churchmen were provoked into taking the law into their own hands. When the Despenser forfeiture took place, the priory in the confusion of the moment entered its former holdings on its own initiative and resumed possession.[45]

In general, the crown does not appear to have courted this type of behaviour by granting confiscations to third parties until later in the fourteenth century, at which point a change in practice appears to have taken place. In 1366, for example, holdings at Tannington and Wilby (Suffolk) forfeited by the abbey of West Dereham were granted for life to a royal servant.[46] The citation of the 1344 ordinance as a reason for giving Maxstoke Priory a pardon in 1360 may also signify a more intransigent royal attitude, since it implies reluctant concession rather than normal procedure.[47] By this latter date, the crown had grown accustomed to rewarding its servants with farms from the forfeited property of the alien priories.[48] A further extension of the practice to ecclesiastical holdings confiscated for other reasons is not difficult to credit.

Some overall ideas about crown policy towards confiscations at this date can be obtained from the subsequent history of fifty forfeitures of London property after new regulations concerning amortisation within the city were introduced in 1364. About twenty were granted to other ecclesiastical bodies, chiefly St Mary Graces. Fifteen were restored, usually after a fine. The rest either

[44] *Cal. Fine*, 1272–1307, pp. 295–6; 1307–19, p. 12; *Cal. Pat.*, 1307–13, pp. 315–16.
[45] *Cal. Close*, 1327–30, pp. 319–20.
[46] *Cal. Pat.*, 1364–7, p. 236.
[47] *Ibid.*, 1358–61, pp. 363–4.
[48] M. M. Morgan, 'The Suppression of the Alien Priories', *History*, 26, 1941, pp. 205–6.

remained in royal hands or were granted to laymen, mostly for a life term only. This distribution is of some significance. Although the original holders of the property were often unsuccessful in securing its return, the church as a whole was not markedly the loser. The king had a special interest in St Mary Graces, a Cistercian house of his own foundation. He therefore took every opportunity to augment its endowment from confiscations. The new house thus prospered at the expense of older-established transgressors. Moreover, even the holdings granted to laymen often found their way back to the church. A grant of 1364 to John de Romeseye, a royal servant, later reverted to the king, who granted it to St Mary Graces (1366); while in 1367, property confiscated from Tortington Priory was given to Richard earl of Arundel, who immediately secured a licence to restore it to its former holders, although this did not actually take place until later in the century.[49] One cannot perhaps draw too many conclusions from this evidence since the circumstances surrounding the confiscations were abnormal. There was considerable dispute as to whether or not the Londoners were wrong in making their alienations, which may have made the crown reluctant to deprive the church entirely of their grants. Furthermore, Edward III was under some pressure to make good the promised endowment of St Mary Graces. Unequivocal infringements of the law might expect less sympathetic treatment. With this in mind, the most telling aspect of the London experience is the low success rate in recovering forfeitures shown by their original tenants. If less than half of the London alienations found their way back to their former ecclesiastical holders, how much more difficult might it have been for an offender who could plead nothing in mitigation.

Although ecclesiastics might reasonably hope that the discovery of illicit dealings would not mean permanent forfeiture, they had to contend with a real chance that the loss would not be made good. Furthermore, even if recovery were made, it might be at the cost of a fine considerably higher than that which would have been incurred by more orthodox procedures. Exactly how much higher is difficult to know. A fixed scale of charges is no

49 Chew, *E.H.R.*, 1945, pp. 10–12.

more in evidence for fines paid for pardons than for those for licences to alienate in the approved manner. Few were as swinge-ing as the two-hundred-pound fine exacted from the abbot of Cirencester in 1313 for illicit acquisitions from fifty-seven dif-ferent grantors or the five hundred marks demanded from the prior and convent of Ely to atone for their attempted appropriation of Wisbech and Foxton churches (Cambs.) in 1298. Moreover, the 1291 Taxation of Pope Nicholas valued the two churches at fifty-eight marks, so even allowing for some under-assessment, especially in the rich fen region, the fine was steep if not exces-sive.[50] Other evidence suggests a relatively mild fining policy on the part of the crown. Just over a third of recorded fines for pardons granted by the first two Edwards exceeded the sum of ten marks. The majority therefore were of quite a modest nature, although the illicit gains may have been equally modest. This picture perhaps appears too rosy since details of many fines are not supplied,[51] nor were there many which fell into the half-mark or charitable category so frequently found in licences to acquire in the approved manner. Where they do occur, as with licences, they tend to concern mendicants. In 1315, for example, the friars preachers of Athy in Ireland were pardoned their unlicensed expansion in return for five hundred masses and were also excused the sealing fee.[52] Sometimes, as in the 1440s under Henry VI, the crown was mercifully inclined, but this could not be relied upon. Churchmen were obviously in a weaker position as sup-pliants for a pardon than as petitioners for a licence. They had more capital invested in a confiscated holding and more to lose through failure to proceed.

Pursuit of unlicensed alienations shows a chronology as dis-tinctive as the grant of licences.[53] Indeed in some ways they were closely interwoven, since both were governed by the church's eagerness to acquire. Royal activity can be gauged chiefly from

[50] *Cal. Pat.*, 1292–1301, p. 365; 1313–17, pp. 7–8; *Taxatio Ecclesiastica* (Rec. Comm., 1802), pp. 64, 265; Graham, *English Ecclesiastical Studies*, pp. 285–8, 295.

[51] Notably for the last seven years of Edward I's reign and the first two of his son's.

[52] *Cal. Pat.*, 1313–17, p. 303.

[53] See below, pp. 155–6.

the escheators' accounts and chancery records, although neither of these sources is straightforward to use. Changes in the geographical scope of the escheators' office and the random survival of their accounts mean that systematic analysis on the lines undertaken by Stevenson for the account roll of William Trussel, escheator south of the Trent for the first year of Edward III's reign, is not practicable on a country-wide basis over a long period of time.[54] Poor legibility and repetitiousness also make any less ambitious analysis confined to the accounts for a single county, such as that undertaken for this study, somewhat unrewarding. Inquisitions into illicit alienations are another potential source of information, but they too have not always survived. Nor are the patent rolls a reliable index of governmental energy, in spite of their excellent run. Pardons were affected by changes in royal policy towards restitution; any drop in the number recorded on the patent rolls is open to two different interpretations. It could signify laxity on the part of the crown towards illegal activity, or it could imply the opposite: a more intensive policy of detection and greater reluctance to return forfeitures to their original holders in exchange for a fine.

From 1313, if not earlier, an article concerning the searching out of illicit alienations into mortmain was included in the *capitula itineris* for eyres.[55] An interesting sidelight on the seriousness with which churchmen took enquiries by the justices and escheators is thrown by the chapter accounts of Lincoln Cathedral. Those ending in September 1313 record a gift of one hundred shillings to John Abel, the escheator, and a mark to his chief clerk 'on the occasion of his visit to Lincoln to enquire into mortmain holdings and other matters touching his office'. Lesser minions, such as squires, grooms and other clerks, also received subventions, each according to status. Similar payments on a smaller scale were made to Matthew Broun the sub-escheator and his aides. In all, £8 14s 4d was expended, and effectively. Although property confirmed to the dean and chapter in 1315 was in unlicensed

---

[54] P.R.O., E136/2/1; Willard, Morris, Dunham, Strayer, *English Government at Work*, vol. II, pp. 144–9.

[55] H. M. Cam, *Studies in the Hundred Rolls* (Oxford Studies in Social and Legal History, 6, 1921), pp. 65–6.

possession before 1313, no confiscation appears in Abel's account for 1312–13. A less liberal disbursement may explain why the only recorded Lincoln confiscation by John Abel concerned a plot in the suburb taken from the abbot of Vaudey in October 1314.[56]

Pardons recorded on the patent rolls, with all their ambiguities, probably reflect to some extent attempts to enforce the law, particularly in the earlier fourteenth century. Table 3 suggests that activity reached a peak in the early 1320s. This picture may be distorted somewhat by the constitutional wrangle over amortisation within the city of London, but a good deal of evidence can be adduced in its support. The Lincolnshire escheators' accounts, selected because of the size of the county and density of its religious settlement, show a flurry of confiscation in the decade after 1314. Unfortunately, missing accounts make it impossible to tell how closely this coincided with the more numerous pardons granted nationally between 1314 and 1316 and again between 1320 and 1321.[57] The high proportion of ill-based confiscations throughout the country at this time also argues for more rigorous enforcement of the law. So too does the panic reaction evident at this date of churchmen fearing persecution over legitimate accessions and the pursuit of alienations of land held in chief from as far back as the reign of Henry III.

This extreme vigilance on the part of royal officials probably owed something to the financial needs of Edward II. Fierce enforcement of the law yielded revenue as welcome in the acute financial crisis of 1321 as in the ensuing years of his miserly hoarding.[58] The illicit inclinations of churchmen must also have played their part, however. The profile of pardons at this time correlates quite closely with that of licences for acquisition in the approved manner, implying that land hunger was common to both.[59]

---

[56] Lincs. Archives Off., Bj/2/4, f86; *Cal. Pat.*, 1313–17, pp. 361–2; Major, *Registrum Antiquissimum*, vol. VII, pp. 135–9; vol. IX, pp. 177–9; vol. X, p. 124; P.R.O., E136/1/25; E136/1/28, m7.

[57] P.R.O., E136/1/20–5; E136/1/28; E136/1/30–1; E136/1/36; E136/1/38.

[58] N. Fryde, *The Tyranny and Fall of Edward II* (Cambridge, 1979), p. 88 et seq.

[59] See below, Table 3; and Graph 6, p. 155.

Table 3. *Pardons and confirmations of illegal acquisitions taken from the patent rolls 1279–1400*

1279	—	1310	6	1341	2	1372	— (half year)
1280	—	1311	5	1342	4	1373	5
1281	5	1312	4	1343	3	1374	4
1282	1	1313	8	1344	6	1375	2
1283	—	1314	20	1345	8	1376	3
1284	3	1315	14	1346	4	1377	1
1285	5	1316	16	1347	8	1378	1
1286	3	1317	9	1348	7	1379	1
1287	—	1318	9	1349	3	1380	1
1288	—	1319	9	1350	4	1381	—
1289	1	1320	13	1351	4	1382	3
1290	3	1321	28	1352	6	1383	1
1291	5	1322	6	1353	3	1384	3
1292	14	1323	8	1354	3	1385	5
1293	4	1324	7	1355	6	1386	5
1294	5	1325	9	1356	2	1387	3
1295	3	1326	10	1357	1	1388	1
1296	1	1327	8	1358	1	1389	2
1297	3	1328	12	1359	—	1390	1
1298	3	1329	21	1360	3	1391	1
1299	2	1330	12	1361	4	1392	5
1300	7	1331	17	1362	—	1393	4
1301	6	1332	12	1363	2	1394	7
1302	3	1333	3	1364	2	1395	3
1303	9	1334	4	1365	—	1396	3
1304	6	1335	8	1366	2	1397	4
1305	16	1336	6	1367	9	1398	—
1306	11	1337	5	1368	2	1399	3
1307	8	1338	6	1369	4	1400	—
1308	—	1339	4	1370	1		
1309	7	1340	3	1371	4		

Pardons dwindled to almost nothing after 1400.

The extent to which changing standards of enforcement led to the declining incidence of pardons on the patent rolls in the second half of the fourteenth century is even more difficult to assess. If Lincolnshire was typical of the country at large, Edward III's reign witnessed a slackening of official activity. Few items were added to the annual returns from old escheats until the latter part of the reign, and the two confiscations made between 1335 and 1345 suggest concern over alienation of land held in chief rather than amortisation. A toft in Whitton (Humberside), lost by Welbeck Abbey in 1343 and still in royal keeping in the last medieval account for Lincolnshire, belonged to royal fee.[60] So too did a messuage and thirteen acres of arable in Swaton (Lincs.) which appeared in the accounts for the first time in the 1340s and disappeared in the 1360s; Castle Acre Priory had acquired the tenement from the abbey of 'Exagnio', which had in turn acquired it from Henry de Lacy, tenant-in-chief of the crown.[61]

The decline in confiscations at this time may be attributable to difficulties encountered by the escheators in the pursuit of miscreants. From the 1340s the crown periodically directed special commissions to enquire into unlicensed alienations into mortmain or alienations which exceeded the value set in licences which had been obtained. Escheators also continued to seek out offenders *ex officio*.[62] Both argue a sustained interest in evasion of the statute. It is likely, however, that action was increasingly frustrated by the growing exploitation by the church of a device designed to circumvent the law. Instead of acquiring property themselves, churchmen arranged for the enfeoffment of their nominees. Since such feoffees thus became the legal owners, the church had no estate in the property although the income from it passed into ecclesiastical hands by private agreement. Technically no alienation into mortmain had taken place, so no licence was required. Providing that care was taken at intervals to replace elderly or deceased feoffees, these enfeoffments to use could be maintained indefinitely.

Escheators appreciated that arrangements such as those made by Elsham Priory in enfeoffing William Brikell and others in this way to the use of the prior, so that the feoffees took no profit to their own use, were done 'by craft' in order 'to defraud the king'. In raising the question of Elsham's dealings, the escheators were in the 1360s explicitly claiming such enfeoffments to be in

[60] P.R.O., E136/10/2, m6; E136/10/3; E136/119/8, m1.
[61] P.R.O., E136/10/1a–1b; E136/11/6. The tenement does not feature in the next legible account; E136/11/8.
[62] E.g. *Cal. Pat.*, 1343–5, pp. 97, 281–2, 399, 512; *Cal. Close*, 1360–4, p. 381; *Cal. Inq. Misc.*, vol. III, p. 191.

breach of the statute, but it is unlikely that this was established.[63]
Not many obviously collusive transactions feature among their
confiscations and where they are found the outcome was not
usually encouraging to officialdom. Elsham licensed the queried
holdings in 1365, but otherwise seems to have escaped penalty.[64]
An inquisition had vindicated Crowland Abbey in similar circumstances in 1334, improbable though its verdict seems.[65] Louth
Park, in 1387, also won a victory in equally suspicious circumstances. The presence of John de Hagh and Albinus de Enderby,
active on behalf of many other religious houses, among the
feoffees makes it hard to credit that the abbey had not been in
receipt of profits from the confiscated tenement.[66] The infrequent
examination of enfeoffments to use by inquisition suggests that
the fruitlessness of the exercise was recognised. Such arrangements may in any case have been more difficult to detect than
straightforward acquisition. It is not without significance that one
of the feoffees involved in the Elsham Priory dealings appears
to have been the son of the escheator responsible for their very full
exposure.[67] The strongest argument that royal officials had been
hampered in their proceedings was the legislation required in
1391 in order to outlaw the practice unequivocally.[68]

Attempts to enforce the 1279 statute must have been dispiriting
once enfeoffment to use became common.[69] The bustle of activity
manifested in the Lincolnshire escheators' accounts from the
1370s, twenty years before the legislation came to their rescue,
argues that loss of morale, rather than complete impotence had
played some part in their previous quiescence.[70] Perhaps increasingly vocal public resentment of the abuse of mortmain controls,
of corruption among royal officials and of rigged inquisitions
goaded the escheators into renewed effort, although this did not
apparently express itself in parliament until 1376.[71]

[63] *Cal. Inq. Misc.*, vol. III, p. 231, no. 621; p. 307, no. 812.
[64] *Cal. Pat.*, 1364–7, p. 174.
[65] *Cal. Inq. Misc.*, vol. II, p. 348, no. 1424.
[66] P.R.O., E136/117/5, m5; see below, p. 124.
[67] *Cal. Inq. Misc.*, vol. III, pp. 231–2, no. 621.   [68] See below, pp. 127–8.
[69] For the chronology of enfeoffments to use, see below, pp. 157–8.
[70] P.R.O., E136/11/12–14; E136/117/1–5.
[71] *Rot. Parl.*, vol. II, pp. 356, 368; vol. III, p. 19.

The appearance of legislation in 1391 had a pronounced effect, not only in stimulating an exceptional number of retrospective licences of 1392, but also in maintaining a relatively high level of formal amortisation in the immediately succeeding years. Not until the turn of the century was the underlying decline in the grant of licences resumed.[72] If the Lincolnshire escheators' accounts are typical, the effectiveness of the statute owed little to official coercion. There are no signs of unusual activity in the county between 1391 and 1394, at which point the record is broken.[73] Short runs of accounts in the fifteenth century show that confiscations still took place, but circumstances no longer warranted the relentless pursuit of illegal alienation of the late thirteenth and early fourteenth centuries.[74] Enquiries were still commissioned and property still impounded, sometimes on ill-based suspicions, as in the past, but a more relaxed attitude towards amortisation became increasingly evident as time progressed.[75] Prior to Henry V's reign, general pardons specifically excluded mortmain offences, but in 1414 the king granted a special pardon to those guilty of unlicensed acquisition (to the explicit relief of Harrold Priory at least) and thereafter illegal amortisation was included in general pardons along with other infringements of the law.[76] In 1453, when John Merston, royal official and founder of a chantry at Epsom (Surrey), received a personal pardon, mortmain offences too were included.[77] From 1457, religious houses were also granted general pardons for illegal accessions.[78]

Even more indicative of a slackening interest in the control of amortisation was the appearance of licences, general and specific, permitting alienation without a preliminary inquisition *ad quod damnum*. Such was that granted to William Swayne, a merchant

---

[72] See above, Graph 1, pp. 42–3; and below, p. 128, and Graph 6, p. 155.

[73] P.R.O., E136/117/7–8; E136/118/3.

[74] P.R.O., E136/117/12–18; E136/119/1–8. A number of other surviving accounts are illegible.

[75] E.g. *Cal. Pat.*, 1441–6, pp. 203, 393; 1446–52, pp. 79, 138.

[76] *Rot. Parl.*, vol. II, p. 365; vol. III, pp. 202, 369; vol. IV, pp. 7, 332, 505; vol. V, pp. 283–4; ed. G. H. Fowler, *Records of Harrold Priory* (Beds. Historical Rec. Soc., 17, 1935), p. 178.

[77] *Cal. Pat.*, 1452–61, pp. 109, 111.

[78] *Ibid.*, p. 417; 1467–77, pp. 21, 272, etc.

of Salisbury, in 1468, permitting alienation of lands, rents and possessions to an annual value of twenty marks for his chantry foundation there.[79] Another general licence, granted to John Elryngton, treasurer of the royal household, in 1482, authorised alienations to his newly-founded chantry but failed to specify any limit as to their value.[80] The most liberal licence of all was granted to William Huse, chief justice of the king's bench, in 1484, permitting alienations of land and rent to an annual value of twenty pounds to his chantry foundation in Old Sleaford church (Lincs.) without any further inquisition *ad quod damnum* or licence.[81] Licences of this kind struck at the very base of mortmain control, although they were not granted indiscriminately. Most recipients had reason to stand high in royal favour. Nevertheless, such action by the crown was worlds away from the decades after 1279, when each proposed alienation was scrutinised and weighed with parsimonious care.

Concern for the amount of land passing into mortmain arose when it appeared to be running at a threatening level. For an explanation of the fifteenth-century *volte-face* one must turn to the low level of demand for licences which had succeeded the lively land hunger of former times. Only a continuing enthusiasm for chantry endowment provoked fears on the earlier scale, leading to fresh legislative measures in the 1530s. Even then, it was perhaps as much the feebleness with which mortmain legislation had come to be enforced as any excessive increase in accessions which led to the harsh limitation of gains to a twenty-year term.[82]

Even when mortmain requirements were most stringently enforced, evidence for unlicensed alienations can be uncovered without difficulty in surviving cartularies and from the patent rolls, indicating that many ecclesiastics were undeterred by the risks involved. It is important to assess how significant this evasion of the statute was, not only for its intrinsic interest but also because, if it attained extensive proportions, it would negate

[79] *Ibid.*, 1467–77, pp. 90–1.
[80] *Ibid.*, 1476–85, p. 304.
[81] *Ibid.*, p. 385.
[82] Kreider, *English Chantries*, pp. 83–6, 238–9, n. 49; *Statutes of the Realm*, vol. III, p. 378, cap. 10.

any conclusions about the ecclesiastical land market based on licences to alienate through normal channels.

Certain houses reveal a persistent willingness to flout the law. Ely Cathedral Priory showed no disposition to learn by its past mistakes. In addition to the huge fine of 1298, the prior and convent paid a fine again in 1311 for illicit acquisitions in Eriswell (Suffolk) and once more in the early 1320s.[83] They were more fortunate in 1303, when Stephen the reeve bought part of a messuage in Sutton (Cambs.) 'for the use of the prior on the prior's order' and the deal escaped attention.[84] They also managed to conceal two other illicit acquisitions by using leasehold tenure as cover. Beginning at Christmas 1293, the prior and convent were granted a forty-year lease on forty-five acres of arable and four acres of wood in Stetchworth (Cambs.) for a nominal rent of a rose. An undated grant in perpetuity from the lessor is also entered in the priory's cartulary, as is his quitclaim of 1309. Thus the lessor had surrendered his interest in the holding long before the expiry of the term, without any backing from a licence.[85] The ruse was employed again with equal success in the fifteenth century. Thomas Martyn of Ely expressed a wish in his last will and testament drawn up on 6 August 1461 that his tenement in Cambridge should be granted to the monks if a licence could be procured. No trace of such a licence is to be found, but the priory received the property at farm from Martyn's feoffees for thirty-three years on 14 September 1461, and on 20 October following they too quitclaimed their rights.[86]

Examples of this device are not confined to Ely. Thornholme Priory had suffered confiscation for a similar arrangement before 1307.[87] In 1369, Barnwell Priory paid out a twenty-pound fine in order to recover possession of a tenement in London forfeit to the crown because the same deception had been exposed. John Noket of Barnwell had leased the holding to the priory for fifteen years and then surrendered all his rights, leaving the

---

[83] *Cal. Pat.*, 1307–13, p. 387; 1317–21, p. 555.

[84] C.U.L., EDC 1B/5, no. 299, dorse.

[85] B.L., Egerton 3047, ff140v–1v.

[86] Oxf., Bodl., Ashmole 801, ff92v–5. Thomas Martyn died on 1 September 1461.

[87] See above, p. 72.

convent in control.[88] Much the same plan is likely to have crossed the minds of the monks of Thorney Abbey in 1325. Their cartulary contains three parallel deeds drawn up on the same date (18 March) with the same witnesses given in the same order. Each grants property in Bolnhurst (Beds.) and Yaxley (Cambs.), but for differing periods: for twenty years, two hundred years and in perpetuity respectively. In the event their nerve failed and they conformed to the law in a licence of 1327.[89]

Although the Thorney monks were law-abiding on that occasion, it was not a deeply ingrained habit. Indeed, at that house illegal acquisition was a calculated extension of the territorial policies of the previous generation. Free tenements on demesne manors in what was then north Huntingdonshire had been gradually eroded before 1279.[90] A further major step was taken in 1304 with the alienation under licence by William Waldeschef of one messuage and two virgates in Woodston, leaving only one substantial free tenant in the village.[91] Abbot William of Clapton, who was in office between 1305 and 1323, elected to act less formally than his predecessor. Instead of seeking licences, he employed his nephew Robert and William de Spanneby, rector of an abbey living at Stanground, to make surreptitious acquisitions. This is explicitly stated in a rubric to one of the charters involved. Property was granted:

to Robert of Clapton nephew of Lord William II abbot of Thorney, which land and meadow with the land and tenements recorded below the abbot bought with the goods of the monastery. And he arranged that the aforesaid Robert should enter those lands and tenements in the name of the monastery and that at an opportune moment, the tenements should be converted to the use of the monastery.[92]

By this means, between 1307 and 1312, further tenements were recovered in Woodston, Yaxley and Stanground (Cambs.) and

---

[88] *Cal. Pat.*, 1367–70, p. 281.
[89] C.U.L., Add. MSS 3020–1, f332–v; *Cal. Pat.*, 1327–30, p. 159.
[90] S. Raban, *The Estates of Thorney and Crowland* (University of Cambridge, Department of Land Economy, Occ. Paper 7, 1977), pp. 62–3.
[91] C.U.L., Add. MSS 3020–1, ff26v–7, iii–iiii; *Cal. Pat.*, 1301–7, pp. 236, 292; *Rot. Hund.*, vol. II, p. 643.
[92] C.U.L., Add. MSS 3020–1, f126, xxxviii.

also on other demesne manors in Northamptonshire and Cambridgeshire.[93] Some precautions were taken to avoid the rigour of the law. The pattern of tenure was confused, certainly at Stanground, and perhaps elsewhere, by permitting Robert of Clapton to take back the recently surrendered holdings on a life lease.[94] It is also possible that the general licence obtained in 1314, but not acted upon until after Abbot William's death, was designed to provide a thread of justification should the necessity arise. There can be little doubt that the abbey was involved in a carefully planned programme of illegal activity at this date. Nor was it an entirely isolated lapse, although it is distinguished by its ambitious scale. Minor unlicensed acquisitions were made in Enfield (London) after 1279 to round out accessions made immediately before the statute, rather in the same way as at Alvingham Priory.[95] There were also more unlicensed gains at Sawbridge and Willoughby (Warws.) in the fifteenth century.[96] The significance of these alienations lies not so much in their existence as in the fact that they were undetected. While neighbouring Crowland struggled through legal proceedings to recover property which had been wrongly confiscated by the escheators, Thorney, either through bribery or luck, transgressed with impunity. If such evasion was happening on a large scale, it negated the whole purpose of the 1279 statute.

By the nature of the offence, no quantitative assessment can be made of undetected infringements of the mortmain laws. Every instinct on the part of those involved dictated concealment. Conveyances belonging to the period before 1279 were commonly undated, so it was an obvious precaution to adhere to this old-fashioned practice in later illicit dealings. Thus many of them

---

[93] C.U.L., Add. MSS 3020–1, ff126–v, xxxviii, 126v–7, xl, 127–8v, xlii–xlvi, 75v, 106–7, lxxvii–lxxxi, 65v–8, xcviii, c–ci, ciii–cvi, 226–v, xxvi–xxviii, 202v–3; Northants. Rec. Off., Westmorland Coll. Box 2, parcel v, no. 1, A8; no. 2, A5; Raban, *Estates of Thorney and Crowland*, p. 72.

[94] C.U.L., Add. MSS 3020–1, f107, lxxxi, rubric. Other possibilities arise because this lease is only fortuitously exposed.

[95] C.U.L., Add. MSS 3020–1, f344–v, v–vi, 349–v, xxiiii. Letters of attorney show that these transactions occurred after 1279; C.U.L., Add. MSS 3020–1, f368v, 369v. The abbey had acquired considerable holdings in the vicinity during the 1270s; C.U.L., Add. MSS 3020–1, f343 et seq.

[96] C.U.L., Add. MSS 3020–1, f243v (1422).

will be overlooked unless indirect evidence, such as dated letters of attorney, brings them to light. The haphazard survival of private archives also militates against any statistical approach. A more fruitful line of enquiry lies in defining which sorts of illegal alienations were likely to escape notice and which were habitually exposed.

Although strategically significant, in that they furthered a coherent policy towards freeholding within the abbey fee, none of Thorney's unlicensed gains was substantial. Robert of Clapton's efforts in Woodston brought the abbey only about six acres of meadow and two acres of arable in four transactions spread over three years. In more urbanised Yaxley, his gains were similarly modest.[97] Not only were these relatively minor accessions, but they were also confined to demesne manors. As such, the business assumed an almost domestic character. The danger of discovery was far greater where the church was intruding on the fee of another. The immediate overlord, as well as the escheator, then had a motive for vigilance, and the tenantry and potential jurors were less vulnerable to intimidation.

It is instructive in this context to analyse Ely's relative failure as an illegal alienee in comparison with Thorney's success. The abortive appropriation of Wisbech and Foxton churches hardly requires explanation. As a focus of village life and subject to the twin jurisdiction of church and state, a parish church did not lend itself to clandestine activity. The Eriswell alienation was sufficiently large (a messuage and one hundred and sixty acres) to draw attention to itself. The two pardons obtained in the 1320s related to more limited enterprises, but that of 1321 concerned a London property held directly of the crown. The holdings featured in the 1322 pardon come nearest to the pattern of behaviour followed by Thorney. In Reach (Cambs.), only two messuages had been acquired, but it was not a demesne manor. At Stetchworth, the monks were recovering their own fee but in larger quantities than Thorney had considered prudent: forty-one acres were involved, thirty of which belonged to a single grant. In contrast to these unsuccessful attempts at acquisition, it is

[97] They were confined to two messuages, some rents, a shop and a garden from three separate grantors again over a three-year period.

worth observing that Stephen the reeve's undetected alienation took place on a demesne manor and was confined to part of one messuage. The chief danger attaching to small acquisitions on demesne manors was that, while they were individually inconspicuous, cumulatively they might attract attention. Perhaps for this reason, Ely, unfortunate or over-ambitious as usual, found many small gains in Ely itself and in Sutton, Witcham and Haddenham (Cambs.) called into question in inquisitions of 1370 and 1371.[98]

The inference to be drawn from the experience of both Thorney and Ely is that, providing illegal activities were kept to insignificant proportions and confined to demesne manors, they could expect a reasonable chance of success, particularly if precautions were taken. Minor infringements of the law, restricted in this way, did not always escape notice, but the number of mistakes made by the escheators in dealing with cases of this type is an eloquent comment on the difficulties of enforcement. Conversely, it was begging for trouble to undertake major acquisitions whose very size attracted attention or to become unduly conspicuous by venturing outside existing demesnes. Thus, while it is likely that there was quite widespread and successful evasion of the statute, the dangers inherent in the more ambitious type of enterprise are some guarantee that the amounts of property concerned were insufficient to undermine the efficacy of the statute.

Less complacency attaches to the dealings of chantries and allied institutions. Their multiplicity of number and form made it difficult to supervise them adequately, especially when some were founded in perpetuity and others merely for a term of years. In the south-west and in the northern counties, arrangements were apparently made regardless of mortmain law in many cases. The picture was not markedly encouraging elsewhere. In Essex, for example, less than a third of the provision for souls in perpetuity existing at the dissolution had been established under licence, though some arrangements were not wholly illegal.[99] It is perhaps not surprising that the quality of law enforcement at the extremities of the realm fell short of standards nearer to

---

[98] *Cal. Inq. Misc.*, vol III, pp. 293–6, no. 784.
[99] Kreider, *English Chantries*, pp. 73–8.

Westminster. Monastic malpractices too may have escaped attention more easily in these areas. However, the basic explanation for the greater amount of evasion noted in chantry endowments lies in the differing chronology of gains by chantries and by the religious. The impetus for chantry endowment continued into the period when monastic acquisition and the consequent vigilance of the escheators were on the wane. Mortmain legislation was not framed with chantries in mind, so it is likely that their gains were not a prime object of attention until they replaced those of the religious as a source of concern in the late fifteenth and early sixteenth centuries, at which point a growing reluctance to concede licences may have driven founders into illegality.[100]

Mortmain legislation demanded efficient policing if it was to have any appreciable effect. Self-interest dictated watchfulness by mesne lords, but ultimately responsibility for enforcement rested with the crown. Unless there were officials constantly on the watch for evasion, and unless offenders believed that they were likely to be exposed, the whole idea of limiting ecclesiastical accessions fell to the ground. On the whole, medieval officialdom proved adequate to the challenge. Constant and all-embracing supervision was not possible, but surviving records nevertheless bear witness to much activity. Desmond estimated that nearly half of the Cistercian houses were investigated for fraudulent gains at one time or another, while houses like Ely, Crowland and Spalding, once suspected of illegal action, were investigated time and again.[101] Lincolnshire escheators' accounts survive for about half of Edward II's reign only, but even so ten houses have confiscations recorded, approximately one in five of the institutions in the county known to have expressed an interest in amortisation after 1279.[102] Enquiry was intermittent, but this promoted feelings of insecurity among the guilty. Moreover, when investigation did take place, it could be thorough to the point of injustice. The tools for ensuring observance of the law were blunt. Some innocents had to be sacrificed in the interests of effective royal

---

[100] *Ibid.*, pp. 83–91.
[101] Desmond, *Cîteaux*, 1974, p. 154.
[102] P.R.O., E136/1/22–5; E136/1/28; E136/1/30–1; E136/1/36. The parish priest at Irby, the prior of Durham and the prioress of Broadholme also lost Lincolnshire property.

administration. If fear was thereby engendered, it served merely as an additional disincentive. Although there were undoubted cases of hardship, few amounted to scandal. The church was not made a victim on any widespread scale, nor deliberately persecuted over amortisation except where a handful of personal grievances were involved. There is no suggestion that mortmain laws were openly flouted until long after the religious had withdrawn from the land market, and a good deal to show that elaborate precautions were taken to avoid discovery where consciences were not clear. The practice of enfeoffment to use caused insuperable problems for royal officials for much of the fourteenth century, but the overall impression is of a restrictive law, firmly and successfully administered so long as mortmain tenure was felt to be a contentious issue.

Chapter 4

MANIPULATION OF THE STATUTE

Perhaps one reason why outright evasion of the Statute of Mortmain never reached uncontrollable proportions was that there existed a good many ways of manipulating it more or less legally into something less restrictive. Some, such as leasehold or enfeoffment to use, enabled the church to dispense altogether with licence procedure. Others, notably the employment of nominees to acquire property with a view to ultimate amortisation, mitigated the inconveniences caused by the legislation. Few of these devices were new. Some had been foreseen by the drafters of the statute, who clearly hoped that its terms would preclude their fraudulent use. In practice, however, it was difficult to draw the line between what was permissible and what was an abuse. Consequently, the church was left with considerable room for manoeuvre. Indeed, so great were the opportunities for modifying the legislative controls that statutory revision of the position was required on several occasions. Thus, there was a far greater risk that the spirit of the 1279 statute would be negated by tactics of nominal legality than by total evasion, which could be pursued and punished.

The first and most radical way in which immunity from the statute could be secured was by claiming exemption from its provisions. A long and bitter dispute arose between the crown and the city of London over this issue. The evidence was thoroughly examined by Miss Chew in her article 'Mortmain in Medieval London', upon which the following account largely depends.[1] The quarrel centred on the liberties of the city and in particular the freedom to devise, which its citizens had painstakingly established earlier in the thirteenth century. Far from championing the cause of the church, Londoners initially wel-

[1] *E.H.R.*, 1945, p. 1 et seq.

comed the statute. Like laymen elsewhere, they had long been concerned about ecclesiastical encroachment on lay tenements. Their enthusiasm for royal control waned, however, when it became clear that the king was prepared to concede more licences than their interests would dictate. Amortisation could be controlled more effectively if the right lay in their own hands. As disenchantment set in, the constitutional implications of the statute assumed greater significance. In defiance of the law, Londoners continued to bequeath their property to the church as freely as before, but by the 1290s their right appears to have been called into question. In 1293, a list of all such alienations since 1279 was drawn up, suggesting that punitive action was intended. The hustings courts of 1295–6 paid great attention to the matter but finally decided in favour of existing custom. There the issue rested for a generation.

In 1321, the conflict resumed when alienations of this type became a subject of enquiry in the *iter* held at the Tower. The escheator's account for that year shows a number of tenements in royal custody pending investigation. A compromise was effected insofar as none of the forfeitures seems to have been permanent. Indeed, the patent rolls record a crop of pardons, usually without fines.[2] A more lasting settlement was made in favour of the city in 1327, when the freedom to devise in mortmain was formally recognised by Edward III on his accession. This might well have been a solution acceptable to both sides, but for the fact that it created a bigger loophole in the 1279 statute than was originally foreseen.

Attracted by the prestige of the metropolis, and the absence of restrictions, outsiders flocked into London to make their benefactions. Some idea of the impact can be gained from the estimate that an average of twenty-eight perpetual chantries were established in every decade between 1300 and 1402. Faced with this enthusiasm, the crown again attempted to curb the city's freedom to devise in mortmain. Outright denial was no longer feasible, so the king now aimed at limiting the numbers of those who could exercise the right. It was decided in 1364 that hence-

---

[2] *Cal. Pat.*, 1317–21, pp. 586–9, 591, 593, 595, 597–600; 1321–4, pp. 1, 5, 7–11, 13–14.

forward only freemen of the city qualified. An enquiry was again held to determine how many retrospective infringements had taken place. The terms of this investigation were particularly harsh in that the right to devise was deemed to have been in abeyance between 1279 and the royal confirmation of 1327. The results of the enquiry were acted on at intervals between 1364 and 1388, culminating in fifty forfeitures. As a deterrent, the purge was not a great success. Outsiders continued to operate in London, but were now forced to act through freemen of the city when they wanted to transfer their gains to the church. This stratagem was made illegal in 1391 under the general legislation intended to curb enfeoffments to use, but bequests continued in large numbers.[3] Between 1400 and 1450, three hundred and sixty citizens made three hundred and eighty-two grants. That some of these remained irregular may be inferred from further restrictive measures. In 1434, it was arranged that the common council of London should examine all bequests before their enrolment in the hustings court. In 1457, it was ordered that all devises should be subject to scrutiny and, if necessary, a fine. Yet, notwithstanding the growing web of restrictions and the confusion as to their rights exhibited by a few testators, the city ultimately gained its point.[4] Its liberty was conceded and in 1482 again reaffirmed.

Other boroughs also put forward claims of a similar nature. The customs of Winchelsea, Rye and Hastings asserted that alienations into mortmain required only the licence of the mayor and commonalty and not that of the king, while the customs of Lincoln claimed the same privileges as London.[5] In 1389, three of the Northampton gilds in agreed returns argued that the townsmen were entitled to bequeath their lands freely to whom they pleased, including the church, because the town was an ancient royal borough.[6] Godmanchester burgesses also claimed to 'give,

---

[3] See below, pp. 127–8.

[4] J. M. Jennings, 'London and the Statute of Mortmain: Doubts and Anxieties among Fifteenth-Century London Testators', *Medieval Studies*, 36, 1974, pp. 175–7.

[5] Ed. M. Bateson, *Borough Customs*, 2 vols. (Selden Soc., 18 and 21, 1904–6), vol. II, p. 202 n.

[6] P.R.O., C47/45/380–2.

bequeath, or sell their lands without hindrance of the king or any other' in an inquisition of 1361 following the confiscation of tenements granted to some chaplains, but since emphasis was laid on the fact that the latter held for life rather than in mortmain, there was perhaps some doubt as to how far claims of burghal privilege might be pushed.[7] It is also noticeable that, whatever their claims, the Northampton burgesses were equally cautious in making bequests, preferring to leave property in the hands of feoffees.[8]

Where townsmen claimed to amortise freely, they seemed to lack the courage of their convictions in practice. Even in London, the freedom to devise in mortmain had been limited to freemen of the city acting in good faith. Although it remained a constitutional victory on a matter of principle, the final privilege was a long way from the blanket freedom envisaged in the thirteenth century. In spite of these reservations, however, it is likely that some sort of burghal privilege regarding amortisation was recognised by the crown. The sixteenth-century legislation designed to tighten the mortmain laws specifically excepted 'such cities and towns corporate, where by their ancient customs they have good and lawful authorities to devise into mortmain'.[9]

Although less conspicuous, religious houses were not entirely without initiative when it came to seeking exemption from the 1279 statute. In the mid-fourteenth century, Glastonbury Abbey urged that its special position as the 'fount and origin of all the religion of England' deserved greater freedom than that enjoyed by other religious houses and that its existing banlieu jurisdiction was some recognition of this. Interpreting their privileges somewhat liberally, the monks were already resuming land granted to tenants and acquiring other unspecified holdings without a royal licence. In the face of confiscation, however, they began to doubt the wisdom of proceeding unless backed by a more specific concession. Thus, in 1355, they sought 'by express words' a pardon for their past activities and the right to acquire further property within the banlieu without resort to a licence. The weight of their case and the one hundred marks which the abbot was

---

[7] *Cal. Inq. Misc.*, vol. III, pp. 148–9, no. 414; *Cal. Close*, 1360–4, pp. 183–4.
[8] P.R.O., C47/45/380–2.   [9] *Statutes of the Realm*, vol. III, p. 378.

prepared to pay into the chamber sufficed to sway the crown in their favour, but unlike general licences, this was not a privilege which came to be distributed on a wide scale.[10]

There was no real need for ecclesiastical institutions to single themselves out for immunity from the 1279 statute even supposing that they had any special claim to it. The most modest institution could avoid the rigour of the law with very little effort. An early device which proved so effective that it provoked almost immediate legislative repression was for the church to bring a fictitious property dispute into the royal courts. By prior agreement, the prospective grantor of the holding failed to answer the case. As a result of this default, the church was awarded possession without a licence and with the full panoply of the law. A halt was called to this practice by the second Statute of Westminster of 1285. In future, where churchmen were left in possession for this reason, a careful enquiry was to be held as to whether they really had any pre-existing right in the property. Where fraudulent intentions were exposed, the holding devolved on the next lord of the fee if he claimed it within a year of the inquest. Failing this, his overlord had six months in which to make his claim and so on up the feudal ladder to the king in much the same way as was provided for in the Statute of Mortmain itself.[11]

Several examples of this law in action can be found in the year books for 1338–9, while in 1341 a prior recovering his debts under Statute Merchant was also subject to enquiry about possible fraud.[12] Daventry Priory found its title under investigation under both Edward I and his grandson. On the first occasion it was challenged over property in West Haddon and on the second in Hanging Houghton (both Northants.).[13] On two other occasions, Pipewell Abbey, also seeking to recover holdings in West Haddon, was likewise subject to enquiry.[14] Such measures were doubtless

[10] *Cal. Pat.*, 1354–8, pp. 212–14.
[11] *Statutes of the Realm*, vol. 1, p. 87, cap. 32.
[12] Ed. L. O. Pike, *Year Books XII and XIII Edward III* (Rolls Series, London, 1885), pp. 114–17, 124–7, 334–5; *Year Books XV Edward III* (Rolls Series, London, 1891), pp. 424–7.
[13] B.L., Cott. Claud. D xii, ff94–v, no. 5, 119v–20, no. 33.
[14] B.L., Cott. Calig. A xiii, ff182–4.

necessary, but they represented considerable inconvenience for those about their legitimate business. In both Daventry cases, the prior's right was upheld, but his recovery was delayed until this was established.

If fictitious actions enjoyed a short life as a means of avoiding mortmain restrictions, leasehold, as such, was never seriously challenged, although attempts to use it to cloak illegal gains were successfully prosecuted. For those subject to mortmain controls it had several attractions. Short-term leases could be used either as an end in themselves or as a prelude to full amortisation, while long-term leases could be arranged to leave their holders with advantages akin to perpetual tenure.

There are some indications that short-term leases gained in attraction once acquisition in fee was restricted. This is especially true of the period before the mid-fourteenth century, when many religious houses were still actively interested in land. Leasehold of this type enabled them to assuage their hunger and possibly afforded them some flexibility in the rather more unsettled economic conditions of the second decade. Several of the fenland monasteries were recipients of major crown leases and for most of them it was a novel enterprise. In 1291, Peterborough Abbey was granted custody of the manors of Torpel and Upton (Cambs.) during the king's pleasure in return for one hundred pounds per annum.[15] Neighbouring Thorney began what was probably a five-year term as lessee of the royal manor of Apethorpe (Nor-thants.) at Michaelmas 1302, rendering £39 19s 3d per annum; while in 1314, Abbot William of Clapton (d. 1323) secured the lease of Glatton (Cambs.) for his lifetime at one hundred pounds per annum.[16] Ely also took advantage of a royal lease. The earliest firm evidence comes from the mid-fourteenth century. In 1369, the convent was granted the manor of Soham (Cambs.) for thirteen years, again for an annual payment of one hundred pounds. This was merely the renewal of earlier provisions, how-ever. In 1358, Queen Philippa had conceded a twelve-year lease on the same terms, and the acquittance of all arrears on a farm which she gave at the same time suggests that the priory's interest

[15] *Cal. Pat.*, 1281–92, p. 421; *Cal. Fine*, 1272–1307, p. 289.
[16] P.R.O., E372/149 et seq.; *Cal. Pat.*, 1313–17, p. 199.

can be antedated still further.[17] It is likely that Crowland Abbey too was involved in leases of this type. Two estates, Holywell (Lincs.) and Stretton (Leics.), figure briefly in the account rolls between 1303 and 1307. Both these manors were assigned to Queen Margaret's dower at this time, so it is likely that they were on the leasehold market. The idea that they were not a normal part of the abbey's demesne is reinforced by an atypical note about profits at the end of the first account.[18]

The barriers to purchase erected by the 1279 statute may well have directed the church into avenues hitherto unexplored. It was unlikely that royal estates would ever be available on other than restricted terms, so while more permanent accessions were possible the benefits of leasing royal property escaped attention. Apethorpe and Glatton had been on the leasehold market before, but Thorney does not appear to have taken them up despite their geographical advantages.[19] The lease of Glatton ensured control of a large estate of eleven hides immediately to the south of the abbey's existing manors in Huntingdonshire and a further extension of influence within its private hundred of Normancross. The appurtenant hamlet of Holme had shown some slight capacity for urban growth in the late thirteenth century, its eight burgages in the Hundred Rolls swelling to twenty-three by 1297, with a corresponding increase in rents.[20] This doubtless added lustre to the estate in the eyes of the abbot although, in the event, it represented little lasting commercial potential. Apethorpe was less closely integrated into abbey holdings than Glatton, but was nevertheless conveniently placed within reach of the monks' main properties in north Huntingdonshire. Crowland too was leasing in the vicinity of its manors at Langtoft and Baston (Lincs.), while Soham fell within Ely's sphere of influence. The position with regard to Peterborough was slightly different in that Torpel and

---

[17] *Cal. Fine*, 1369–77, p. 30; B.L., Egerton 3047, ff253v–4.

[18] C.U.L., QC Box 2, 21–3; ed. W. Page, *V.C.H. Rutland*, 2 vols. (1908–35), vol. II, p. 147.

[19] Ed. W. R. D. Adkins et al., *V.C.H. Northamptonshire*, 4 vols. (1902–37), vol. II, p. 543; P.R.O. E372/149, m5d; Midgley, *Ministers' Accounts of the Earldom of Cornwall*, vol. II, p. 185.

[20] Midgley, *Ministers' Accounts of the Earldom of Cornwall*, vol. II, p. 177; *Rot. Hund.*, vol. II, pp. 650, 652.

Upton were already held of the abbey in knights' fee. They had been alienated to the crown by their tenant because of debt.[21] In other circumstances, the abbey might well have wished to buy back direct control of this part of its ancient endowment.

There were also advantages in short-term leases of a more modest nature, designed as a prelude to full ownership. They permitted leisured evaluation of a property before the more extreme step of formal alienation was taken. At the same time, they provided security while negotiations were pending. In some cases, they could be exploited to lure sitting tenants deeper into debt, making ultimate sale a necessity. Probably all three motives were involved in Thorney Abbey's dealings with William Waldeschef in Woodston (Cambs.) in the early fourteenth century. He was one of the few surviving free tenants of any consequence on a manor which had long been a focus of the abbey's policy of resumption.[22] In 1296, he conceded the monks a lease for thirty years in return for a flat payment of forty marks for the first ten years and forty shillings per annum for the following twenty. Then, in 1304, the tenement was bought and alienated under licence for a further disbursement of one hundred marks.[23] Ely also used leasehold to edge out tenants in financial distress. During the first three decades of the fourteenth century, the convent acquired holdings piecemeal in Sutton, Witcham and Over (Cambs.) from the Pelryn family. The tension between the desire of the monks and the desperate reluctance of the tenant is depicted in a succession of leasehold agreements with the convent. In 1304, John Pelryn granted the monks nine acres of land and a fishery in Witcham for his lifetime and a further eight years after his death in return for a much needed fifty-pound loan. In 1308, he was in the midst of a six-year lease of his lands in Witcham and wished to vary the terms. Yet another leasehold

---

[21] King, *Peterborough Abbey*, pp. 39–40.

[22] *Rot. Hund.*, vol. II, p. 643; C.U.L., Add. MSS 3020–1, ff114v–15v, iiii–v, 128v, xlvii; Northants. Rec. Off., Westmorland Coll. Box 2, parcel II, no 1B. A note on the dorse of this last deed reveals it as a sale by Martin le Freman.

[23] C.U.L., Add. MSS 3020–1, ff26v–7, iii–iiii, 123v–4, xxx; *Cal. Pat.*, 1301–7, pp. 236, 292; Northants. Rec. Off., Westmorland Coll. Box 2, parcel II, no. 1C.

agreement was made in 1312. In that year he granted all his lands in Witcham, with the exception of his capital messuage, for a ten-year term. In this case, the arrangements were particularly complex and not easy to follow. The surviving indenture is so damaged that it is difficult to read, and judging by the obscurities of the cartulary copy it presented some problems in its pristine state. What is evident is that Pelryn required an immediate payment of twenty marks and a robe and that his lands lay uncultivated. His bond for a hundred-mark loan in the same month suggests that he had reached the limits of his financial resilience. Significantly, he sold twenty acres of arable in Witcham to a convent nominee within a few weeks. Uncultivated lands, and leasehold terms which anticipated his death, argue that debility was as much a threat as monastic greed, though he apparently lived until at least 1326. It is noticeable that laymen as well as ecclesiastics benefited from his woes: several deeds allude to outstanding leases other than to Ely. Even if the monks cannot be held entirely responsible for his undoing, however, there can be little doubt about the speed with which they seized the opportunity it presented.[24]

Less traumatic dealings at Peterborough illustrate the convenience of leasehold as an interim measure. In 1288, Elias of Bekingham granted the abbey the manor of Southorpe (Cambs.) expressly 'to have and to hold to the same abbot and convent at my will until I and the aforesaid abbot and convent have obtained permission from the lord king for them to retain the aforesaid tenement in perpetual alms'. The arrangement proved all the more useful because of the delays and difficulties occasioned by the king's absence in Gascony and the ill will of the former owner. The abbey did not secure its licence until 1291. Monastic capital had been tied up in the acquisition since at least 1287, so the grant at will permitted the abbey a return on this several years before it could have been otherwise achieved.[25]

---

[24] B.L., Egerton 3047, ff2, 64 et seq.; *Cal. Pat.*, 1313–17, p. 121; C.U.L., EDC 1B/4, nos. 265, 305, 738, 747–8, 752, 754, 762, 770, 773–4, 803. On a lesser scale, in 1293, the acquisition of another debtor's tenement had been preceded by a lease to the convent. B.L., Cott. Vesp. A. vi, ff106v–7v.

[25] Mellows, *Henry of Pytchley's Book of Fees*, p. 62 et seq. See also above, pp. 58–9.

The undoubted advantages of short-term leases could not altogether compensate for some very real disadvantages. Tenure was limited, with renewal uncertain. A lessee was in an invidious position at law. Unless he held a life tenancy, he was not a freeholder. Consequently, if he were expelled from the tenement, it was the lessor and not the lessee who had to take action to recover seisin. The lessee's only direct redress lay through the action of trespass. Even without malicious intent, a lease could be disrupted by wardship or dower rights if the lessor happened to die.[26] Such insecurity inevitably placed the lessee in a weak position, as the monks of Crowland had found in the thirteenth century. Their experience is instructive. Burgeoning interest in the rich fenland vill of Gedney (Lincs.) led them to take out a five-year lease on a manor belonging to Walter de Thurkelby. The dowager countess of Aumale, tenant-in-chief of the fee, viewed this insinuation of the dead hand with misgiving. As a result of her harassment, the monks demanded full enfeoffment or nothing and negotiations for their purchase of the manor were begun in the same year.[27] It is probable that permanent transfer of the estate was envisaged from the start and that appreciation of this provoked the dowager. Nevertheless, the monks rightly felt that they would be better placed to defend themselves if they held in perpetuity. Once the worst had happened and the enfeoffment had taken place, there would be little purpose in an overlord attempting to frighten ecclesiastical intruders away.

Problems such as these were not sufficient to dissuade churchmen from using short-term leases to pave the way to full ownership, but they may have acted as a deterrent to short-term leases as an end in themselves. It certainly appears that the fen monasteries enjoyed a fairly brief flirtation with crown leases, although this probably owed more to their dubious profitability than to interrupted tenure. Accounts for Glatton in 1296–7 suggest that, even without any problems of arrears, the abbot of Thorney would be lucky to make much profit after rendering one hundred pounds to the crown.[28] The Peterborough manors

---

[26] F. Pollock, F. W. Maitland, *History of English Law*, 2 vols., 2nd edn (Cambridge, 1968), vol. II, pp. 106–8.   [27] W.P.C., ff116v–18.

[28] Midgley, *Ministers' Accounts of the Earldom of Cornwall*, vol. II, p. 176 et seq.

of Torpel and Upton, owing the same farm, were valued at eighty pounds per annum in 1281 and the abbey account rolls suggest that this may have been an overestimate.[29] Perhaps the fenland houses were peculiarly tempted by leasehold opportunities since their proximity to each other limited the scope for purchase, but they were not unique in resorting to such tenure. In 1280 the abbess of Shaftesbury was granted a twelve-year lease on crown land in Shaftesbury, while in 1302 Sempringham Priory was granted a seven-year lease on the Lincolnshire manors of Folkingham and Edenham.[30] Again it appears that proximity rather than profit was the main attraction.

The appeal or otherwise of short-term leases would be much better established by examining those granted by other landlords, since an element of coercion cannot be ruled out in the case of potentially extortionate crown leases. Unfortunately very few leases granted by other landlords are known. The grant by Philip de Kyme of a manor at West Torrington (Lincs.) to Bullington Priory for a twenty-year term from October 1318 highlights the problem of leasehold records. Whereas most medieval deeds are found in cartulary copies, this lease belongs to the much more perishable category of surviving originals.[31] Because leases lasted for a limited period, deeds recording them were of no permanent value. There was consequently little incentive to copy them into cartularies. Thorney Abbey's scribe included all William Waldeschef's quitclaims, grants in perpetuity and related licences in his Red Book, but the preceding lease is known only because the agreement itself happens to survive. The Apethorpe lease is not recorded anywhere in the abbey archive. Similarly, Crowland's Holywell and Stretton leases can only be inferred from the account rolls since they did not merit inclusion in the Wrest Park Cartulary. It is arguable, but quite incapable of proof, that many leases have disappeared without trace, while others will only yield themselves to patient excavation. This may well obscure

---

29 *Cal. Close*, 1279–88, p. 81; Northants. Rec. Off., Fitzwilliam Accs. 233, mm17–18; 2388, mm21–v. The latter references were kindly supplied by Dr King of Sheffield University.

30 *Cal. Pat.*, 1272–81, p. 375; P.R.O., E372/149, m16d.

31 The lease may have been a prelude to full alienation. B.L., Harley Charter 52 H 20; *Cal. Pat.*, 1317–21, pp. 345–6.

a significant interest in short-term leasehold up to the mid-fourteenth century stimulated by the controls imposed in 1279.

Longer-term leases were less disadvantageous than those for short periods in that they reduced uncertainty about renewal. Where successful, they could obviate or postpone the need for a licence. In 1366, Ely took out a twenty-five-year lease on property in Foxton (Cambs.). Full acquisition was clearly mooted since a mesne lord licence had been secured in 1362, but no royal licence can be traced.[32] Obviously the lease was proving a satisfactory alternative. When the term stretched to sixty-six years, as in a Witcham lease to the same convent in 1379, or to one hundred years, as in a lease to Daventry Priory in 1318, leasehold was largely conceived as a substitute for formal alienation.[33] Any doubts on this score dissolve in the face of Mullicourt Priory's two-thousand-year lease on three acres in Outwell (Norfolk/ Cambs.) of 1306.[34] Agreements of this sort were sailing very close to the wind. Royal disapproval may explain why they are not to be found in great number, although the length of their terms made them as worthy of inclusion in cartularies as grants in perpetuity.

Leasehold of whatever term offered flexibility to those confronted by mortmain restrictions. Ambiguity as to its legality expressed in the terms of the statute was reflected in practice. Some churchmen chose to use it to obscure their illicit dealings. Others deliberately extended terms so that their interest approximated to tenure in perpetuity. Even more found it a convenient means of enjoying property for a short period or until negotiations for formal acquisition could be completed. To add to this variety, a distinctive local version of the same principle appeared in the Welsh Marches. Here *prid* deeds offered effective ownership by means of mortgage agreements arranged for limited terms but perpetually renewable if repayment was not made.[35] By this means, Haughmond Abbey was able to buy out peasants

---

[32] C.U.L., EDC 1B/19.
[33] B.L., Egerton 3047, f63v; B.L., Cott. Claud. D xii, f137v, no. 153.
[34] C.U.L., EDC 1B/15, no. 856.
[35] L. B. Smith, 'The Gage and the Land Market in Late Medieval Wales', *Ec.H.R.*, 2nd ser., 29, 1976, p. 538.

in Aston and Hisland (Hereford and Worcester), notably in the crisis years between 1314 and 1317, without resorting to licensing procedure.[36] Thus, in *prid* agreements, as in leasehold, landlords found that pre-existing practice offered added advantages in the years after *De viris religiosis*. The benefits were all the greater in that the multiplicity of form, term and motivation to be found in leasehold and allied arrangements made it difficult for the crown to legislate against either evasion or avoidance of the law. As a result, individual cases involving illegal acquisition were prosecuted, while the general position remained loosely defined. Thus, the church was able to retain a welcome measure of freedom in the face of restrictive regulations.

A practice which was sometimes used in conjunction with lease-hold was the employment of nominees. This offered great scope for mitigating the worst rigours of the statute. The lengthy delays imposed by licence procedure left the church at a marked dis-advantage in a land market where vendors were often character-ised by their urgent need for a sale. Nominees could act swiftly to buy up a holding and could then afford to wait for the due processes of law to effect the final transfer. If, as often occurred, a religious house was recovering its own fee piecemeal, nominees could also assemble a collection of small holdings before proceed-ing to a licence, thus avoiding an expensive procedure for each petty accession.

The advantages were so manifest that the device was often used. Thorney Abbey provides a fully documented example. A number of holdings in Bolnhurst (Beds.), Yaxley and Stanground (Cambs.) were alienated under licence to the abbey by Thomas of Deeping in 1327. The grant represented the fruits of at least four years of careful preparation. In 1323, he had received the entire holding of Thomas de Myvile in Bolnhurst. In the follow-ing year, Walter de Upton, Richard de Haunes and Henry de Malverne granted further tenements there; and a year later still, Thomas gained another from Robert Grym. Shortly before the

---

[36] I am greatly indebted to Mrs U. Rees for generously making available part of her unpublished work on Haughmond Abbey, together with transcripts of *prid* deeds. Conventional mortgages were also used by this house, but I have not found examples elsewhere.

licence was taken out, he also secured two acres of meadow from Peter de Paston and his wife Emma. Meanwhile, in Yaxley, he had negotiated the reversion of a messuage from Richard of Clapton. Thorney's position as *éminence grise* is emphasised by the way in which some of the deeds were executed at the abbey. Thomas de Myvile drew up his conveyance and appointed his attorney there in 1323. Thomas of Deeping himself appointed an attorney there in December 1323 and again in February 1324. The interest of the monks can be the only reason for conducting such business at Thorney, which was far from convenient for Bolnhurst. Furthermore, it all occurred three years before the abbey acquired any official standing in the matter. It is also revealing that the rubric to the grant of Peter de Paston and his wife attributes the gain to Abbot Reginald although the nominal recipient was Thomas.[37]

A more sophisticated version of the same procedure can be seen at the same house before 1343. In that year, John of Yaxley granted the monks holdings at Yaxley, Stanground, Whittlesey (Cambs.), Bolnhurst and Husborne Crawley (Beds.) under licence. He was merely the final link in a chain of nominees. Much of the groundwork had been done by John of Newton. He in turn had made over his gains to Roger of Stanground, who then granted them to Robert of Thorney. Robert added further to this nucleus of property before surrendering it all to John of Yaxley in 1336. John continued in possession for the remaining seven years until the licence was obtained. As in the earlier transactions of Thomas of Deeping, some of the business was conducted at Thorney itself.[38] By no stretch of the imagination could this series of conveyances have been fortuitous. Thorney was clearly gathering land for a decade before the royal licence was granted, and employing chosen nominees to that end.

The use of single nominees placed a great premium on their trustworthiness. It was safer therefore to employ several. Not only did this provide greater security against a breach of faith,

---

[37] *Cal. Pat.*, 1327–30, p. 159; C.U.L., Add. MSS 3020–1, ff330v–2, 109v, 73; Raban, *Past and Present*, 1974, pp. 10–11.
[38] *Cal. Pat.*, 1343–5, p. 136; C.U.L., Add. MSS 3020–1, ff36, 334v–5v, 110v–12v, 201–2; Raban, *Past and Present*, 1974, p. 11.

but also it obviated certain practical difficulties which might arise should the nominee die. Where one man alone was involved, the church had scant legal grounds on which to oppose his heirs' claim to possession. This danger was especially marked when a minority transpired. Even if the exact situation could be established, an overlord might find it in his interest to claim the wardship and ignore the church's stake. The convent of Ely appreciated this point. Early in the fourteenth century, it had arranged for single nominees to secure property in Ely, Downham, Sutton and Witcham (Cambs.),[39] but under Edward III it preferred to use at least two people. In the middle years of the century, a notable partnership emerged between Richard de Barenton and William Broun of Wisbech. Together, they granted substantial Cambridgeshire holdings to the priory under licence between 1357 and 1363.[40] The most important of these was the manor and advowson of Mepal (Cambs.). The estate was initially granted to five priory nominees in July 1361. Two months later, these were replaced by six further nominees, including Broun and Barenton. The other four quitclaimed their interest on 6 November, leaving Broun and Barenton to surrender the holding to the convent in April of the following year.[41] Their rôle was by no means passive; William Broun handled both the purchase of Mepal and its subsequent amortisation. His accounts of the necessary expenditure survive in both original and cartulary copy.[42] It was he who paid the expenses of Thomas de Elteslee senior and Nicholas West, two of the nominees engaged in the initial transfer. Again, it was he who rode to London to obtain the writ for an inquisition *ad quod damnum* and then made all the arrangements with the escheator. He later returned to London, accompanied by the sacrist, to secure the licence itself. He is also to be found engaged in various associated legal tasks. When the convent, like other religious houses, anticipated full tenure of the

[39] *Cal. Pat.*, 1313–17, p. 121.
[40] *Ibid.*, 1354–8, p. 545; 1361–4, pp. 171, 344.
[41] Oxf., Bodl., Ashmole 801, ff128v–30v; C.U.L., EDC 1B/23, nos. 1135, 1137–8, 1142–3, 1145. The royal licence to alienate is dated 12 March 1362. *Cal. Pat.*, 1361–4, p. 171.
[42] Oxf., Bodl., Ashmole 801, ff132v–4v; C.U.L., EDC 1B/23, unnumbered. They have also been edited by Evans, *E.H.R.*, 1936, p. 113 et seq.

property with a lease, it was William Broun who acted as one of
the attorneys for the livery of seisin. He was also deputed to
visit Cambridge to persuade John Chene to sell a further
tenement in Mepal. These dealings reached a successful conclusion
in 1363.[43]

Nominees like Broun and Barenton could be satisfactorily
employed on a wide range of business. The growing popularity
of the use in the fourteenth century enabled the church to extend
their utility still further.[44] Feoffees could remain the tenants in
law, while ecclesiastics enjoyed the fruits of the holding. This, it
was hoped, rendered formal amortisation an expensive superfluity.
Barton noticed that Oxford colleges were accustomed to manage
their property in this way. Merton habitually retained holdings
'in use' for twenty to thirty years before proceeding to amortisation, while Oriel only resorted to licences under duress of the
1391 statute.[45] The canonesses of Harrold Priory were equally
alive to the possibilities of enfeoffments to this end. Their
arrangements are most explicit for a croft in Stagsden (Beds.). A
memorandum in the priory cartulary records that it was given
to the convent by Margery Cane in order to provide candles.
The deeds show that in 1349 she granted it not to the canonesses
but to Sir John de Grey. After his death a few years later, she
granted it to John Rysle and William Yeldon. The croft then
passed from hand to hand over the next forty years without any
moves towards amortisation. Like Oriel, the canonesses took out
a licence only when they were forced to do so under the legis-

---

43 Oxf., Bodl., Ashmole 801, ff130v–1; C.U.L., EDC 1B/23, nos. 1132, 1147.
It is possible that both Broun and Barenton also represented the convent on
business of another sort. Amongst the Ely archives there is an interesting
obligation for a hundred marks. This was a straightforward business loan
in 1351 to John Sturdy of Sutton *ad mercandisandum ad commodum et
proficuum* of the grantors, who were Broun, Barenton and Robert de
Wilburton of Ely. Robert de Wilburton had lent thirty pounds for the
same purpose shortly beforehand. B.L., Egerton 3047, ff85v–6; C.U.L., EDC
1B/24, no. 290. Some monastic involvement is suggested by the care with
which the agreement was preserved and copied into the convent cartulary,
as well as by the later activities of Broun and Barenton on its behalf.
The monks' reluctance to appear as principals is perhaps attributable to
the fear of appearing to be usurers.

44 Bean, *Decline of English Feudalism*, p. 114 et seq.

45 J. L. Barton, 'The Medieval Use', *L.Q.R.*, 81, 1965, p. 565.

lation of 1391.[46] Clearly it was external pressure rather than shortcomings in their nominees which forced them to modify their position.

It is interesting to note that nominees proved just as useful to the church in parallel circumstances in the nineteenth century, when the monastic revival once more posed the problem of acquisitions in the face of mortmain restrictions. Mark Pattison's memoirs recorded how Rosminian nuns evaded the 'Mortmain Act by vesting property legally in the name of a member, while really it is at the disposal of the general'.[47] The same procedure was followed by the community at Llanthony in Wales.[48] The canon law ban on the ownership of private property by religious probably precluded medieval houses from adopting this ruse on a wide scale. There is one example, however, of a monk acting in this way. An inquisition of 1372 showed that a monk of Walden had acquired land worth two shillings per annum to the use of the abbot in Thorley and Sawbridgeworth (Herts.).[49]

The employment of nominees offered a very real flexibility to the church, but it was not without hazard. Although enfeoffment to use was practised by churchmen on a wide scale, questions were raised as to its legality, and confiscation could occur, if only rarely.[50] Quite apart from possible transgression of mortmain legislation, there were legal difficulties attaching to enfeoffment to use in itself. Since the practice was not recognised in common law, the church had no remedy against fraud.[51] Early in Richard II's reign, chancery took some cognisance of disputes over enfeoffments to use, but it was not altogether wise for the church to advertise its activities in that quarter.[52] In view of this vulnerability, the choice of nominees was of the utmost importance.

Barton suggests that church courts may have exercised a measure of control over clerical nominees, thus making them

---

[46] Fowler, *Records of Harrold Priory*, pp. 156–8, nos. 263–73; p. 178, no. 316; p. 216. For other feoffees, see *ibid.*, p. 137 et seq.; *Cal. Pat.*, 1391–6, p. 164.
[47] M. Pattison, *Memoirs* (London, 1885), p. 192.
[48] A. Calder-Marshall, *The Enthusiast* (London, 1962), p. 192.
[49] *Cal. Inq. Misc.*, vol. III, p. 319, no. 843.
[50] E.g. *ibid.*, vol. IV, p. 21, no. 30.
[51] Bean, *Decline of English Feudalism*, p. 162.
[52] Barton, *L.Q.R.*, 1965, p. 569.

an ideal choice.[53] Certainly surviving records show a marked preponderance of secular clergy amongst those employed for this purpose. William Broun of Wisbech and Richard de Barenton were described respectively as a chaplain and a clerk, while Thomas of Deeping, who featured in the Thorney dealings of the 1320s, was parson of East Deeping. Of those involved in the transactions preceding Thorney's 1343 licence, John of Newton was rector of Bolnhurst, while the others were chaplains.

The coercive power of canon law was not the only reason why the secular clergy proved attractive. They were less likely than laymen to have obstructive heirs. Moreover, patronage was a time-honoured and inexpensive way of paying for their services. Bolnhurst and East Deeping were both Thorney livings. Elias of Bekingham, who handled the purchase of Southorpe for Peterborough, was rector of the abbey's church at Warmington.[54] Hopes of preferment were likely to offer a more potent incentive to loyalty than fears of ecclesiastical sanction.

In some cases it was not so much clerical status which recommended potential nominees as the expertise often associated with it. Bekingham was a royal justice, 'in whom the abbot and convent had great confidence'. Thorney also harnessed the talents of a man of wider experience by rewarding him with its living of Stanground early in the fourteenth century. William de Spanneby, who aided Robert of Clapton in illicit acquisitions from abbey tenants, was employed on a variety of business by the crown. In 1303, the vacant abbey of Crowland was committed to his keeping, and in later years he was appointed guardian of the Templars' lands in Lincolnshire. He also served on several commissions of *oyer* and *terminer*. The monks of Thorney were not alone in appreciating his merits. He was also involved in alienations to Bourne Abbey under a licence of 1314.[55]

---

[53] *Ibid.*, p. 566.
[54] Mellows, *Henry of Pytchley's Book of Fees*, p. 62.
[55] C.U.L., Add. MSS 3020–1, ff106–v; *Cal. Fine*, 1272–1307, p. 484; e.g. *Cal. Pat.*, 1307–13, p. 438; *ibid.*, 1313–17, pp. 78, 313, 594. He was probably acting for Thorney at about the same time as he was administering Crowland. His final conveyance is dated on the conversion of St Paul, 36 Ed. I. Since Edward died in his 35th year, this is probably a scribal error for 33 Ed. I.

It is likely that family relationships or local ties rather than clerical status dictated Ely Priory's choice of nominees in the same period. Prior John de Fressingfield (1303–21) employed Geoffrey de Fressingfield, clerk, and William de Fressingfield, chaplain, in a series of Cambridgeshire acquisitions. The part played by personal association is emphasised by the involvement of Geoffrey's brother Alexander, who was not in holy orders, and also of Robert Gold, who hailed from Fressingfield even if he was not a relative.[56] There can also be little doubt that it was the family relationship which made Abbot William of Clapton select his nephew Robert for Thorney's illicit activities.[57]

Some churchmen felt able to trust their lay officials in this rôle too, notwithstanding the possible interference of heirs. Reginald de Celario, who granted Crowland Abbey property in Crowland, Langtoft and Baston (Lincs.) in 1300, is probably the same official who presented the grange and stock account at Crowland between 1265 and 1267. In the following century, Walter de Somerby, abbey steward, was almost certainly employed in a similar way: he acquired a tenement at Bucknall (Lincs.) in 1336 in company with a more traditional kind of nominee, John of Surfleet, vicar of Crowland's church at Wellingborough. Three years later he quitclaimed his interest and nothing further is recorded. The combination of a Crowland official and the incumbent of a Crowland living, neither of whom had any known connection with Bucknall or each other, strongly suggests that they were abbey representatives. It is likely that John of Surfleet continued to hold the property to the use of the monks.[58] A similar combination of clerks and lay officials as chosen nominees has also been observed on the Westminster Abbey estates.[59] The prior of Ely also reposed confidence in select lay nominees. William Castleacre, who figured as one of a group of feoffees

---

[56] B.L., Egerton 3047, ff2, 49 et seq., 64 et seq., 95v; Cott. Vesp. A vi, ff109–11; C.U.L., EDC 1B/3, 4, 8, passim.

[57] See above, p. 96.

[58] *Cal. Pat.*, 1292–1301, p. 492; C.U.L., QC Box 2, 2; Lincs. Archives Off., 6 Anc. 1/32–8; W.P.C., ff191–v, xii–xiii; Raban, *Past and Present*, 1974, p. 12.

[59] B. Harvey, *Westminster Abbey and its Estates in the Middle Ages* (Oxford, 1977), pp. 184–5.

in a 1392 licence, was steward of the bishop's courts from the 1360s to 1381.[60]

Sometimes it sufficed that the layman was an old friend or a local notable. The bishop of Ely enjoyed the services of Sir Guy Brian on the former basis, while the canonesses of Harrold Priory drew upon the Braybrook family on the latter.[61] Small houses with no great reserves of patronage had especial need to be circumspect over their choice of nominees. The evidence of Harrold shows that all likely resources were tapped. Not only were the Braybrooks, father and son, harnessed to the priory interest, but also their relatives by marriage. By this means, Harrold, like richer Peterborough, secured the aid of a royal justice, in this case Sir William Thirning.[62] Apart from the Braybrook connection, its feoffees showed the usual preponderance of secular clerks. The most active of these was Robert Lary, who 'chopped' churches as readily as he engaged in priory business. He handled part of the final transfer of property under licence to the house after 1391 and was also entrusted with the acquisition of holdings.[63] Although he and other clerks employed by the canonesses were not priory incumbents, Fowler suggests that many were clients of the Grey family, members of which were patrons and benefactors of the priory at this period. Even the Grey family itself was called into service on occasion.[64] Thus with imagination and opportunism, even houses with little apparent power or influence could call upon adequate help.

So ubiquitous were nominees during the fourteenth century that it is worth investigating whether demand ever called forth a class of professionals. Men featuring in the licences of more than one foundation can certainly be found. About thirty such individuals are recorded for the East Midlands and Lincolnshire

[60] M. E. Aston, *Thomas Arundel* (Oxford, 1967), pp. 141, 239; *Cal. Pat.*, 1391–6, pp. 106–7.

[61] Aston, *Thomas Arundel*, p. 18; Fowler, *Records of Harrold Priory*, pp. 128, 160 et seq., 212.

[62] Fowler, *Records of Harrold Priory*, pp. 147–9, 215.

[63] *Ibid.*, pp. 126–7, 137–40, 171–2 no. 301; *Cal. Pat.*, 1391–6, pp. 164, 343. He was successively parson of part of Walton, Stoke Goldington (Bucks.) and Thurleigh (Beds.).

[64] Fowler, *Records of Harrold Priory*, pp. 11–12, 146, 156–7, 172 et seq., 211–12, 216.

during this period, but this number is hardly significant in the overall context of grantors; nor were they all necessarily acting for churchmen. Confusion between men acting on their own behalf and those acting for the alienor rather than the alienee can easily take place. Moreover, nothing suggests that such activities were mutually exclusive. The record of Master Simon of Islip, then canon of Lincoln, later archbishop of Canterbury, is instructive in this respect. Between 1348 and 1349 he arranged grants to Thorney Abbey to establish a family chantry.[65] Shortly before this he was associated with two more licences of a less personal nature. In company with two others, he granted an advowson to the Cistercian nuns of Heynings, while at Lincoln Cathedral he combined chapter business with provision for the soul of Master Hugh de Walmesford.[66] In 1347 he and Richard de Whitewell, another canon of Lincoln, granted a small holding in Louth to the monks of Louth Park.[67] In addition, Crowland Abbey is known to have retained him although there is no evidence that he ever acted for the monks in land dealings.[68]

Busy though Islip was with the affairs of several houses, it is doubtful whether he could justifiably be called a professional nominee. His were tasks which inevitably fell to men of note in the local hierarchy. Canons of Lincoln were an obvious choice for those seeking honest feoffees or executors and for minor religious houses needing help. Islip was not the only canon to act in this way. John de Warsop (d. 1386) was one of several grantors in licences to the canons of Newbo in 1373 and 1379 and again in a licence to the nuns in Legbourne in 1384.[69] Similarly, Thomas la Warre (d. 1427) assisted in the transfer of substantial holdings to Barlings Abbey in 1390 and 1398 and to Swineshead in 1400. A further grant to Sixhills in 1407 concerned the endowment of a personal chantry.[70] Laymen of

---

[65] *Cal. Pat.*, 1348–50, pp. 127–8, 422. For this and family connections with this house, see Raban, *Estates of Thorney and Crowland*, p. 45.

[66] *Cal. Pat.*, 1345–8, p. 450; 1348–50, p. 112.

[67] *Ibid.*, 1345–8, pp. 336–7.

[68] B.L., Add. MS 5845, f24–v.

[69] *Cal. Pat.*, 1370–4, p. 325; 1377–81, p. 406; 1381–5, p. 472.

[70] *Ibid.*, 1388–92, pp. 192–3; 1396–9, p. 340; 1399–1401, p. 285; 1405–8, p. 334.

comparable standing show much the same pattern of involvement. The chief justice Sir William Thirning, whose family connections associated him with Harrold Priory, also lent his aid to the Warre chantry and the Thorp chantry in Peterborough Abbey as well as to St Mary's Priory, Huntingdon.[71]

The strongest case for calling these men professional is that they were professional men of affairs, who became feoffees as a consequence of other, more important activities. Professional nominees, if ever they existed, should more properly be sought among the comparatively obscure men who also performed this service. One such minor feoffee, chosen at random, was Thomas Claymond, who was involved in grants to several religious houses and chantries between 1382 and 1392.[72] Neither knight nor clerk, he appears to have come from a minor Lincolnshire landed family. His brother Alan, who held land in Wyberton (Lincs.), is several times referred to as an esquire.[73] Thomas himself is sometimes described as Thomas Claymond of 'Hale' or 'Hole', a place variously identified, but probably Great-Hale-by-Sleaford. The first record of his career appears in 1367, when he acted as attorney for two other Lincolnshire men who were going abroad.[74] Thereafter he became gradually more active on royal business, receiving commissions of *oyer* and *terminer*, array and peace, overwhelmingly in Lincolnshire and usually in Kesteven. For a few months in 1385 he served as sheriff.[75] The high point of his career was reached in the late 70s and early 80s and he is recorded as having died by 1397.[76]

Interestingly, Claymond only emerged as a feoffee in his later years, although it is likely that some of the ecclesiastical grants with which he was involved between 1389 and 1392 had long antecedents. It is known, for example, that the grant to Barlings in 1390 was the culmination of an enfeoffment made in 1378. His career pattern suggests a minor county figure whose growing administrative expertise recommended him to other locals in

[71] *Ibid.*, 1385–9, pp. 313–14; 1396–9, p. 30.
[72] *Ibid.*, 1381–5, p. 115; 1388–92, pp. 38, 192–3, 427; 1391–6, pp. 17, 140.
[73] *Cal. Close*, 1385–9, pp. 105, 594.
[74] *Cal. Pat.*, 1367–70, p. 34.
[75] *Ibid.*, 1370–96, passim; *Cal. Fine*, 1383–91, pp. 93, 106–7.
[76] *Cal. Pat.*, 1396–9, p. 71.

need of a feoffee. Far from appearing as a professional land dealer, his services as a nominee marked the climax to a long career of public service. In this he was probably typical enough. At various points in his career, he was associated with John de Hagh, Philip le Despenser, Robert de Cumberworth, Henry Malbussh parson of Willoughby (Lincs.), John Amory of Horncastle and Albinus de Enderby, all of whom had records similar to his and sometimes acted for the same houses.[77] There are, however, few instances of the same combinations of feoffees regularly recurring or of any consistent involvement with one house. Rather, the impression is of a pool of suitable men, well known to local churchmen, who were employed on a random basis as the need arose.

Much the most vivid account of a transaction involving feoffees concerns the grant by Henry le Vavasour of his manor at Cockerington (Lincs.) to Louth Park in 1342. Fascinating details of the arrangement have survived because it became a *cause célèbre* after his death. The story began with le Vavasour, in failing health at Cockerington, summoning the abbot of Louth Park to hear his confession. Either spontaneously or under pressure from the abbot, he conceived a desire to augment the endowment of the house by giving the monks his manor. On Wednesday, 27 November 1342, he asked to be transferred to the abbey. His doctor may even have recommended it in the interests of his well-being. The request was granted and the abbot sent a covered cart to fetch him. The abbot later swore that, on arrival, he was fit enough to walk to his chamber and demand constant attention. Fit or not, as le Vavasour pointed out to the abbot, he was worth pampering since the latter might never 'take such a fish in his net again'. It had been agreed that four feoffees, two chosen by each party, should effect the transfer of the manor, and care was taken to see that le Vavasour's heirs should be compensated for their lost inheritance. Constance, his wife, was to receive one hundred marks per annum for her lifetime, and after her death one of her sons was to receive twenty marks per annum as long as he lived. Their opposition to the gift was foreseen and

[77] *Ibid.*, 1381–5, pp. 115, 134, 140, 245, 250, 284; 1385–9, p. 389; 1388–92, pp. 3, 38; 1391–6, p. 140; 1396–9, p. 71.

countermeasures taken. A deed was drawn up giving one of le Vavasour's life tenants elsewhere full tenure. This quitclaim was only to be used in an emergency. Should the family bring legal action against the abbey, the tenant was to be sold the deed, thus, at one blow, financing the defence and depriving the family of further property. Provision was also made for bad faith on the part of the monks. The abbot agreed to make a bond for one thousand pounds as security that le Vavasour's spiritual directions would be carried out within two years. The sheaf of deeds required to effect all these arrangements was drawn up by le Vavasour's steward and by the abbot in consultation with his counsellors. The matter then went ahead. On the Saturday morning, the feoffees and attorneys appointed to deliver seisin assembled in le Vavasour's chamber. The sick-room was already packed with members of the family, servants and monks. Amongst this throng a controversial scene was then played out.

Constance later claimed that her husband had not been in his right mind since the preceding Thursday and even that the hand set to the seal at the crowded Saturday gathering was that of a corpse. She maintained that she had been hoodwinked over the documents, believing that they were to enfeoff her with part of the manor. All the other witnesses, including the two feoffees nominated by le Vavasour, took a more charitable view of the proceedings and agreed that he was perfectly lucid. The most moving account of what took place was given by Alice, le Vavasour's servant. She had not paid much attention to what was happening because she was 'standing before the fireplace in the chamber of the abbey, sad on account of the sickness of her master'. However, she heard some deeds read aloud and saw one of the monks present heat wax for the seal over the fire. Constance herself brought over the seal, 'understanding all that was being done if she would'. Other depositions clothe Alice's picture. One of the feoffees was excused the sealing, but the other three remained and took an oath on the Gospels that they would faithfully transfer the manor to Louth Park. Le Vavasour, and perhaps even Constance, then urged them to pursue the business in all haste. Accordingly, they hurried with the attorneys to Cockerington and took seisin before sunset. All three spent the

Saturday night at the manor, where they were joined the following morning by the fourth feoffee. Together they took attornment of the free tenants and then returned to the abbey. Meanwhile, le Vavasour's condition had worsened and the abbot had been summoned to give him extreme unction. Finally, in the early hours, with Alice sitting with 'her cheek against his cheek', he died.

The weight of evidence suggests that le Vavasour was in full possession of his faculties when he made provision for the gift, even if the abbot may have played on his death-bed fears. In the stress of the moment, Constance appears to have been equally eager for the grant, but in retrospect appreciated her loss and attempted to rectify it. The fact that everything had been hastily arranged on le Vavasour's death-bed gave her a lever. Nor did she stop at litigation. The abbot claimed that Constance and her henchmen had subsequently burgled the abbey close, assaulted him and carried away a muniment chest. She doubtless hoped to recover the precautionary quitclaim. In retaliation, the monks seized and imprisoned her at Louth Park and made free of her goods. Eventually, the matter was heard before the royal justices in spring 1345. Perhaps the abbey triumphed in the end since le Vavasour's son was licensed to alienate considerable holdings in Cockerington to Louth Park in 1347 and steps were taken to complete the matter after his death.[78] However, as an inquisition following the death of William Vavasour in 1369 revealed continued family possession of a manor in Cockerington, there must be some doubt about this.[79]

Little is known about the feoffees in this case apart from Robert de Yerdeburgh. They fulfilled the basic qualification, however: they remained loyal to the grantor's intention. The precise relationship of a nominee to his principal was not important. The sole requirement was that the bond should be sufficiently strong. For some, kinship offered the greatest security, while others depended on the ambition of servants or clients. Few nominees can have found it worthwhile to cheat their

[78] *Cal. Pat.*, 1343–5, pp. 490, 573; 1345–8, pp. 1–7, 336–7; 1348–50, pp. 437–8.
[79] *Cal. Inq. Post Mortem*, vol. XIII, p. 5, no. 6; pp. 107–8, no. 134.

principals in spite of the church's precarious position at law. Challenges, as at Louth Park, were more likely to issue from disappointed heirs. The satisfactory nature of most arrangements can be gauged from the speed with which they were adopted. Those which enabled nominees to hold property until negotiations for a licence were complete were a convenience but of little fundamental significance. Enfeoffments to use were more far-reaching in their implications. By the later fourteenth century, they had become so popular that they had driven a coach and horses through mortmain legislation.

Churchmen were not the only members of society to perceive the manipulative possibilities of such enfeoffments. Lay landlords also made copious use of them to evade feudal incidents. By Richard II's reign, the need for legislation against a variety of abuses had become clear. In 1376, a statute forbade debtors to avoid their obligations by disposing their property amongst feoffees to their own use. In the following year, a further statute was enacted so that plaintiffs in property disputes should not be thwarted in the same way.[80] Petitions in the parliaments of 1376 and 1377 demanded redress against the church too, but on both occasions the crown refused to make any changes.[81] Action was finally taken, in response to another petition, in 1391. An attempt was then made not only to halt the exploitation of uses, but also to compel those churchmen who had benefited from property held by this means to amortise it before the following Michaelmas:

all they that be possessed by feoffment, or by other manner to the use of religious people, or other spiritual persons, of lands and tenements, fees, advowsons, or any manner other possessions whatsoever, to amortise them, and whereof the said religious and spiritual persons take the profits, that betwixt this and the Feast of St. Michael next coming, they shall cause them to be amortised by the licence of the king and of the lords, or else they shall sell and aliene them to some other use between this and the said feast, upon pain to be forfeited to the king, and to the lords, according to the form of the said Statute of Religious [1279 Statute of Mortmain], as lands purchased by

---

[80] Bean, *Decline of English Feudalism*, p. 125; *Statutes of the Realm*, vol. I, p. 398; vol. II, pp. 3–4.
[81] *Rot. Parl.*, vol. II, p. 368; vol. III, p. 19.

religious people: And that from henceforth no such purchase be made, so that such religious or other spiritual persons take thereof the profits, as aforesaid, upon pain aforesaid.[82]

Clearly some thought had been given to the whole issue of mortmain tenure, because the same statute also extended the field within which restrictions were to operate. The church was no longer the only perpetual corporation affected; boroughs and gilds were also to be subject to licensing procedure:

from henceforth. . .the same statute extend and be observed of all lands, tenements, fees, advowsons, and other possessions purchased or to be purchased to the use of gilds or fraternities. And moreover it is assented, because mayors, bailiffs, and commons of cities, boroughs and other towns which have a perpetual commonalty, and others which have offices perpetual, be as perpetual as people of religion, that from henceforth they shall not purchase to them, and to their commons or office, upon pain contained in the said statute *de religiosis*; and [whereas others be possessed] or hereafter shall purchase to the use, and they thereof take the profits, it shall be done in like manner as is aforesaid of people of religion.[83]

The results of the 1391 enactment were spectacular. From an average of 41.6 licences per annum in the previous decade, licences in 1392 rose to an all-time record of 378.[84] Institutions like Oriel College, Oxford, and Harrold Priory hastened to regularise their position. Bodies newly brought within the purview of the law were also well represented. In September 1392, the borough authorities of Leicester, Colchester, Thetford and Great Yarmouth all obtained licences to acquire in mortmain. The purposes of the resulting income ranged from the funding of pious works and chantries to the repair of walls and bridges.[85] Gilds were equally assiduous in their efforts to conform to the new regulations. The quay and profits from a ferry across the harbour impart a marine flavour to the licence granted to the aldermen and brethren of the merchant gild of Holy Trinity at

---

[82] *Statutes of the Realm*, vol. II, pp. 79–80; *Rot. Parl.*, vol. III, p. 291.
[83] *Ibid.*
[84] See above, p. 42. 365 of these licences related to specific alienations. The previous record had been 104 in 1336.
[85] *Cal. Pat.*, 1391–6, pp. 154, 162, 170.

Bishop's Lynn in the same month.[86] Gilds at Leicester and Coventry both sought to revive earlier privileges which had suddenly assumed fresh relevance and each won a new general licence. Significantly, accessions to the full value of these were made within a few weeks.[87]

This flurry of activity marked the full development of medieval mortmain legislation. Henceforward, the acquisitions of all perpetual bodies were under external control, while the most effective and widespread method by which the church might avoid restriction was abolished. Nor did ecclesiastical ingenuity succeed in devising further methods of negating the mortmain statutes. In theory the situation was highly satisfactory; in practice less so, since attitudes towards amortisation grew more lax during the fifteenth century. Nevertheless, the third and last mortmain enactment before the Dissolution suggests that evasion was mainly confined to chantry foundations and that widespread abuse of mortmain law by the religious was indeed a thing of the past.[88]

[86] *Ibid.*, p. 149.
[87] *Ibid.*, pp. 131, 136, 155, 161–2.
[88] *Statutes of the Realm*, vol. III, p. 378, cap. 10. No mention was made of the religious. The statute was directed against parishes, gilds and boroughs.

Chapter 5

PATTERNS OF ECCLESIASTICAL ACCESSION

That mortmain legislation was keenly enforced for much of the period after 1279, and that churchmen were at pains to circumvent its restrictions, is beyond doubt. What may be questioned is whether all this activity resulted in any significant distortion of the pattern of acquisition which would otherwise have prevailed. Statutory obstacles were only one factor governing the church's territorial accessions. Changes were taking place both in the economy and in popular religious expression, so it could be argued that each contributed in some measure towards a diminution of landed accessions. To understand how much real restrictive power was exercised by mortmain legislation, it is necessary to examine its effects in relation to the complex independent pressures already confronting the church as a landlord.

The church had been accumulating property for centuries before the 1279 Statute of Mortmain and indeed owed its greatest wealth to the patrons of the tenth-century monastic revival. Archbishop Dunstan, bishops Aethelwold and Oswald and interested laymen like ealdorman Aethelwine made over whole villages or even districts to their nascent foundations. Professor Raftis calculated that nearly 50% of vills featuring in the Huntingdonshire Domesday changed hands at this date.[1] Although many of these grants were later challenged, particularly following the death of King Edgar and the Norman Conquest, the broad disposition of land achieved by the church before 1066 was maintained until the Dissolution. Moreover, individual losses were sometimes made good by later donations, and the property of the church as a whole was considerably augmented by gifts to the new orders entering England in the twelfth century.

[1] J. A. Raftis, *The Estates of Ramsey Abbey* (Toronto, 1957), p. 7.

By the late twelfth century, therefore, religious houses both collectively and individually were among the richest and most influential landholders under the medieval crown. Yet already, long before any royal attempts to curb accessions, there were signs that the flow of land into ecclesiastical hands was slowing. Neither individual houses nor the orders to which they belonged were able to sustain their original ideals over a long period, a dilemma neatly summed up later by a Protestant in the observation that 'God's word has seldom tarried in one place longer than forty years'.[2] In consequence, existing foundations forfeited much external support, which flowed instead to the latest experiments in reform. In the twelfth century, enthusiasm was increasingly reserved for the Cistercians together with the new orders of canons and in the thirteenth century for the mendicants. This preference for novel expressions of spirituality accorded well with the other major development in patronage: a reduction in the size of gifts. Inevitably, as society became more settled, the opportunities for patronage on the earlier scale declined. It was the simplicity of their needs, as well as their fervour, which favoured the swift expansion of the Cistercians.[3] More sparing grants were also a reflection of the prevalence of increasingly less aristocratic donors, to whose resources they were better suited. Southern showed how Henry I's men raised 'from the dust' sought to consolidate their elevation through pious gifts, while King traced the same ambition down to the lesser knights later in the twelfth century.[4] Gradually the habit of patronage filtered down through society to the peasantry.[5] By the thirteenth century, religious houses were likely to find men of extremely limited means amongst their most typical benefactors. So far as gifts to the older foundations were concerned, therefore, the Statute of Mortmain appeared long after most of their property had been

2 G. Strauss, 'Success and Failure in the German Reformation', *Past and Present*, 67, 1975, p. 31.
3 B. D. Hill, *English Cistercian Monasteries and Their Patrons in the Twelfth Century* (Illinois, 1968), pp. 52–3.
4 R. W. Southern, 'The Place of Henry I in English History', *Proc. Brit. Acad.*, 48, 1962, pp. 137–8; E. King, 'Large and Small Landowners in Thirteenth-Century England', *Past and Present*, 47, 1970, pp. 47–8.
5 Raban, *Estates of Thorney and Crowland*, pp. 38–9.

received. At most it could accelerate the decline in gifts which was already taking place for other reasons.

The broad picture of smaller gifts from less prestigious donors never entirely precluded large-scale patronage on traditional lines. Indeed, the gifts of the nobility remained sufficiently numerous to permit a study of their incidence in the later Middle Ages. Although licences permitting grants to the church by this section of society showed the same fifteenth-century decline as those permitting grants by society at large, individuals continued to make outstanding gifts.[6] There were even new foundations. The Carthusian order owed almost all its English houses to the piety of fourteenth- and fifteenth-century magnates. Sheen, the largest and wealthiest of them, was founded by Henry V along with the Bridgettine abbey of Syon.[7] The need for display ensured that the crown at least continued the practice of ecclesiastical patronage. Even Edward IV, supposedly disinclined to pious largesse, added further to the endowments of Sheen and houses associated with royal residences as well as introducing the Observant Franciscans into England.[8] Prominent among aristocratic patrons was Mary de St Pol, countess of Pembroke. She established a house for Franciscan nuns at Denney (Cambs.), although not without some opposition from the inmates, who resented their upheaval from nearby Waterbeach. She also founded Pembroke Hall at Cambridge and a chantry in the hermitage at Cripplegate, and planned two Carthusian houses which never came to fruition.[9] Her contemporary and friend Elisabeth de Burgh transformed the penurious University Hall at Cambridge into Clare Hall and founded a chantry in Anglesey Priory as well as a Franciscan house at Walsingham.[10]

Although gifts of this kind persisted, a closer examination of

6 Rosenthal, *Purchase of Paradise*, pp. 135–6.

7 D. Knowles, R. N. Hadcock, *Medieval Religious Houses: England and Wales*, 2nd edn (London, 1971), pp. 133–6, 202.

8 C. Ross, *Edward IV* (London, 1974), pp. 273–5.

9 H. Jenkinson, 'Mary de Sancto Paulo, Foundress of Pembroke College, Cambridge', *Archaeologia*, 66, 1915, p. 418 et seq.

10 *Ibid.*, p. 428; ed. L. F. Salzman et al., *V.C.H. Cambridgeshire*, 6 vols. (1938–78), vol. III, pp. 340–1; *Cal. Pat.*, 1330–4, p. 39; 1345–8, pp. 135, 255; 1348–50, p. 7.

them underlines the disquieting implications evident in the general trend away from benefactions. Both Mary de St Pol and Elisabeth de Burgh were unusual. Each enjoyed a long and wealthy widowhood, distinguished by religious enthusiasm. Mary lived childless for fifty-three years after the death of Aymer de Valence in 1324, while Elisabeth, who buried her third and last husband in 1321, lived until 1360. In addition to their dower property, Elisabeth was a major heiress in her own right. After her brother's death at Bannockburn, she received a third of the Clare estates, worth about £2,500 per annum.[11] These ladies therefore were among the most affluent as well as the most active benefactors of the later Middle Ages. Accordingly it is the more significant that their gifts, and also those of the crown, show signs of financial constraint and changing preferences.

In founding Sheen and Syon, Henry V drew not on his own reserves of land but on the confiscated property of the alien priories, just as in the previous century Edward III had used the disputed bequests of Londoners to fulfil promises to his Cistercian foundation of St Mary Graces. Similarly, many of the royal benefactions to Westminster Abbey in the late Middle Ages involved merely the transfer of estates from one religious body to another.[12] In each case, permanent retention of the property in lay hands might have provoked public criticism. Neither Mary de St Pol nor Elisabeth de Burgh could make gifts quite so painlessly; indeed, it is noticeable that they deliberated at length and frequently changed their minds before actually bestowing a property. The advowson of Great Gransden (Cambs.), destined by Elisabeth in 1336 for the dean and chapter of St Paul's, was granted in a new licence of 1343 to her friend's foundation at Denney. Then, three years later, she finally dictated that it should be given to Clare Hall.[13] In a similar fashion, Mary de St Pol caused the cancellation of a licence authorising the grant of property in Repton (Derb.) and Whissendine (Leics.) to West-

[11] Jenkinson, *Archaeologia*, 1915, p. 406; G. A. Holmes, *The Estates of the Higher Nobility in Fourteenth-Century England* (Cambridge, 1957), pp. 35–7, 109.

[12] Morgan, *History*, 1941, p. 210; Chew, *E.H.R.*, 1945, p. 11; Harvey, *Westminster Abbey and its Estates*, p. 31.

[13] *Cal. Pat.*, 1334–8, p. 245; 1343–5, p. 3; 1345–8, p. 135.

minster Abbey in order to found a chantry, and made the gift instead to Pembroke Hall. She also obtained several licences allowing her complete discretion in choosing to whom she should give certain properties, thereby establishing her freedom to alienate while keeping her options open.[14] Indiscriminate giving had never been characteristic even among benefactors of this wealth and status,[15] but such hesitancy when allied to quite exceptional piety indicates how tight the resources of donors had become.

Causes chosen for sponsorship are as revealing as the grants made. Only the Carthusians among the enclosed orders exercised a continuing attraction. For the most part the crown and the two widows favoured the mendicants, chantries or educational provision. Such preferences accord well with the survey undertaken by J. A. F. Thomson into the bequests of Londoners between 1401 and 1530. Although roughly 40% of testators left something to the regular orders, a high proportion of these legacies went to the mendicants, while the remaining grants went increasingly to the Carthusians. Many bequests were also designed as the foundation grants for chantries, although often they were only able to provide finance for a limited period. Other popular causes were hospitals and sundry public works.[16] Surprisingly enough, only 3.5% of Londoners favoured educational bequests, although like Mary de St Pol and Elisabeth de Burgh they showed a preference for the universities.[17] Some of their chantry bequests may have involved contributions to schooling, however, since the country at large witnessed a growing enthusiasm for endowed schools in the wake of the first known chantry school at Wotton-under-Edge in 1384.[18] Licence figures in general also show that parish churches were increasingly a focus of local wealth and pride.[19] Thus, at a period when overall gifts to the church were

[14] *Ibid.*, 1340–3, p. 529; 1343–5, p. 568; 1345–8, pp. 61–2, 86; 1348–50, p. 349.
[15] Raban, *Estates of Thorney and Crowland*, pp. 36, 41–2.
[16] 'Piety and Charity in Late Medieval London', *The Journal of Ecclesiastical History*, 16, 1965, p. 186 et seq.
[17] *Ibid.*, p. 186.
[18] N. Orme, *English Schools in the Middle Ages* (London, 1973), pp. 194–7.
[19] Rosenthal, *Purchase of Paradise*, p. 136; see also below, p. 169.

declining, laymen continued to drift away from the old orders and at all levels of society became more secular and self-assertive in their tastes.

Old foundations could only share significantly in later medieval patronage if they were prepared to adapt to contemporary needs. There is little evidence that they responded to the demand for wider education, their chief concern remaining the schooling of their inmates. Monastic houses sometimes became patrons of grammar schools, as at Cirencester in the fifteenth century, and they also provided for poor scholars in their almonry schools, but only at Bury St Edmunds, Reading and Evesham could they be seen to foster the free grammar schools which attracted later medieval patronage.[20] By contrast, the acceptance of formal chantry obligations enabled the religious to offer a service currently in vogue and one which also accorded well with their established ideals.

Whether chantries also secured an appreciable augmentation of ecclesiastical endowments is somewhat doubtful. The very popularity of such foundations encouraged founders whose means were inadequate. It was not unusual for religious houses to find themselves out of pocket, a problem which was exacerbated when the undertaking was perpetual.[21] Even if funds sufficed to pay for the services, no additional benefits would necessarily accrue to the house which administered them. This was evident to the monks of Christchurch Cathedral Priory at Canterbury in 1368, when they refused a Beauchamp chantry because they were expected to do too much for too small a return.[22] The meagre financing of many chantries is illustrated by the bequest of William Fleet, a London merchant, to Thorney Abbey in the mid-fifteenth century. He left the monks endowments designed to yield four pounds per annum, two pounds of which was to be spent on a parochial chaplain. A further one pound was to support a singing chaplain, with 6s 8d for distribution among the poor. This left 13s 4d for distribution among the convent. The abbey rental shows that the monks could probably extract a

[20] Orme, *English Schools in the Middle Ages*, pp. 206, 233 et seq.
[21] Wood-Legh, *Perpetual Chantries in Britain*, pp. 148–54.
[22] *Ibid.*, p. 145.

further 11s 4d from the property, but it was a relatively small sum to offset against the responsibility which they had incurred.[23]

Chantries figure prominently in the accounts of the common property of the dean and chapter of Lincoln, making it possible to form some assessment of the financial benefit they conferred. In the second decade of the fourteenth century, there are signs of shortfall in the rents assigned to the chantries of William de Thornton and William de la Gare. The difficulty was due partly at least to houses standing empty. The problem was not acute, but it was chronic, and in 1323–4 measures had to be taken to safeguard the foundations for the future. Various properties were bought by the provost of the common and granted to the dean and chapter under licence. As a result, the following years saw a small surplus of about five pounds on this account.[24] Other chantries at Lincoln had a healthier record, yet even to think in terms of a surplus on chantry obligations of this sort is misleading. They were founded by members of the chapter or its officials with wealth supported, in part at least, by their office. The prebendal system at Lincoln and the opportunities for continued possession of private property preclude certainty about this, but less doubt attaches to the endowments commonly set aside by the heads of religious houses from the resources of their houses for the care of their souls. The most that many such founders could contribute from their own reserves was sufficient acumen to increase the existing wealth of the body. All too often, therefore, there was a parasitic relationship between chantries and their hosts. Thus, even chantries which appeared to pay their way may in reality have absorbed wealth which would otherwise have accrued, unencumbered, to the house.

The disabilities attaching to chantries can be overstated, however. Few houses gained as much as Westminster Abbey was able to draw from its royal chantries,[25] but the more usual small annual sum was the more valued because outright gifts were so few. Moreover, surplus apart, a chantry might make a genuine con-

[23] C.U.L., Add. MSS 3020–1, ff39v, 292v–3; Add. MS 4401, f43; *Cal. Pat.*, 1446–52, p. 502.

[24] *Cal. Pat.*, 1321–4, p. 406; Lincs. Archives Off., Bj/2/4, ff90v, 97v, 135; Bj/2/5, ff1v, 11v, 66v, 89–v, 112.

[25] Harvey, *Westminster Abbey and its Estates*, pp. 28–30, 33–6.

tribution to the economy of a house if a member of the community served it and its endowment could thereby be used in his support. Arrangements of this sort were popular with the regular canons in particular, although it is noticeable that many founders, like Fleet, insisted on the employment of secular chaplains.[26] Perhaps they feared that endowments and prayers of chantries served by the religious themselves would be assimilated too readily into the general life of the house. The principal aim of a founder was to provide as effectively as possible for the souls of himself and his family. Unless he were a member of the community, the well-being of the house administering the chantry was not his concern. Indeed, conspicuous poverty might not inspire his confidence. On balance, therefore, the most that the religious could hope to gain from a chantry was a modest surplus, the goodwill of the laity and an acceptance that the enclosed orders had something to offer to late medieval society.

That some justification for their continuance was desirable had become evident by the later fourteenth century. Far from wishing to swell the endowments of the ancient foundations, a vocal body of opinion was calling for their dispossession. The fact that they became known in popular parlance as 'possessioners' is some indication of the disproportionate importance which their temporal wealth had come to assume in the eyes of the laity. Criticism and satire had long been directed at the enclosed orders, as is evidenced by the accusations of greed levelled at the Cistercians by their rivals in the late twelfth and thirteenth centuries.[27] The Statute of Mortmain itself indicated that lay generosity had turned to suspicion and a wish to limit ecclesiastical accessions. Now a more radical spirit suggested that limitation was not enough: the accumulated wealth of ecclesiastical bodies could be put to better use in the parishes or even among the laity.

Hostility was expressed in varying degrees and in a variety of circumstances. In parliament, tensions over taxation fuelled fierce attacks. When the clergy refused to make a grant without the

---

[26] Wood-Legh, *Perpetual Chantries in Britain*, p. 130 et seq.
[27] C. V. Graves, 'The Economic Activities of the Cistercians in Medieval England (1128–1307)', *Analecta Sacri Ordinis Cisterciensis*, 13, 1957, pp. 46 et seq.

prior approval of convocation in 1371, two Austin friars returned a forthright statement of the popular view. With appropriate citation of the Fathers and canon law, they denounced the example set by churchmen in being so wicked and ill-natured as to refuse to come to the aid of the crown and people in their hour of need, more especially since it was the laity who had provided their endowments. They further argued that in an emergency both natural and divine law ordained that all possessions should be held in common.[28] Similar views were put forward by a lay lord in the form of an elaborate metaphor casting the clergy as an owl whose protective plumage had been provided by the other birds. When a hawk threatened and the birds reclaimed their gifts, they were refused; the feathers could only be recovered by force.[29] Arguments were even more extreme in similar circumstances in 1385. Certain members of the commons called for the confiscation of the church's temporalities and Walsingham recorded in outrage how he had heard with his own ears how his house of St Alban's was to yield one thousand marks per annum.[30] The most far-reaching plans to be aired in parliament were presented in a petition of 1410 thought to have been inspired by Lollard teaching. This attempted to value ecclesiastical temporalities and to suggest how they could be assigned more usefully. The authors of the petition estimated that church wealth could fund fifteen new earls, one thousand five hundred knights and six thousand two hundred esquires, as well as supplementing the king's income and providing for fifteen thousand priests, one hundred almshouses and five universities.[31] That these grandiose schemes resulted in so little practical action can in part be ascribed to the Peasants' Revolt of 1381. According to the Anonimalle Chronicle, Wat Tyler asked at Smithfield:

[28] V. H. Galbraith, 'Articles Laid before the Parliament of 1371', *E.H.R.*, 34, 1919, pp. 579–82.

[29] Ed. W. W. Shirley, *Fasciculi Zizaniorum* (Rolls Series, London, 1858), p. xxi; W. Stubbs, *The Constitutional History of England*, 3rd edn, 3 vols. (Oxford, 1887), vol. II, pp. 440–1.

[30] Ed. H. T. Riley, *Historia Anglicana*, 2 vols. (Rolls Series, London, 1863–4), vol. II, p. 140.

[31] M. E. Aston, 'Lollardy and Sedition 1381–1431', *Past and Present*, 17, 1960, p. 16; ed. V. H. Galbraith, *The St. Alban's Chronicle* (Oxford, 1937), pp. 52–5.

that the goods of holy church should not be in the hands of the religious, nor of parsons and vicars, nor others of holy church, but that those holding office should have adequate sustenance and the rest of their goods should be divided amongst parishoners; and there should be one bishop only in England and only one prelate, and all the lands and tenements of the possessioners should be taken away from them and divided amongst the commons, saving to them their reasonable sustenance.[32]

In proposing this, he effectively associated the redistribution of ecclesiastical wealth with rebellion, thereby alienating those whose support was needed to enforce any change.[33] The religious orders thus gained a reprieve, but the fact that this owed more to fear of social unrest than to any acceptance that demands for disendowment were fundamentally misplaced remained ominous for the future.

The hostility of late-fourteenth-century society to the wealthiest elements in the church can of course be exaggerated since, inevitably, extremists impressed their mark most forcibly on the records. Nevertheless, patterns of giving also suggest that the sympathies of more moderate men were no longer aroused by the older and richer institutions. Radical and moderate alike were united in respect for the Carthusians, hospitals and many parish priests, the one favouring them with gifts and the other, as instanced by the 1410 petition, exempting them from reform.[34] Thus, in considering either benefactor or aspiring despoiler, one thing is clear: whereas individual sanctity or local loyalty might secure some continued patronage for the ancient enclosed foundations, it was no longer the social norm.

Even so, to chart the declining gifts of land and the change in their distribution is not to tell quite the whole story. There were still some reserves of piety among the laity and other ways in which it could be expressed. McFarlane suggested that the Statute of Mortmain deflected alms from landed endowment to building and altar funds.[35] This merits serious consideration. Gifts

---

[32] Trans. from ed. V. H. Galbraith, *The Anonimalle Chronicle* (Manchester, 1927, repr. 1970), p. 147.

[33] Aston, *Past and Present*, 1960, pp. 8–9.

[34] Galbraith, *St. Alban's Chronicle*, p. 55.

[35] McFarlane, *Nobility of Later Medieval England*, p. 95.

of cash and precious objects had always been highly valued by the church and there are reasons, quite apart from restrictions concerning amortisation, for thinking that they may have become more popular. As donors descended the social scale, their capacity to give land diminished too. Modest gifts of cash or moveable goods were more easily within their reach and permitted the sharing of their resources among several recipients. There was the added advantage that gifts of this sort were acceptable to the much favoured mendicants, by whom land would normally be refused.

Some of the best evidence for such gifts comes from bequests. The testamentary bar to the devise of land outside boroughs emphasises gifts of cash and chattels, but this is a welcome corrective to the more usual bias in favour of real property offered by licences and title deeds. To return once more to Mary de St Pol: her testament of 1377 shows that, in addition to the holdings and other gifts transferred during her lifetime, she left something over one thousand three hundred marks shared between twelve individual houses and the four leading orders of mendicants. She also bequeathed assorted relics, jewels, plate and books to bodies such as Westminster Abbey, St Paul's Cathedral and her own foundations. Fifty years earlier and at a humbler level, the testament of Avice de Crosseby of Lincoln, another widow, shows exactly the same predilections. Whereas Mary left one hundred marks to each order of friars, Avice left half a mark to the Austin friars in Lincoln and twelve pence each to the Carmelites, Franciscans and Dominicans. Small sums were also left to the canons of Torksey and Barlings. The hundred marks Mary devoted to the fabric of Bruisyard echoes the two shillings left by Avice to the fabric of Lincoln Cathedral. While Mary naturally favoured her own foundations, Avice turned principally to her parish church: half a mark went towards its fabric, two shillings to its clerks and ten pounds for anniversary celebrations. She also gave a funeral pall and gifts to various altars.

In the particular context of mortmain tenure, it is interesting to note that both women made provision either for the purchase or for the disposal of land. Avice, in accordance with the custom of Lincoln, instructed her executors to sell property to fund anniversary prayers, while Mary left three hundred marks to Westminster Abbey, where her husband was buried, expressly to buy rents to fund a chantry, and a further one hundred marks to Latton Priory towards the purchase of lands or rent.[36] Such arrangements probably commended themselves on practical grounds, but they may also reflect constraints imposed by mortmain legislation. Certainly the influence of the statute can be detected in the provisions of wills elsewhere. Many London testators in the first half of the fifteenth century, fearing that their gifts to religious houses would be frustrated, made alternative plans tending towards less contentious public works.[37]

The store set by churchmen on gifts other than landed property is evident. The author of the *De gestis abbatum* of Thorney Abbey, when writing of his own abbot, supplemented the usual panegyric on newly won estates and magnificent building projects with a dazzling account of recently acquired vestments. Rich colours abound amidst admiring phrases like *magni precii* and *opere mirifico*. For this contemporary, the long-term benefits of land were almost overshadowed by the immediate spectacle of cloths embroidered with gold stars, leopards or griffons.[38] The cost and conspicuousness of such precious items were sufficient to satisfy even the most prestigious of benefactors. So, for the rich, too, there was ample incentive to turn from landed gifts. The extent to which this became general and the amount which any such change owed to difficulties placed in the way of alienating real property cannot be quantified. Apart from testaments, record of such gifts depends on the whim of chroniclers and on other chance accounts. Yet the lack of such evidence should not encourage us to underrate a major and highly valued form of ecclesiastical patronage and the rôle it may have played in absorbing the shock of mortmain controls.

Whether before or after 1279, land was only one of a number of gifts which a benefactor might bestow on the church, and by the later thirteenth century it was offered ever more sparingly. How

[36] Jenkinson, *Archaeologia*, 1915, pp. 432–5; ed. C. W. Foster, *Lincoln Wills* (Lincoln Rec. Soc., 5, 1914), vol. 1, pp. 5–7.

[37] J. M. Jennings, 'The Distribution of Landed Wealth in the Wills of London Merchants 1400–1450', *Medieval Studies*, 39, 1977, pp. 264–5.

[38] C.U.L., Add. MSS 3020–1, ff460v–1.

much such a decline owed to a general disinclination to patronise the religious and how much to a preference for other types of gift remains obscure. What is clear, however, is that if *De viris religiosis* was designed to curb gifts of land to the church, the crown had chosen to lock the stable door long after the horse had bolted. The statute cannot be justified or explained as a rein on galloping generosity. It appears much more convincingly as a response to the rising scale of land purchased by the church. That this aspect of ecclesiastical acquisition was of greater concern to contemporaries may be inferred from the version of the Provisions of Westminster preserved in the Burton Annals, which suggested that mesne lord licences were to be required for purchases only, with no mention of a restriction on gifts.[39]

There are reasons for thinking that the church felt the need to buy more intensively in the century before the statute, though even then the practice was far from new. There is the suggestion that, as early as the tenth century, monastic refoundation was achieved through purchase as well as piety.[40] Nonetheless, buying tended to play a subordinate rôle in the early accumulation of wealth. Prior to the end of the twelfth century, the greatest ecclesiastical landlords could rely on a steady augmentation of their income through patronage, and if this proved inadequate they could develop existing estates through more intensive settlement and colonisation. After about 1200, neither of these options was so readily available. Moreover, inflation and rising commitments made greater demands on increasingly finite resources. One well observed reaction to this predicament was the resumption of manorial demesnes in order to produce directly for the market. A second and less adventurous measure entailed the purchase of additional property for the sake of the extra income it might bring.

Evidence of buying on a large scale is not far to seek; the dealings of individual houses are often well documented. Whether the transfer of land into ecclesiastical hands represented a sig-

[39] Ed. H. R. Luard, *Annales de Burton* in *Annales Monastici*, 5 vols. (Rolls Series, London, 1864–9), vol. i, pp. 474, 482. 'Item provisum est quod nullus religiosorum aliquam terram emat sine voluntate domini capitalis, videlicet propinquioris praeter medium': Standen, 'Administration of the Statute of Mortmain', p. 37.

[40] Raban, *Estates of Thorney and Crowland*, pp. 9–12.

nificant encroachment on lay fee is more difficult to evaluate. However full each monastic archive, its evidence divorced from a regional context is almost meaningless. There are relatively few areas where thirteenth-century purchases can be assessed in relation both to long-term ecclesiastical endowment and to the pattern of tenure in society at large. The most promising of these is the East Midlands, home of the great fenland abbeys, where the availability of good modern studies permits a general picture of tenurial conditions to emerge.

Already in 1086, the area comprising modern Cambridgeshire, north Northamptonshire and south Lincolnshire was dominated at the level of tenant-in-chief by a handful of monastic institutions. Where laymen held land, it was more often than not by knight service to the larger of these houses. Against this background of limited lay tenure substantial ecclesiastical purchases took on a threatening aspect. By the mid-thirteenth century, large sums of money were involved; between 1253 and 1274, Prior John the Almoner of Spalding Priory paid out about £1,450 on properties chiefly located in Lincolnshire, while William de Godmanchester of Ramsey Abbey spent £1,666 13s 4d on a single transaction c. 1275.[41]

In terms of the intention behind the 1279 Statute of Mortmain, the possible erosion of knightly tenure is more important than the scale of expenditure. Apart from piecemeal surrenders, which in themselves amounted to a sizeable onslaught on free tenements in the area, several knightly families lost estates large enough to be called manors. The Tivills sold a Gravenhurst estate (Beds.) to Ramsey in 1266, while Berengar le Moyne sold major holdings centred on Barnwell, Hemington and Crowethorpe (Northants.) to the same house in a transaction c. 1275 and more at Holywell cum Needingworth, Woodhurst, Walton and Fen Drayton (Cambs.) sometime after 1267.[42] A William le Moyne, who was probably no relation, also featured as one of the most conspicuous

[41] E. D. Jones, 'Some Economic Dealings of Prior John the Almoner of Spalding, 1253–74', *Lincolnshire History and Archaeology*, 12, 1977, p. 41; Raftis, *Estates of Ramsey Abbey*, p. 109.

[42] Hart, Lyons, *Cartularium Monasterii de Rameseia*, vol. II, pp. 337–40, 345–6; P.R.O., Ancient Deeds A 128, B 3869; Raftis, *Estates of Ramsey Abbey*, pp. 109–10.

vendors to Prior John of Spalding. Financial difficulty and political miscalculation almost certainly precipitated his sale of land and rent in Spalding, Pinchbeck and Whaplode (Lincs.).[43] The misfortunes of the Peterborough knights have been described by Dr King. The Northborough family was bought out during the first half of the thirteenth century, while Geoffrey of Southorpe sold his manor of Gunthorpe (Cambs.) *c.* 1277.[44] Crowland Abbey had by 1271 acquired the interests of two of three Oyry heiresses in Gedney (Lincs.), and in the following year Thorney Abbey bought a Kingsthorpe estate (Northants.) which had recently belonged to Joanna and Alan de Chartres. This latter purchase was only one of Thorney's ventures, which included a nearby Clapton (Northants.) estate acquired from William Hay as well as others further away.[45] The transfer of these substantial holdings into monastic hands in a confined geographical area over a short space of time on the eve of the statute suggests that lay anxiety on the score of ecclesiastical acquisition may not have been misplaced.

The advance of mortmain tenure was not quite so relentless as it seems, however. Perspectives are easily warped by undue dependence on ecclesiastical archives. Surviving feet of fines present a contrasting view. Those for Northamptonshire in the decade before the statute reveal six major purchases, each involving a cash payment of over one hundred pounds. Clearly they were exceptional in their magnitude: only one other transaction involved anything approaching this sum, and the majority of feet of fines record payments of less than ten pounds. Of the six outstanding purchases, just two concerned alienations into mortmain. Both took place in 1272 and record the abbot of Thorney's purchase of Kingsthorpe lands for three hundred and thirty marks and the purchase of various properties in the neighbourhood of Brackley for six hundred pounds by the hospital of SS. James and John there.[46] Of the four remaining purchases, two at least were made

[43] Jones, *Lincolnshire History and Archaeology*, 1977, pp. 42–3.

[44] King, *Peterborough Abbey*, pp. 40–3; ed. T. Stapleton, *Chronicon Petroburgense* (Camden Soc., 47, 1849), p. 25.

[45] Raban, *Estates of Thorney and Crowland*, pp. 66–8; C.U.L., Add. MSS 3020–1, f379–v.

[46] P.R.O., CP 25(1)/174/50/902; CP 25(1)/174/50/912.

by members of a group which might equally well be singled out for self-aggrandisement: men whose fortunes had been made in the service of king and aristocracy. One such was Hervey de Borham, who sold the Kingsthorpe estate to Thorney, having first acquired it from Joanna and Alan de Chartres in 1270 in return for relaxing their debt of two hundred marks.[47] What thus appears as a speculation in land crowned a successful career as a royal servant and steward of Westminster Abbey and the honour of Clare.[48] Another notable purchaser was Robert Burnell, soon to become bishop of Bath and Wells. In 1274, he bought a manor at Wootton from John de Beauchamp for two hundred pounds.[49] Although he no longer possessed this estate at his death, his surviving investments ranging over nineteen counties give some idea of the scale on which he had been operating. By coincidence, one of his earlier speculations, Chamberlain's fee in Enfield, was purchased in 1271 by Thorney Abbey.[50] Little is known about the two remaining purchasers, William de Bradene and Michael son of Simon de Houctton, but the former at least appears to have aspired to a modest local prosperity. In addition to an estate held for a quarter of a knight's fee in the village from which he took his name, he held a second in Easton Neston (Northants.) for two parts of a knight's fee, as well as the Wappenham (Northants.) holdings purchased from John de Wahull and his wife in 1276 for one hundred pounds.[51] From the feet of fines for this county, therefore, it would appear that buyers acting in their own interest played at least as active a part in the market for larger properties as churchmen adding to the endowment of their houses. It is important to remember, however, that feet of fines can be just as misleading as monastic cartularies. There is no guarantee that all transactions were recorded. Indeed, it is evident from the absence of any record of Ramsey's dealings

---

[47] P.R.O., CP 25(1)/174/49/895.

[48] M. Altschul, *A Baronial Family in Medieval England: The Clares* (Baltimore, 1965), pp. 227–8; F. Pegues, 'The Clericus in the Legal Administration of Thirteenth-Century England', *E.H.R.*, 71, 1956, p. 556.

[49] P.R.O., CP 25(1)/174/51/11.

[50] *D.N.B.*; C.U.L., Add. MSS 3020–1, f360 et seq.

[51] P.R.O., CP 25(1)/174/49/896; CP 25(1)/174/51/36; J. Bridges, *The History and Antiquities of Northamptonshire*, 2 vols. (Oxford, 1791), vol. 1, pp. 236, 290.

at Barnwell, Hemington and Crowethorpe and Peterborough's purchase of Gunthorpe (then in Northamptonshire) that they were not. Nor is it easy to evaluate the payments for property where annuities had been arranged. Nevertheless, the fines remain useful in showing that competition might be expected between lay and ecclesiastical purchasers when desirable properties became available.

It is not without significance that both at Kingsthorpe and at Enfield, Thorney Abbey had been preceded in the market by men of affairs. Much the same had happened at Gedney. One of the Oyry heiresses sold first to Roger de Thurkelby, one of the most prominent lawyers of his day with properties scattered throughout Lincolnshire, Yorkshire and Norfolk, before the estate passed finally to Crowland Abbey in 1262.[52] Peterborough was swift to recover its Gunthorpe fee directly from Geoffrey of Southorpe, but Stephen of Cornhill, a London merchant, was the first purchaser of his Southorpe manor.[53] Peterborough was able to recover Southorpe later in the century, but the monks of Ramsey totally missed the opportunity to recover estates which Geoffrey held of them in Hemingford and Yelling (Cambs.). Late in 1278, Geoffrey and his wife sold them to Reginald de Grey for three hundred marks, thereby enabling another rising family to consolidate its landed base.[54] Thus, although much of the land coming on to the market in this area ultimately fell to the church, it does not appear that knightly families were coerced into selling by direct monastic pressure. Rather, the monks entered the market late and, indeed, often found difficulty in raising the cash needed to exploit the opportunities open to them. It is known that part of the vast purchase price paid by Abbot William de Godmanchester of Ramsey for the Barnwell, Hemington and Crowethorpe estates *c.* 1275 was an annuity of one hundred marks per annum and a lease of the manor of Chatteris (Cambs.) for the remaining eleven years of Berengar le Moyne's life.[55] Thorney too arranged a life lease of its manor at Twywell (Northants.) rather than pay

[52] *D.N.B.*; Raban, *Estates of Thorney and Crowland*, p. 76.
[53] King, *Peterborough Abbey*, p. 43.
[54] *Ibid.*; P.R.O., CP 25(1)/93/14/12.
[55] Ed. W. D. Macray, *Chronicon Abbatiae Rameseiensis* (Rolls Series, London, 1886), p. 348 n. 3.

William Hay in cash for his manor at Clapton. The instalment arrangement by which Crowland paid Walter de Thurkelby, brother of Roger de Thurkelby, for his Gedney manor also argues that large sums of money were not readily available.[56] Whether these shifts were due to problems of liquidity or to more serious underlying weaknesses in the economy of the houses concerned is a moot point, but they certainly do not suggest bodies replete with the profits of demesne farming in ruthless pursuit of investment opportunity.

The importance of monastic gains is further diminished when it is recalled that, not only were they confined to a very few rich houses, but most of these accessions already belonged to the lordship of one or other of them. The church was only resuming possession of land already held in chief. Gunthorpe and Berengar le Moyne's estates each represented knights' fees held of their purchaser. Thorney's acquisitions at Kingsthorpe and Clapton were both held by knight service of Peterborough.[57] Some of these monastic purchases could therefore be seen as a positive attempt by the church to reassert control over estates which had long ceased to yield a realistic return. Taken in conjunction with the campaigns of Peterborough, Ramsey, Thorney, and to a lesser extent Spalding to recover freeholds on demesne manors, it was yet another way in which thirteenth-century landlords might seek to increase the attenuated revenues from their estates.[58] Equally, the purchases could be regarded as essentially defensive. As older knightly families encountered difficulties, monastic overlords were faced with the choice of stepping in themselves or allowing the estates to fall to newcomers of far greater consequence. The advent of men like Hervey de Borham or Roger de Thurkelby may have encouraged monastic landlords to make more determined efforts to purchase their own or neighbouring fee when the occasion arose. Benefits to be gained by harnessing the new-

---

[56] Raban, *Estates of Thorney and Crowland*, pp. 68, 75.

[57] King, *Peterborough Abbey*, pp. 41–3; ed. W. Page et al., *V.C.H. Huntingdonshire*, 3 vols. (1926–36), vol. II, p. 176; *V.C.H. Northants.*, vol. III, pp. 72, 127, 105–6.

[58] King, *Peterborough Abbey*, pp. 66–9; Raftis, *Estates of Ramsey Abbey*, p. 112 n. 60; Jones, *Lincolnshire History and Archaeology*, 1977, p. 42; Raban, *Estates of Thorney and Crowland*, pp. 62–5.

comers' *savoir-faire* and influence were perhaps outweighed in the minds of the monks by the potential challenge to their hitherto all-pervading dominance of the area. At best the new arrivals represented a transient speculative interest; at worst, like Reginald de Grey, they were destined to buy their way into long-term prominence.

Thus, although it may be superficially plausible to picture the church as a land-hungry predator in the East Midland region, there are sufficient grounds to query such a view. Moreover, the religious were only one constituent of the clergy, however wealthy. Nor did their acquisitions necessarily imply continued possession by churchmen. While Crowland incorporated Gedney into its sheep-farming enterprise, Peterborough appears to have rented Gunthorpe out.[59] The ambitions and pressures governing monastic purchases were clearly complex, permitting wide latitude in their interpretation. Yet whatever the motives for such purchases and whatever the use to which they were put, it must be recognised that, once the monastic houses were embarked upon a course of purchase, their wealth in this area was likely to make them conspicuously, even alarmingly, successful in the eyes of contemporaries.

The fen region and neighbouring uplands were clearly exceptional in the density and wealth of their monastic settlement. One might question the extent to which the pattern of ecclesiastical purchase prevalent in this watery English Athos was duplicated elsewhere. Strong echoes might be anticipated in the vicinity of other great houses and their estates and these can indeed be found. At Battle Abbey the monks coveted farmland for demesne cultivation and also profitable burgage tenements. Like fenland monks, once involved they quickly dominated the land market, and again older knightly families were among the common vendors.[60] Both Glastonbury and Westminster Abbeys yield similar evidence. At Westminster, a major programme of land purchase began with the abbacy of Richard de Berking in

---

[59] Raban, *Estates of Thorney and Crowland*, p. 78; King, *Peterborough Abbey*, p. 97.

[60] E. Searle, *Lordship and Community: Battle Abbey and its Banlieu 1066–1538* (Toronto, 1974), pp. 133, 144, 154–5.

1222. Although the abbey's estates were scattered over a wide area, its main aim, like that of the fen abbeys, was to recover control of its own fee. Similarly, the monks rarely had enough cash in hand to pay immediately for their gains and again old-established families were common vendors. The abbey's single major venture outside its own fee, the purchase of Great Amwell (Herts.) in 1269, dislodged the Limsey family, whose tenure went back to the time of the Domesday Survey.[61] Worcester Cathedral Priory and Winchcombe Abbey were also known to be buying out financially embarrassed minor landlords from the late twelfth century.[62] For many such families Jewish moneylenders were the first resort, although continuing misfortune often presaged foreclosure and the ultimate transfer of their holdings to churchmen. Yorkshire religious were conspicuously alert to this possibility. Meaux, Malton and Fountains each assumed the lands and obligations of several debtors simultaneously in the earlier thirteenth century, arrangements complicated enough to suggest a deliberate policy of acquisition. Lincolnshire houses showed comparable initiative and further instances can be found in London and elsewhere.[63] The rôle of the church in assuming these encumbered estates cannot be denied, but as in the case of the fenland recoveries, it may not have been wholly rapacious. Where the debtors were their own tenants, religious houses had no acceptable alternative. It is unlikely that Thorney Abbey was alone in rescuing a subtenancy from the Jews in order to retain close control over those who held its land.[64]

Studies of religious houses throughout the country demonstrate that the fen houses were not the only ones to buy estates from lesser lay landlords from the late twelfth century, albeit in manner and motive far short of naked territorial aggrandisement. Yet this was only one aspect of the land market and, in terms of source material, the most readily accessible to modern scholars. When the affairs of lay magnates and successful career officials

[61] Postan, *Medieval Economy and Society*, p. 162; Harvey, *Westminster Abbey and its Estates*, p. 65; ch. 6.
[62] R. H. Hilton, *A Medieval Society* (London, 1966), pp. 51–2.
[63] H. G. Richardson, *The English Jewry under Angevin Kings* (London, 1960), pp. 94–9.
[64] C.U.L., Add. MSS 3020–1, f74, cxxxiii.

are examined, much the same pattern of buying emerges. Records of Richard de Clare and William de Valence show the lay aristocracy under Henry III engaged in purchase and, in clause 25 of the Petition of Barons in 1258, it was 'magnates and other persons powerful in the kingdom' who were said to be taking over Jewish debts to the disadvantage of minors. Whilst these magnates may have included churchmen, it is significant that they were not singled out for complaint.[65] Relatively little work has been done on land acquisition by the baronage, however, more attention having been concentrated on the activities of self-made men.[66]

Even where ecclesiastical influence was strong, Hervey de Borham and Roger de Thurkelby managed to compete successfully for land on the market. Where there were few notable houses, in counties like Bedfordshire, Oxfordshire and Warwickshire, the opportunities were much greater. Robert Braybrook, servant respectively to Richard I and the earl of Leicester, built up a holding of more than fifteen hides, his original two-hide estates in Braybrook (Leics.) swelling to land in five counties. In Bedfordshire, where he was sheriff from 1205, it was he rather than churchmen who bought up lands mortgaged to the Jews.[67] The plea rolls of the Exchequer of the Jews show that he was by no means the only layman to seize such opportunities.[68] Paulinus Pever, steward of the household of Henry III, described by Matthew Paris as an 'insatiable buyer of lands', in his turn acquired a substantial estate scattered throughout Buckinghamshire, Bedfordshire, Hertfordshire and Essex, not always by the most scrupulous methods.[69] Geoffrey de Langley, ultimately chief

[65] P. R. Coss, 'Sir Geoffrey de Langley and the Crisis of the Knightly Class in Thirteenth-Century England', *Past and Present*, 68, 1975, p. 23; Sanders, *Documents of the Baronial Movement of Reform and Rebellion*, pp. 86–7.

[66] For Henry de Lacy's land dealings later in the thirteenth century, see below, pp. 164–5, 178; and above, p. 91.

[67] K. S. Naughton, *The Gentry of Bedfordshire in the Thirteenth and Fourteenth Centuries* (Leicester University, Department of English Local History, Occ. Paper, 3rd ser., 2, 1976), p. 14; G. H. Fowler, *Cartulary of the Abbey of Old Wardon* (Beds. Historical Rec. Soc., 13, 1930), p. 324; Richardson, *English Jewry under Angevin Kings*, pp. 100–2.

[68] Richardson, *English Jewry under Angevin Kings*, p. 102.

[69] Naughton, *Gentry of Bedfordshire*, pp. 13, 17, 60; Luard, *Chronica Majora*, vol. v, p. 242.

justice of the forest and steward to the Lord Edward, enjoyed similar success in his buying. By 1258, he had acquired estates worth some two hundred pounds per annum, chiefly in Warwickshire.[70] The purchases of these men happen to be well documented; those of Walter de Merton or Adam de Stratton could also be cited and there are doubtless many more about whom we are not yet fully informed.[71] Thus, what might initially appear as an ecclesiastical onslaught on small landlords turns out on closer inspection to involve laymen on a comparable scale. Indeed, the most systematic investigation to date confirms this by showing that knightly families in thirteenth-century Oxfordshire lost estates in roughly equal measures to the religious and other laymen if one discounts pious gifts.[72]

It was perhaps the volume of transactions rather than any disproportionate share of the market which threw ecclesiastical buying into such sharp relief. Although those with larger fees were well cushioned against the harsher effects of inflation, distress severe enough to be termed crisis among some of the older and poorer knightly families seems to have been prevalent.[73] Enforced sales from this quarter, together with land values lower than those prevailing in the later Middle Ages, suggest that transfers of smallish estates may have attained an exceptionally high level at this date.[74] The church was not buying more than its fair share, but it may have been buying more than would normally have been available. This must remain a matter of speculation. It is hard to be certain about trends in the movement of lay land because holdings were in a constant state of flux due to marriage and family settlement or failure of the male line. Although inconvenient, the kaleidoscopic character of lay landholdings in contrast to the stable, cumulative nature of mortmain tenure explains why the church as a body formed a more readily identifiable focus for unease than individual lay purchasers, however acquisitive. The steady accretion of church property also

---

[70] Coss, *Past and Present*, 1975, pp. 4–5, 19–20.

[71] *Ibid.*, pp. 23–4.

[72] D. A. Carpenter, 'Was there a Crisis of the Knightly Class in the Thirteenth Century? The Oxfordshire Evidence', *E.H.R.*, 95, 1980, p. 728.

[73] *Ibid.*, pp. 729–32; Coss, *Past and Present*, 1975, pp. 1, 22–5.

[74] See below, pp. 177–8.

made ecclesiastical buying less tolerable, even if the church's rate of gain was well balanced against that of the laity. This was emphasised in that certain mitigating factors such as the enfeoffment of knights and the 'farming out' of manors were no longer commonplace by the thirteenth century. Thus, the likelihood of estates newly purchased by the church finding their way back into lay hands, as would have happened in the eleventh and twelfth centuries, was now in doubt. Renting remained a possibility, but new rents were likely to reflect the market rate whereas, by the later thirteenth century, older arrangements favoured the tenant to a marked extent. It is in this combination of circumstances that mortmain legislation becomes an understandable response. By 1279 there were few excessive gifts to the church needing control, but it is likely that the statute came hot on the heels of a land market in which the church had come to take an active interest and which was perhaps abnormally brisk. Its effects therefore should be seen primarily in relation to this phenomenon.

Chapter 6

THE IMPACT OF MORTMAIN LEGISLATION
ON THE CHURCH

The availability of licences to alienate in mortmain after 1280
raises the possibility of assessing the impact of the legislation on
the church over a long period of time. But, as is so often the
case when records are used for purposes other than those for
which they were designed, there are pitfalls for the unwary. The
chief disadvantage attaching to licence evidence is its resistance
to statistical treatment except in the most rudimentary way. In
calculating the number of licences granted in any one year,
arbitrary decisions have to be made as to inclusion. This is
especially true of the early years after the statute, before a
common form was firmly established. Since the overriding
concern in compiling the graphs for this study has been the
pattern of accessions in the late medieval period, royal grants of
land and rent which were not couched as licences have nonetheless
been included, while vacated entries (except where they relate
to general licences vacated upon completion), confirmations of
land already held in mortmain, cash grants and exchanges have
all been left out. Grants to borough corporations, which were
few in number, have however been included and pardons for
illicit acquisition have been recorded separately. Even with these
criteria clearly defined, the scope for individual discretion remains
such that no two scholars are likely to arrive at exactly the same
figures, although the discrepancies should not be great enough
to promote disagreement as to broad trends.[1]

Methodological problems apart, there remain severe limitations
on what licence figures can yield in the way of information. A
licence recorded only the occasion on which permission for an
alienation was given. There is no assurance that any transfer ever

---

[1] Compare for example my figures for the period 1280–1306 with those of
Bean, *Decline of English Feudalism*, p. 55.

took place and sometimes there is evidence to the contrary. Furthermore, licences can be used to calculate only the number of grantees in a given year, not the amount of property involved; the range of different sorts of land, rents, advowsons and reversions defies computation. Trends in the numbers of licences granted therefore need careful interpretation. It cannot be stressed too forcefully that a trend upward in the number of licences granted need not indicate an increasing flow of property to the church. An increase in licences is entirely compatible with a fall in the size of individual transfers and an overall diminution in the flow. The reverse situation is equally possible. Even allowing for these particular difficulties, there remain the twin icebergs of avoidance and evasion of the law. Allowance has to be made for these also.

Not all problems are inherent in the nature of licences. External political considerations could affect markedly the number granted in certain years. The absence of the king abroad has already been shown to account for the fluctuations in the number of licences conceded before 1300 and this continued to be a feature of the figures throughout the later Middle Ages.[2] The sizeable drop in grants in 1339 can be attributed to the absence of Edward III in the Netherlands, Germany and France between July 1338 and February 1340. Similarly, Henry V's spells abroad between July 1417 and February 1421 and again between June 1421 and September 1422 are quite accurately reflected in the number of grants made.[3] The character and quarrels of individual monarchs are also reflected in the figures. Very few licences were granted early in 1322, when Edward II was playing out the last scenes in his struggle with Thomas of Lancaster. In a different vein, the rise of grants evident after 1437 owed a good deal to Henry VI's personal piety, although this was somewhat dampened by the Acts of Resumption and attendant fuss in 1450 and 1455.[4] It is not always possible to proffer a neat explanation for fluctuations in the annual grants of licences, but except in 1392 the

---

[2] See above, Graph 3, p. 53.

[3] See above, Graph 1, pp. 42–3; ed. F. M. Powicke, E. B. Fryde, *Handbook of British Chronology*, 2nd edn (London, 1961), pp. 36–7.

[4] *Rot. Parl.*, vol. v, pp. 183 et seq., 300 et seq.; see above, Graph 1, pp. 42–3; p. 67.

extremes almost certainly owed more to mundane external factors than to marked variation in the number of petitioners coming forward.

The most striking feature to emerge from a count of licences, as Graph 6 shows, is their relative paucity in the decades immediately after 1279. When the impersonal figures of the graph are

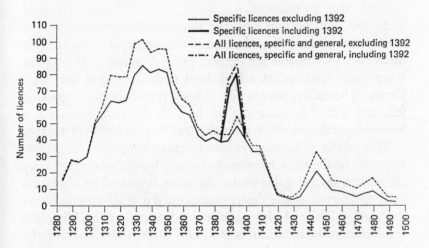

Graph 6 Running averages of licences to alienate into mortmain in England and Wales from the patent rolls

translated into individual houses, the picture is reinforced. Of the fen houses, so busily acquisitive before 1279, only Peterborough secured a licence in the ten years after the statute.[5] Spalding and Crowland each received one licence in the 1290s, but Ely, Ramsey and Thorney obtained nothing until the early years of the following century.[6] In Lincolnshire, a county well provided with religious foundations, an analysis of the date at which each house received its first licence reveals a similar if less dramatic situation. Almost all, unless they were alien priories or cells, received a mortmain licence sooner or later. Yet only seven of them had obtained their first by the tenth anniversary of the

[5] *Cal. Pat.*, 1281–92, p. 214 (1285).
[6] *Ibid.*, p. 419 (1291); 1292–1301, p. 481 (1299); 1301–7, pp. 125, 221–2, 236, 291, 292 (1303–4).

statute. Considerably more ventured to secure one in the following decade and by 1320 almost three-quarters of the Lincolnshire religious houses had done so.[7] So, although it is clear that most houses felt the need for a licence after 1279, it is equally evident that there was no rush for them. However active they may have been in purchase on the eve of the statute, Lincolnshire churchmen abstained almost entirely from licensed acquisition for at least a decade after its publication.

As this Lincolnshire evidence shows, such restraint was not maintained for long after the turn of the century. During the first three decades demand for licences grew. Peaking in the 1330s, it was then sustained at a high level until the eve of the Black Death. Thereafter, except for a brief period in the 1390s, it fell, and settled permanently by the early fifteenth century at a level comparable to, or even lower than, that evident before 1299.

This profile of licensees cannot be taken entirely at face value, however. In the early fourteenth century, houses were commonly amortising several gains under the same licence. The cheapness and convenience of this device commended it at all periods, but at this date it enjoyed the additional advantage of enabling the regularisation of unofficial acquisitions made while awaiting the long-term response of the crown towards pressure for the relaxation of mortmain law. As a result of these conflated transactions, the already steep rise in licence figures may understate the rise in the number of accessions.

The prevalence of general licences can also mislead, since they represented permission to proceed to a specific licence rather than permission to make a firm accession. By the fifteenth century in particular, such licences played a large part in the number of annual grants and were infrequently or never invoked. When such general licences are discounted, the reduced demand for licences evident in this period becomes even more marked.[8] Taken together, these difficulties suggest that the pattern of accessions revealed by licence figures masks an even sharper contrast

---

[7] A total of fifty-eight institutions are known to have received one or more licences at some time. This figure includes the mendicants, but excludes hospitals, gilds and parish churches.

[8] See above, Graph 1, pp. 42–3; Graph 6.

between the early fourteenth and the early fifteenth centuries than might otherwise appear.

The most serious distortion of the picture of recipients afforded by licence statistics, however, arises from the practice of enfeoffment to use. There can be no doubt that this was a popular means of by-passing mortmain requirements until it was forbidden in 1391. Yet, although it is clear that most of these arrangements were terminated under licence in 1392, it is much more difficult to trace them back to their inception, even in well documented cases. Of those concerning Harrold Priory, for example, only the Stagsden (Beds.) gift of Margery Cane can be traced back to a firm date (1349).[9] The priory's interest in a Pertenhall (Beds.) holding, which Robert Lary conveyed under licence in 1392, had been acquired over twenty years earlier, but the deed of gift is known only by allusion. Its date is therefore conjectural, though unlikely to be much earlier than 1360.[10] Lary and Sir Gerard Braybrook together conveyed rents held in use to the priory in Wooton Bourne and Carlton (Beds.) under the same licence. The history of these is also shrouded in mystery. Fowler suggested that the grantor was John Rycher, in which case the enfeoffments had a relatively short life, with 1380 as a *terminus a quo*.[11] Such uncertainties in the context of a single house demonstrate the impossibility of any analysis of gains in the period before 1392 from church archives in general.

Public records are not much more illuminating about the chronology of enfeoffments. The inquisition held into those of Elsham Priory in 1364 showed that some had been undertaken thirty years earlier, while others were recent in origin.[12] In 1372, Maxstoke Priory was said to have enjoyed a similar arrangement for the past twenty years.[13] Fewer confiscations by the Lincolnshire escheators from as early as the 1330s may indicate that enfeoffments to use were already impeding them in their work.

---

9 Fowler, *Records of Harrold Priory*, pp. 156–8, nos. 263–73; p. 178, no. 316; p. 216.

10 *Ibid.*, pp. 151–4, no. 255 et seq.; p. 178, no. 316; *Cal. Pat.*, 1391–6, p. 164.

11 Fowler, *Records of Harrold Priory*, pp. 160–4, no. 278 et seq.; p. 217; *Cal. Pat.*, 1391–6, p. 164.

12 *Cal. Inq. Misc.*, vol. III, p. 231, no. 621.

13 *Ibid.*, vol. III, p. 318, no. 839.

One could argue from this scant evidence that enfeoffments to use became common at any time between the stabilisation of licence grants in the 1330s and their decline in the second half of the century. Such inexactitude is the more unfortunate since it obscures the point at which the tide of accession turned. The levelling out of licences in the 1330s and 1340s may belie continued accession by less approved methods. Equally, it may represent a true plateau in the number of recipients. That a decline must have occurred sooner or later is certain, since the enfeoffments regularised in 1392 were too few to permit the extension of the peak demand of the 30s and 40s throughout the intervening five decades. On balance, a later date for the widespread appearance of enfeoffments to use is the more likely. Attempts by the escheators to establish their illegality in the 1360s and the parliamentary petitions against their abuse in 1376 and 1377 suggest that they had come to be recognised as a nuisance by this date, even though they may have existed for a long time. A late emergence of the practice on a large scale would also account for the more marked decline, evident in Graph 6, in licences granted after 1360, and perhaps cancel out the trough in grants between 1360 and 1394 which is clearly visible if the exceptional grants of 1392 are excluded from calculation. A late date carries added conviction in that it coincides with Bean's conclusion that the device first became popular with lay landlords during the latter part of Edward III's reign, even though it had been evolving over the preceding century.[14] If a late date is correct, it appears that the number of occasions on which the medieval church made accessions did indeed reach a peak in the decades before the Black Death, but that the apparent decline revealed by licences thereafter was not entirely echoed by reality.

Enfeoffment to use, together with other forms of avoidance and evasion of the law, must constitute the largest question-mark over the profile of accessions revealed by licences. Kreider's recent work on medieval chantry foundations is therefore particularly useful in offering an independent view of the significance of such attempts to mitigate the rigour of mortmain law by one type of ecclesiastical body. Licences for the foundation of chantries and

[14] Bean, *Decline of English Feudalism*, pp. 117–26.

similar institutions follow roughly the same pattern as other licences to alienate into mortmain, except for a tendency towards a rather less sharp decline in the later fourteenth and fifteenth centuries. This was subject to some regional variation: whereas licences for chantry foundations in Buckinghamshire had peaked by 1350, in Essex and Warwickshire no substantial decline was evident before the second half of the fifteenth century. Most counties fell between the two extremes.[15] This chronology changes when enfeoffments to use and illegal foundations are taken into account. Although Warwickshire foundations still show a late-fifteenth-century decline, those for Essex and Wiltshire appear to have reached their highest point at this date. For three of the four counties examined, the overall effect is to flatten the graph of foundation dates between 1300 and 1548 to a significant extent.[16]

No analogy between chantries and the rest of the church can be exact, so it is unlikely that a true profile of accessions for the whole church would echo this levelling out to the same degree. Different factors governed the accessions of different types of institution and evasion of mortmain requirements by chantry founders is likely to have been greater than average.[17] Moreover, Kreider's figures are not strictly comparable with those of this study, since they cover foundations only, not all additions to endowments. The advantage of good evidence is also counter-balanced by the distortions arising from the decay of other bodies and their consequent exclusion from his calculations.[18] Nevertheless, enough is known about the character of evasion and avoidance of the mortmain law to suggest that a corrected graph of accessions for the church at large would show some revisions of chronology in the later Middle Ages, if not as drastic as the revised profile reveals for the chantries. This is less likely for the first half century after *De viris religiosis* because rigorous enforcement of the law and the absence of enfeoffments to use make it probable that licences bore a closer resemblance to the true position.

Clearly the picture of ecclesiastical accession presented by mortmain licences has serious shortcomings. Even so, it is a great

---

[15] Kreider, *English Chantries*, pp. 72–5.   [16] *Ibid.*, pp. 86–90.
[17] See above, p. 99.   [18] Kreider, *English Chantries*, pp. 87–9.

deal more helpful than no picture at all. Without the framework provided by licence statistics, it would be impossible to gain any coherent sense of development over time. They provide an indispensable foundation, however tentative, for understanding late-medieval ecclesiastical acquisition; without them it would not be possible to pose two crucial questions: how far changes in the demand for licences were a reflection of changing amounts of land passing to the church and what part, if any, mortmain restrictions played in bringing such changes to pass. The answers to these questions cannot be supplied from licences alone, however. It is necessary to turn as well to the licensees and the subtleties of their relationship to society as a whole.

Licence figures baldly argue that *De viris religiosis* exercised a profound effect on ecclesiastical acquisition for the best part of twenty years. The steady rise in licences after 1299 can be attributed to the introduction of fines in that year and the growing realisation that licences were no longer likely to be withheld. The experiences of individual houses suggest that, while true, this is something of an oversimplification. The illicit but undetected activities to be found in their cartularies, together with pardons on the patent rolls, cast doubt on the extent to which the statute inhibited gains.[19] That there was underlying continuity between the aggressive earlier buying in the thirteenth century and the resurgence of activity after 1299 seems plain. The key to any assessment of the success of the statute therefore lies in the nature of these accessions rather than their occurrence. Few unlicensed gains were substantial. Ely was almost alone in attempting anything so provocative as the appropriation of Wisbech and Foxton churches and the acquisition of a large estate in Eriswell; discovery was too easy and the penalties too severe. Concern about the church's encroachment on knightly tenure had contributed to the enactment of the statute and it was at this level, rather than over minor holdings, that a halt may have been called. Indeed, there can be no doubt that the statute imposed a short-term political embargo on large-scale acquisition. The strangled immediacy with which major dealings ceased can be explained in no other way. How far the constraint became permanent and

[19] See above, Table 3, p. 90; p. 94 et seq.

to what extent the statute, as opposed to purely economic considerations, was influential is more problematical.

Most of the fenland houses, so busy in the land market on
the eve of the 1279 statute and then apparently quiescent for a
generation, contributed to the rising tide of licences after 1299.[20]
Spalding alone showed little enthusiasm for formal acquisition
before 1318, but the contrast with its neighbours was superficial,
since a pardon also acquired in that year shows that failure to
amortise did not necessarily mean failure to acquire.[21] A dawning
interest in the possibilities of licensed accession was not confined
to the fens. Battle Abbey, for example, gained its first licence in
1310 and a further two by 1316. Pardons granted in 1313, 1314
and 1315 also bear witness that earlier land hunger had been
satisfied, as at Spalding, by less orthodox means.[22]

At a casual glance it would appear that the interrupted accessions of the 1260s and 1270s had been resumed, but this was not
entirely the case. Peterborough certainly purchased a manor at
Southorpe for five hundred and fifty marks and another at
Luddington (Northants.), but few other houses could match this
in scale.[23] The fen houses were amongst the richest in the country;
yet, Peterborough apart, only Ramsey seemed to be making gains
in proportion to its resources, and even then the evidence is
equivocal.

The abbey received thirteen licences, excluding a general
licence, between 1304 and 1320.[24] Impressive though this appears,
the two largest accessions concerned chantry endowments. Assessment of Ramsey's dealings in the land market in the early
fourteenth century hinges on whether or not these endowments
can be taken at face value. It can be argued that the grantors,
Roger de Nortone and William de Cortone, acted throughout on
behalf of the abbey. Both were associated with other licences to

[20] *Cal. Pat.*, 1292–1301, pp. 481, 492; 1301–7, pp. 221–2, 233, 236, 241–2, 291–2, 372.
[21] *Ibid.*, 1281–92, p. 419; 1307–13, p. 22; 1317–21, pp. 190, 211, 417; 1321–4, p. 34.
[22] *Ibid.*, 1307–13, pp. 268, 597; 1313–17, pp. 29–30, 82, 219, 525.
[23] *Ibid.*, 1281–92, p. 414; 1301–7, pp. 241–2; Mellows, *Henry of Pytchley's Book of Fees*, p. 62 et seq.
[24] *Cal. Pat.*, 1301–7, pp. 221–2, 312; 1307–13, pp. 18, 190, 211, 351, 522; 1313–17, pp. 451, 639; 1317–21, p. 238.

acquire in a manner reminiscent of proven nominees elsewhere and Nortone, like so many of these, was a clerk.[25] There was also something irregular in the circumstances of each grant. Nortone's yielded a good deal more in rent than the monks were obliged to spend on prayers, while William de Cortone acquired John Hauker's manor in Slepe (Cambs.) only a year before he was licensed to grant it to the abbey, and an account of the obits of Abbot Simon Eye (1316–42) suggests that it was the abbot himself who had put up the five-hundred-mark purchase price.[26] It is unlikely that the chantries were wholly fictitious. Numerous agreements were made for their operation and Nortone retained something of a life interest in his endowment, suggesting some stronger association with the property than business alone would dictate.[27] A combination of piety and service to the abbey seems probable. The chantries may have been a form of reward for services rendered or perhaps the monks felt that the crown might look more favourably on large acquisitions, particularly from royal fee as was the case with the Hauker manor, if some spiritual end was in view. If these were not in fact monastic purchases, abbey buying in spite of its frequency was largely confined to piecemeal recoveries on demesne manors. Typical of these were the seven and a half acres in Heathmangrove (Cambs.) granted by John de Suttone and Thomas de Norgrave and the messuages and twenty-pence rent in St Ives and Ramsey granted by Robert de Sautre and Richard de Spaldinge under licences of 1311: a far cry from the grandiose ventures preceding the statute.[28]

Cumulatively such small acquisitions might bring quite large amounts of land into ecclesiastical ownership. This seems to have been the case at Ely, where in 1314 the prior and convent took out a licence permitting substantial accessions from the bishop's fee assembled by nominees in Ely, Witcham, Downham and

---

[25] *Ibid.*, 1301–7, p. 221; 1307–13, p. 18; 1313–17, p. 639; 1327–30, p. 262.

[26] Hart, Lyons, *Cartularium Monasterii de Rameseia*, vol. I, pp. 372–5; vol. II, pp. 104–5, 120, 243; Macray, *Chronicon Abbatiae Rameseiensis*, p. 349.

[27] Hart, Lyons, *Cartularium Monasterii de Rameseia*, vol. I, pp. 373–6; vol. II, pp. 108–9, 113–15.

[28] *Cal. Pat.*, 1307–13, p. 351; Hart, Lyons, *Cartularium Monasterii de Rameseia*, vol. II, pp. 124–6. The rent is recorded as twenty shillings on the patent roll, but twenty pence in the abbey's cartulary.

Sutton (Cambs.).[29] This was, however, the only specific licence obtained before 1320. The convent's disastrous addiction to un-lawful acquisition probably contributed to the debts which may explain this relative restraint.[30] Among the lesser fen houses, Crowland's acquisition of the advowson of Wigtoft church in 1299 marked a new departure, but its gains in 1300, like those of neighbouring Thorney in 1304, were all minor recoveries of free-hold on its own manors.[31] Only the adventurous leases of crown estates during this period bore witness to the continuing interest of these houses in property on the earlier scale.

By 1300, the wealth of the great black monk houses in the fens apparently no longer guaranteed the capacity to undertake frequent major purchase. Only Ramsey's putative investment in Slepe from royal fee ventured outside their own lordship, although this was not in itself significant; the great purchases made by the abbeys in the mid-thirteenth century had also been predomi-nantly from their own tenants.[32] More important was the pre-valence of minor acquisition, which before the statute had been quite overshadowed by more substantial dealings. The wide horizons of the 1260s and 1270s were narrowing in spite of the flurry of licences. Even at Peterborough, other accessions in 1304 and 1305 comprised small properties within the Soke.[33] Another ominous sign was the speed with which the licensing boom spent itself. General licences apart, Crowland gained no licence between 1300 and 1334 and Thorney none between 1304 and 1327. Peterborough withdrew from licensed acquisition between 1305 and 1329, while Ramsey paused for a decade between 1318 and 1328, having perhaps over-extended itself in the preceding decade.[34] The licences of the early fourteenth century thus appear as little more than the expression of a pent-up urge to acquire

29 *Cal. Pat.*, 1313–17, p. 121; B.L., Egerton 3047, ff2, 29–v, 50 et seq.; C.U.L., EDC 1B/3–4.
30 *Cal. Close*, 1288–96, p. 190; 1296–1302, pp. 322, 597.
31 *Cal. Pat.*, 1292–1301, pp. 481, 492; 1301–7, pp. 236, 291–2; Raban, *Estates of Thorney and Crowland*, p. 70.
32 Peterborough's purchase of Luddington in 1304 was from the fee of John Marmion, but he in turn held of the abbey. Mellows, *Henry of Pytchley's Book of Fees*, p. 46; *V.C.H. Northants.*, vol. III, pp. 83–4.
33 *Cal. Pat.*, 1301–7, pp. 233, 372.
34 Hart, Lyons, *Cartularium Monasterii de Rameseia*, vol. II, p. 201.

which had been suppressed during the immediately preceding period. The subsequent lull argues that, for these houses at least, there was no real capacity to return to the practices of the mid-thirteenth century.

This conclusion is necessarily somewhat subjective. Close comparison of the gains of different houses and at different periods is impossible. Purchase price, where known, may be the best index of the importance of an acquisition but even this presents problems.[35] Description of holdings is still less reliable since relatively small estates might be designated as manors. Most difficult of all to assess are the multiple accessions, which could cumulatively bring large amounts of land into ecclesiastical ownership although the individual units were quite small. Such qualifications are all the more important in assessing late medieval ecclesiastical accession outside the confines of the fen houses, where less is known about the composition of individual endowments.

Among the other houses of Lincolnshire and the East Midlands, only the Augustinian abbey of Thornton-on-Humber approached the riches of the fenland monasteries.[36] Its accessions thus make an interesting contrast with those of the black monks. A major purchase, costing some £241 in 1269, shows that the canons were as deeply involved as the monks in the land market on the eve of the 1279 statute.[37] Similarly, leasehold agreements after the statute show parallels with the activities of the fen houses. A plot in Ravenspur (Yorks.) was leased for the lifetime of Isabella de Fortibus and, in 1301, the abbey paid the crown 995 marks for a ten-year lease of woodland rights in Rumwood in Sherwood forest.[38] Unlike most of the monks, however, the canons did not withdraw from large-scale purchase after the statute. In 1292, Henry de Lacy was licensed to grant them the manor of Halton-

---

[35] See below, p. 181.

[36] As a very rough guide, for the purposes of comparison, the valuations given in *Valor Ecclesiasticus* (6 vols., Rec. Comm., 1810–34) are used in the following pages. Most sixteenth-century endowments were substantially complete by the late thirteenth century, so proportionate wealth should be indicated although the actual income figure in the earlier period probably differed substantially. The figures are taken from Knowles, Hadcock, *Medieval Religious Houses*, pp. 53–7, 144, passim.

[37] Oxf., Bodl., Tanner 166, ff9v, 22.

[38] *Cal. Pat.*, 1292–1301, pp. 528, 597.

by-Killingholm (Humberside), for which the cellarer paid him one thousand pounds. One year later, the cellarer gave him a further one thousand marks to secure 'Inkelmor in Marsland' near Swinefleet (Humberside). Like the fen purchasers, Thornton was not able to raise this sum immediately in cash. The agreement was for payment in annual instalments of £66 13s 4d.[39] A royal pardon shows that, while these negotiations were in train, the canons were also busy in a small way with unlicensed recoveries from their own fee.[40] In 1313 the cellarer, active once more, paid Henry Percy £338 6s 8d for woodland rights in Wressle (Humberside). Further important gains were made in 1324 and 1325, when a manor in Barrow (Humberside) was purchased for two hundred pounds and the advowson of Welton church for £80 6s 8d.[41] All told, the abbey received twelve licences between 1292 and 1330, a figure which compares more than favourably with the more active of the fen houses.[42] Rather more of Thornton's acquisitions were drawn from outside its own fee than was evident with the fen houses, probably because its original endowment provided fewer opportunities for fruitful recoveries.

Insofar as one can tell from licences alone, other houses in this region were generally active in proportion to their means. The Premonstratensian abbey of Barlings and the Cistercian abbey of Woburn, both comparatively well endowed, achieved eight and five licences respectively before 1320. For Barlings at least, some of these involved sizeable holdings, although there is nothing to prove that they were purchases.[43] By contrast Sawtry,

---

[39] The cost was further inflated by payment of £60 to Thomas of Lancaster in 1313 for the confirmation of charters. Oxf., Bodl., Tanner 166, ff11–v, 22; *Cal. Pat.*, 1281–92, pp. 466–7. It is not immediately obvious why Henry de Lacy was selling on such a scale. For other dealings with the church, both sale and purchase, see above, p. 91; and below, p. 178.

[40] *Cal. Pat.*, 1281–92, p. 480.

[41] The Welton figure includes the initial purchase price, the cost of making a fine and twenty pounds paid subsequently in confirmation. Oxf., Bodl., Tanner 166, ff11v–12, 22.

[42] *Cal. Pat.*, 1292–1301, p. 597; 1301–7, p. 524; 1307–13, p. 467; 1313–17, pp. 28, 110, 470; 1321–4, p. 12; 1324–7, p. 107; 1327–30, p. 259. The Barrow manor and Welton advowson were not licensed until 1330. *Ibid.*, 1327–30, pp. 492–3, 496.

[43] *C.* 1535 their valuations were *c.* £242 and *c.* £391 per annum net respectively. Knowles, Hadcock, *Medieval Religious Houses*, pp. 115, 184; *Cal. Pat.*,

another Cistercian house characterised as poor but generous in later local doggerel, attempted only one gain at this time: a plot in Fulbourn (Cambs.) next to existing property, licensed in 1310.[44] Even more modest was the Gilbertine priory of Catley, whose endowment yielded a tiny income in the sixteenth century and which apparently made no gains whatsoever after 1279.[45]

Wealth alone did not determine the level of acquisition. The monks of Warden, rich enough in terms of endowment, showed no sign of activity legal or otherwise before the 1340s. It is perhaps not without significance that they were pardoned their taxes in 1338 on account of their depressed circumstances and that entries on the close rolls in the 1320s show debt and the leasing out of manors for life.[46] Just as at Ely, temporary financial embarrassment counted for more than landed assets when it came to playing an ambitious rôle in the property market. At the other extreme, the Gilbertine priory of Newstead-by-Ancholme, with a sixteenth-century income only marginally less exiguous than that of Catley, managed in spite of this to acquire numerous if not large holdings, both licensed and unlicensed, in the decades before 1320.[47]

The religious certainly succeeded in acquiring some large properties between 1299 and 1330, but there is no suggestion even among the richest houses of a return to the inroads on knightly tenure of the mid-thirteenth century. The time when substantial additions might be made regularly to existing endowments was well past. Further important gains continued to be made in the late medieval period, but they appear increasingly isolated and atypical. The details of this progressive withdrawal

---

1272–81, p. 443; 1281–92, pp. 125, 128, 137, 392, 427, 429; 1301–7, pp. 494, 499; 1307–13, pp. 133, 482–3; 1313–17, p. 401. General licences are omitted.

[44] *Cal. Pat.*, 1307–13, p. 285. The abbey's valuation was *c.* £141 per annum net *c.* 1535, poverty in the context of other fen houses rather than in absolute terms. Knowles, Hadcock, *Medieval Religious Houses*, p. 114; *Notes and Queries*, 1st ser., 6, 1852, p. 350.

[45] *C.* £34; Knowles, Hadcock, *Medieval Religious Houses*, p. 194.

[46] *Ibid.*, p. 114; *Cal. Pat.*, 1338–40, p. 46; *Cal. Close*, 1318–23, pp. 317, 705; 1323–7, p. 50.

[47] *C.* £38 per annum; Knowles, Hadcock, *Medieval Religious Houses*, p. 197; *Cal. Pat.*, 1297–1301, p. 127; 1301–7, pp. 311, 462; 1317–21, p. 395.

from the land market are not as well documented as one could wish. Many of the cartularies whose contents flesh out earlier purchases and gifts were drawn up before the mid-fourteenth century. Such was the case, for example, with the Red Book of Thorney compiled under Abbot William of Clapton (d. 1322), the Wrest Park Cartulary of Crowland compiled *c.* 1343 and the principal cartulary of Spalding Priory dated *c.* 1331.[48] Deeds relating to subsequent transactions were sometimes added, but later scribes were rarely as expansive as those responsible for the original compilation. Changes in record-keeping brought about by the abandonment of demesne agriculture in favour of renting also make it more difficult to set late purchases in context. The abbot of Crowland made two large and intriguing purchases around the turn of the fourteenth and fifteenth centuries. What little is known about them comes chiefly from the first anonymous continuator of the Crowland Chronicle, but how the monks were able to afford the purchase price after the financial decay of the mid-fourteenth century and the hostile economic climate thereafter remains a mystery.[49] Equally tantalising is the purchase of a second manor at Longthorpe (Cambs.) by the abbot of Peterborough in 1507–8 for one hundred and eighty pounds.[50] Licences suggest that Thornton Abbey sustained a lively interest in land acquisition longer than most houses but the last reference to purchase in its own surviving records is the one hundred pounds paid for land in Thornton in 1343–4.[51] The dearth of records for the later medieval period is obviously relative rather than absolute. Particularly full accounts happen to survive for the purchase of the advowson and manor of Mepal (Cambs.) by the prior and convent of Ely in 1361, and although there is no late Thorney cartulary, a distressingly frail rental compiled in the 1450s provides some insight into the yield of a chantry endow-

---

[48] C.U.L., Add. MSS 3020–1; Gentlemen's Society, Spalding; B.L., Add. MS 35296; B.L., Harley 742; G. R. C. Davis, *Medieval Cartularies of Great Britain* (London, 1958), pp. 34, 105, 110.

[49] *Cal. Pat.*, 1396–9, p. 319; 1405–8, p. 340; ed. W. Fulman, *Rerum Anglicarum Scriptorum Veterum* (Oxford, 1684), p. 496.

[50] Bridges, *History and Antiquities of Northamptonshire*, vol. II, p. 572; *V.C.H. Northants.*, vol. II, p. 458.

[51] Oxf., Bodl., Tanner 166, f22v.

ment licensed in 1451.[52] Nevertheless, the minute documentation from year to year so often available between 1250 and 1350 rarely lasted for long after this. It is tempting to conclude that a period rich in archival material must have seen more significant activity than one barren in record. Such was not necessarily the case. Although late medieval acquisitions often seem sparse and unimpressive, the extent to which this was true may be more apparent than real.

In the increasing absence of internal evidence, licences, however unsatisfactory, offer the only broad view of the last accessions to the religious. Crowland Abbey gained its last licence in 1412.[53] By the mid-fifteenth century, Thornton Abbey too was defeated although it had responded more aggressively than most houses to earlier openings in the land market. Ely, Thorney and Ramsey all gained their last licence at approximately the same date, between 1449 and 1453.[54] Lincoln Cathedral was slightly more resilient. During the previous century more licences were granted to the bishops or the dean and chapter than to any other body in the county, but at Lincoln too the fifteenth century marked a new era. Just four licences are recorded during the century, the last being that of 1480, and these were largely concerned with chantry endowments.[55] Only an institution as rich and as secular as Lincoln Cathedral could have held out for so long. Of the forty-three Lincolnshire houses known to have taken out licences after 1279, only eighteen received them after 1400, and of these only six received them after 1420. Some of the poorest, like Newstead-by-Stamford or Humberston, gained no licence after 1310, but most contrived occasional bids for acquisi-

---

[52] Evans, *E.H.R.*, 1936, pp. 118–20; C.U.L., Add. MS 4401, f43; *Cal. Pat.*, 1446–52, p. 502.

[53] *Cal. Pat.*, 1408–13, p. 362. A licence of 1428 concerned provision for black monks studying at Cambridge rather than any addition to the abbey's endowment. *Ibid.*, 1422–9, p. 475.

[54] *Ibid.*, 1446–52, pp. 249, 502; 1452–61, p. 74.

[55] *Ibid.*, 1413–16, p. 24; 1436–41, p. 137; 1452–61, pp. 145–6; 1476–85, p. 176; 1494–1509, p. 134. Further accessions are not entirely excluded since the dean and chapter were granted a licence permitting acquisitions to an annual value of twenty-eight pounds without further formality in 1498. Gains made on the basis of this licence would not therefore have found their way on to the patent rolls.

tion until the later fourteenth century. For many of these houses, licences taken out under the exigency of the 1391 legislation represented their last formal accession.

Whether one examines the number of licences granted or the nature of the acquisitions, it appears that religious houses gained progressively less with the passage of time. Since the case for ecclesiastical engrossment of land at the expense of the laity rests mainly on the activities of these institutions, there can be little doubt that the church as a whole experienced a reduction in the growth of landed accessions after 1279, even if this did not happen overnight. Such a contention is further strengthened by

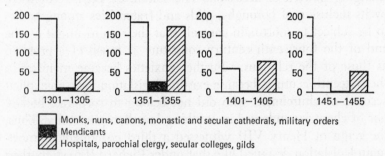

Monks, nuns, canons, monastic and secular cathedrals, military orders
Mendicants
Hospitals, parochial clergy, secular colleges, gilds

Graph 7 Recipients of licences to alienate into mortmain in England and Wales from the patent rolls (all licences)

the changing identity of late medieval alienees. Whereas the enclosed orders dominated the scene in the late thirteenth and early fourteenth centuries, this was far from the case by the mid-fifteenth century. Graph 7 shows that, at the latter date, more than twice as many licences went to the parochial clergy, secular colleges, gilds or hospitals as were granted to the religious.[56] The escheators' accounts for Lincolnshire also reflect this change. Only the parson of Irby amongst the numerous secular clergy of the county had been unfortunate enough to fall foul of the escheators of Edward II.[57] The account of 1423–4, one of the few to survive in immaculate condition complete with its leather bag, shows the

---

[56] Ambiguity about the need to amortise gild endowments before the 1391 legislation may conceal a sharper swing from one type of licensee to the other.

[57] P.R.O., E136/1/22–5; E136/1/28; E136/1/30–1; E136/1/36; E136/1/38.

non-religious in a more prominent rôle. The Irby confiscation was still in royal hands. To it had been added a cottage bequeathed to the incumbent at Bonby (Humberside), the endowments of three parochial chantries, and gifts to parishioners and the fabric of a local church. Confiscations from two more parish clergy were the result of deliberate acquisition, in one case to enlarge the rectory. All were mundane transactions comparable to those undertaken by other non-religious and enshrined more acceptably in licences, but together they involved nine out of the sixteen ecclesiastical alienees on the account.[58]

Legislative changes are yet another convincing sign of a changing pattern of accession. The statute of 1391 recognised, by its inclusion of boroughs, gilds and fraternities among bodies to be subject to mortmain control, that their gains might by the end of the fourteenth century constitute as much of a problem as those of the religious.[59] Further anxieties became manifest in the sixteenth century, because existing legislation took no explicit account of churchmen who did not belong to corporate bodies, nor of chantries endowed in anything less than perpetuity. Thus, the reign of Henry VIII witnessed a third enactment of mortmain legislation designed like that under Richard II to strengthen current mortmain laws and close loopholes created by changing ecclesiastical fashion. As a result, after 1 March 1532, grants were limited to a maximum period of twenty years, and parochial chantries, together with groups associated for pious purposes but not formally incorporated, were brought unequivocally within mortmain law.[60]

The laws of 1391 and 1532 reflect the spiritual aspirations of late medieval society and show that they caused some governmental concern. As with the statute of 1279, one might ask whether this anxiety was misplaced. Recipients of the newly dominant sort commanded far more limited resources than their forerunners and consequently became far less involved in the land market. Not that this is easy to prove. If it is sometimes difficult to assess patterns of endowment in the enclosed orders,

---

[58] P.R.O., E136/119/1.
[59] *Statutes of the Realm*, vol. II, pp. 79–80.
[60] *Ibid.*, vol. III, p. 378.

it is almost impossible to generalise about the possessions of the licensees who supplanted them. The very terms gild, chantry and hospital pose problems since many foundations embraced more than one function or evolved from one to include another. Tattershall College, for example, started life in 1389 as a parochial chantry before a licence of 1439 began its transformation into a college with an adjacent almshouse.[61] So far as gilds were concerned, even the crown found it hard to distinguish between their craft and spiritual rôles when mounting its enquiry into their activities and holdings in 1388-9.[62] Questions about property in what might otherwise seem to be an enquiry into potential sedition, coupled with the inclusion of gilds in the 1391 statute, show that the acquisitions of such bodies were seen as a threat; but this is largely belied by the account they offered of their possessions in the returns to the enquiry, assuming of course that these can be trusted.

Returns survive for 507 gilds, a high proportion belonging to the eastern counties.[63] Recorded Lincolnshire gilds were more than twice as numerous as the religious houses in the county licensed to acquire property after 1279, but their economic significance was infinitely smaller. The return of the members of the fraternity of St John the Baptist at Baston typifies a simple rural expression of popular piety, reporting that:

they have no lands, tenements, rents or possessions amortised or not amortised, either in their own hands or in the hands of others, nor any goods, chattels or cash for the use of the said fraternity other than twenty-eight quarters of malt worth six marks. And they have no charters or letters patent granted by the king or his progenitors.[64]

Most gilds of this sort operated on the basis of entry fines consisting of grain and wax, augmented in many cases by a small annual subscription; they admitted to no territorial holdings

[61] *Cal. Pat.*, 1388-92, p. 38; 1436-41, p. 292; D. M. Owen, *Church and Society in Medieval Lincolnshire* (Lincoln, 1971), p. 99.

[62] W. R. Jones, 'English Religious Brotherhoods and Medieval Lay Piety: The Inquiry of 1388-9', *The Historian*, 36, 1974, p. 653; *Cal. Close*, 1385-9, p. 624.

[63] H. F. Westlake, *The Parish Gilds of Medieval England* (London, 1919), p. 38.

[64] P.R.O., C47/39/76.

whatsoever. None claimed to have more than forty shillings in hand to meet expenses.[65] There were doubtless reasons why they might minimise or deny the extent of their property, and other doubts may arise from the stereotyped language of the returns and the evident collusion in drawing them up, but the resources described seem entirely appropriate to the associations concerned.[66] Nor do they seem to have acquired much property after 1391, when the obligation to seek a licence was unambiguous. Holdings on the scale of the messuage, forty acres of arable and twenty acres of meadow sought by the gild of the Nativity of St Mary in Baston in 1403 were rare.[67] Not surprisingly, the wealthiest parochial gilds were to be found in the large towns. The gild of Corpus Christi in Boston was one of the few to attract more than purely local membership. As early as 1349, it secured a general licence to acquire property to an annual value of twenty pounds and subsequent licences suggest that a reasonable endowment was achieved.[68] Like other religious bodies it probably made use of feoffees before 1391. This was certainly the case with some of the Northampton gilds. In spite of their trenchant assertions that burgesses had a perfect right to bequeath their property to any sort of churchman they wished, their income in fact depended on property held to their use by local laymen. St Mary's Gild in All Saints' Church benefited *inter alia* from an enfeoffment arranged by William of Wykeham worth some forty shillings per annum after maintenance costs, providing that tenants could be found.[69]

It is to rich urban gilds such as these, or merchant gilds like that of Coventry, which reported land, houses and rents worth £37 12s 4d, that one must look when arguing for the territorial aggrandisement of late medieval licensees.[70] Even so, their re-

---

65 This account is based on P.R.O., C47/39/73–100, C47/40/104, C47/41/182, a sample of twenty-five per cent of the 123 surviving Lincolnshire returns.

66 Gilds in the same place made returns in the same format or even on the same parchment. E.g. P.R.O., C47/39/79–81.

67 *Cal. Pat.*, 1401–5, p. 312.

68 Owen, *Church and Society in Medieval Lincolnshire*, p. 127; *Cal. Pat.*, 1348–50, p. 364; 1350–4, p. 101; 1391–6, p. 68; 1396–9, p. 342; 1413–16, p. 290; 1461–7, p. 356; P.R.O., C47/39/83.

69 P.R.O., C47/45/380–3.

70 Ed. Toulmin Smith, *English Gilds* (London, 1870), p. 231.

sources were modest in comparison with those of most religious houses. It must have been the ubiquity of gilds rather than their individual wealth which made them an object of concern.

Much the same applied to chantry endowments. A few with founders of first rank attained considerable wealth. Ralph Cromwell, during his career as royal treasurer, added substantial landholdings to his inheritance. Shortly before his death provision from this was made for both his heirs and his college at Tattershall. His grant formed the core of an endowment yielding a net income of nearly three hundred and fifty pounds per annum in the sixteenth century.[71] If this did not quite establish Tattershall at the forefront of Lincolnshire religious institutions, it nevertheless enabled it to outrank most of the old orders. In this it was atypical. Few colleges in England, unless they were associated with secular cathedrals or minster churches, could boast an annual income of more than one hundred pounds in 1535.[72] Parochial chantries were poorer still. William de Hanlay's interesting endowment of his family chantry at Burgh-on-Baine (Lincs.) in the mid-fourteenth century serves to illustrate the point. In 1345, he obtained a licence to grant a messuage, eighty acres of arable, six acres of meadow and twenty shillings' rent there to provide for two chaplains. Following the Black Death, in 1352, he gained a second licence substituting eleven marks' rent for the proposed landholdings, because he considered the chaplains would be more secure with a fixed rent since land 'in these days requires great anxiety'.[73] In either event the endowment was modest. Parochial clergy attracted similar or even smaller benefactions, often in order to extend their premises. Such was the grant of a messuage authorised to the parson of Conisby (Lincs.) in 1345 so that he could enlarge his manse.[74]

Far from swelling their endowments, many chantries, gilds and allied bodies withered to extinction. In Essex and Wiltshire more than three-quarters of those licensed in the first half of the fourteenth century had vanished by the dissolution.[75] Insofar as

[71] *Cal. Pat.*, 1436–41, pp. 384, 435; 1441–6, p. 66; 1452–61, pp. 161, 195, 199–200; *Valor Ecclesiasticus*, vol. IV, p. 44.
[72] Knowles, Hadcock, *Medieval Religious Houses*, pp. 413–19 and passim.
[73] *Cal. Pat.*, 1343–5, p. 439; 1350–4, p. 358.
[74] *Ibid.*, 1343–5, p. 463.   [75] Kreider, *English Chantries*, p. 89.

generalisation is possible, it appears that late medieval alienees were poorer if more numerous than their predecessors. Thus, not only were there fewer licences in absolute terms during this period, but they were spread among a larger and less affluent constituency.[76] If this brought the question of amortisation home to a wider public, it nevertheless resulted in relatively small amounts of land passing into ecclesiastical hands. The fall in accessions suggested by the decline in licences, albeit somewhat falsified by the large-scale evasions associated with chantries, was therefore equalled if not transcended by the fall in the amounts of land involved. One of the most alarming features of mortmain tenure had been the economic power of the larger religious houses. In this aspect at least, the accessions of the late Middle Ages posed no threat.

It could reasonably be concluded that economic conditions alone would have led to the withdrawal of religious houses from the land market in the late medieval period and that the prevailing pattern of ecclesiastical accession owed little to mortmain legislation. Although resilience depended to some extent on the underlying strength of the economy of each house, the quality of its leadership and the magnitude of its inherited debt, there are signs that even the most prominent ecclesiastical purchasers of the mid-thirteenth and early fourteenth centuries were in increasing financial difficulty.

The plight of later medieval landlords is well known. Marriage, the salvation of so many lay magnates, could bring nothing to the church.[77] Extravagant building programmes, famine and war took their toll on the religious, particularly those located in the north and extreme south. Quarr and Battle Abbeys suffered under the uncertainties of the Hundred Years' War, while Durham and Bolton Priories fell prey to Scottish raids.[78] The effect of such disasters on the life and purchases of the last of these houses was

---

[76] See *ibid.*, p. 8 et seq. for an estimate of the number of chantries and similar arrangements in late medieval England.

[77] McFarlane, *Nobility of Later Medieval England*, pp. 59–60, 184–6.

[78] S. F. Hockey, *Quarr Abbey and its Lands 1132–1631* (Leicester, 1970), p. 134 et seq.; Searle, *Lordship and Community*, p. 338 et seq.; R. B. Dobson, *Durham Priory 1400–1450* (Cambridge, 1973), p. 274; I. Kershaw, *Bolton Priory* (Oxford, 1973), pp. 14–16.

striking. Although their estates lay in the infertile uplands of the Dales, the canons of Bolton were nevertheless sufficiently prosperous to undertake substantial investment in land and appropriated churches between 1299 and 1317. By 1320, however, the threefold onslaught of foul weather, disease and the Scots reduced the community to seeking refuge in other Augustinian houses. Some recovery was achieved, but only two further important gains were made throughout the rest of the priory's history.[79]

Those less exposed to political hazard also showed signs of distress. Thorney Abbey's withdrawal from the land market coincided with the succession of Abbot Reginald to a debt of one thousand three hundred marks in 1323.[80] Crowland Abbey was in such straits in 1344 that it was taken into royal keeping, a fate it shared with thirty-five other houses during the course of Edward III's reign.[81] The depressing cartulary of Pipewell Abbey explains only too readily why this house received so few licences to acquire land.[82] Bodies like Meaux, hoping to compensate for its personal flood disaster in the 1340s by purchase, were just as likely to compound their problems with suffocating debt and high litigation costs.[83] The painful accumulation of the purchase price of Mepal in 1361 by Ely Priory may also indicate something more than the usual shortage of ready cash. The prior made a large contribution of £66 13s 4d to the total of £241 13s 4d, but more typical were gifts of a single pound or less.[84] Credit had been the more usual recourse of earlier generations.

High production costs, low prices and a shortage of tenants prepared to hold land on traditional terms, if at all, were the final undoing of even the very rich, though the process was often slow. Income from the common property of the dean and chapter of Lincoln was falling in the later fourteenth century, but crisis

---

[79] Kershaw, *Bolton Priory*, pp. 13–21, 113–16.
[80] C.U.L., Add. MSS 3020–1, f465.
[81] *Cal. Pat.*, 1343–5, p. 339; Wood-Legh, *Studies in Church Life*, p. 12.
[82] B.L., Cott. Otto B xiv, passim.
[83] Bond, *Chronica Monasterii de Melsa*, vol. III, pp. vii–x, 6 et seq.
[84] Evans, *E.H.R.*, 1936, pp. 118–19; C.U.L., EDC 1B/23. The manuscript figure for the prior's contribution is clearly £66, not £67 as given in the transcript.

point had not yet been reached.[85] Much the same was true of Ramsey Abbey, where acute strain was not evident until the 1390s. Withdrawal from the land market coincided with what has been described as the 'phenomenal' arrears of the mid-fifteenth century.[86] Few houses were as fortunate as Westminster Abbey, which could fall back increasingly on the income from exceptional royal chantry endowments.[87]

Confirmation that the economic climate alone was enough to drive churchmen from the land market comes from a comparison with the fate of lay magnates. The noble families studied by Holmes tended to buy piecemeal in the early fourteenth century before withdrawing altogether from the market towards the middle of the century. Small additions were made to estates in the bailiwick of Clare until *c.* 1330. Earl Humphrey de Bohun, who died in 1322, made some notable gains, but his successors did not choose to emulate him. The activities of the earls of Warwick were on a more subdued scale, consisting of numerous additions to existing manors rather than acquisition of complete new manors, but acquisitions such as these had also virtually disappeared by the mid-1340s.[88] As with ecclesiastical estates, the trend with baronial lands appears to be one of shrinking horizons, preceding almost complete withdrawal from the market around the middle of the century. Royal requirement of a licence to acquire land held in chief, to which members of the baronage were often attracted, may have contributed to this situation, but more probably the explanation can be attributed to the growing gloom emanating from rentals and accounts.

Land purchase, like demesne farming, was a defensive response of landlords confronted by inflation and greater demands on their income. Like demesne farming, it could only provide a solution as long as conditions were favourable to their interest. This was increasingly less the case from the second decade of the fourteenth century. Cash was harder to raise and the returns on capital outlay

---

85 K. Major, 'The Finances of the Dean and Chapter of Lincoln from the Twelfth to the Fourteenth Century: A Preliminary Survey', *Journal of Ecclesiastical History*, 5, 1954, p. 167.
86 Raftis, *Estates of Ramsey Abbey*, chs. 9 and 10.
87 Harvey, *Westminster Abbey and its Estates*, p. 36.
88 Holmes, *Estates of the Higher Nobility*, pp. 113–14.

discouraging. Although the purchase of new estates was a time-honoured way of increasing income, the costs were becoming crippling or even prohibitive. Religious houses were therefore constrained just as powerfully in their withdrawal from the land market by economic weakness as by any legal impediment. This makes it particularly difficult to disentangle the impact of mortmain legislation from more general conditions all tending to the same end. It is arguable, though ultimately incapable of proof, that for those stretched to the limits of their resources, the further burden imposed by the costs of amortisation proved the last straw.

Just how much the legal trappings of amortisation cost potential alienees has never been clarified. Circumstances varied greatly and this has discouraged scholars from embarking on any but the vaguest of generalisations. Indeed, to attempt anything more specific is a thankless and controversial task. It is unavoidable, however, if the effects of mortmain legislation on the church after 1300 are to be fully appreciated.

Although it may be subject to serious criticism, the most useful frame of reference is provided by considering fines in relation to the cost of land. That fines came to bear some theoretical relationship to an agreed multiplier, however often it broke down in practice, has already been noted.[89] The same could be argued, with the same practical proviso, about the cost of land. On several occasions, some widely spaced in time, there are suggestions that land was normally sold at a given number of times its annual value. The first occurs in a letter from Henry III to the king of France in 1267, laying down the terms on which the younger Simon de Montfort might resume his father's lands:

the said Simon shall be bound to sell the said lands to the king or his children or one of them whenever required by the king or them or one of them, the price of which lands the king leaves to the decision of the king of France on condition however that the price of land of the value of one mark a year be not assessed above ten marks, at which price lands are commonly sold in the realm.[90]

[89] See above, pp. 68–71.
[90] *Cal. Pat.*, 1266–72, p. 141; Harvey, *Westminster Abbey and its Estates*, pp. 197–8.

This was echoed in an arbitration by Queen Eleanor of Provence between her son Edmund and Gilbert Talebot in 1270, where it is stated that land valued at ten pounds per annum should, when sold in fee, fetch one hundred pounds.[91] The ten years' purchase of the thirteenth century had risen to fifteen in several versions of an admonitory jingle directed at purchasers between the mid-fifteenth and early sixteenth centuries:

> In xv yere if ye wise be
> Ye shalle ayein your money see.[92]

By the 1540s, if commissions for the sale of monastic lands are to be credited, yet a further rise had brought the norm for sales to twenty years' purchase.[93] This contemporary theory has received some support from modern calculations based on actual transactions. Henry de Lacy was buying at ten years' purchase from an indebted Kirkstall Abbey in 1287.[94] The monks of Battle Abbey were prepared to pay more than this to acquire coveted rent charges on their property, but the usual price tended to be about ten times the annual render.[95] Thorold Rogers recognised a rise from ten years' purchase prevailing until the late fourteenth century to fifteen years' purchase, then a further rise before the mid-fifteenth century to twenty years' purchase.[96] McFarlane, notwithstanding the evidence of the doggerel he cited, also believed that twenty years' purchase had become the accepted rate for the mid-fifteenth century.[97]

Just as the assertion of Burton or Henry Fillongley that fines were assessed at five times the annual value of a holding was not always borne out in practice, so these generalised figures for the price of land were never understood to operate rigidly on all

[91] P.R.O., DL 41/1/19, m2.
[92] K. B. McFarlane, 'The Investment of Sir John Fastolf's Profits of War', *T.R.H.S.*, 5th ser., 7, 1957, pp. 112–13; F.R.H. du Boulay, *The Lordship of Canterbury* (London, 1966), p. 158.
[93] J. Youings, *The Dissolution of the Monasteries* (London, 1971), pp. 120–2.
[94] N. Denholm-Young, *Seignorial Administration in England*, 2nd impression (London, 1963), p. 61.
[95] Searle, *Lordship and Community*, p. 125.
[96] J. E. Thorold Rogers, *Six Centuries of Work and Wages*, 2 vols. (London, 1884), vol. I, pp. 287–8; *idem*, *A History of Agriculture and Prices in England*, 7 vols. (Oxford, 1866–1902), vol. I, p. 688; vol. IV, p. 100.
[97] McFarlane, *Nobility of Later Medieval England*, p. 57.

occasions. Much depended on the location and desirability of the property and on whether or not the supply of suitable land matched the ambitions of potential purchasers. The variety concealed behind a general figure is illustrated by Sir John Fastolf's acquisitions in the mid-fifteenth century. They ranged from eleven to thirty years' purchase. Averaged at 17⅘ years' purchase, however, they fall neatly between the fifteen years' purchase of the poet and the twenty years' purchase of present-day observers.[98] Unless the market is very unstable, estate agents now find it easy enough to assign an appropriate sale price to individual property in the light of a general appreciation of current values, an understanding backed today by sophisticated calculation.[99] Once it is allowed that the concept of so many years' purchase was known in the medieval period, there is no inconsistency in accepting that a broadly valid theoretical notion of land value could exist alongside wide fluctuations in practice at that date too.

Objection might be made to the implication that land became more expensive with the passage of time when late medieval records are full of vacant tenements and tumbling rent rolls. Yet here also there is no inconsistency once it is accepted that the land market was not a single entity, but a series of interrelated markets subject to varying pressures.[100] Peasant tenements, only too often abandoned by their cultivators, could not command high prices in a time of flagging population unless they were very attractive. The same did not necessarily apply to properties large enough to be dignified as estates. Few landlords sold such property unless constrained by lack of heirs or financial disaster. Perhaps fewer landed families were being squeezed out in the later Middle Ages, or possibly the number of aspirants to landed respectability increased. Whatever the explanation, there is the suggestion of a shortage of good properties for wealthy purchasers at this time.[101] Limited supplies of land, sought, as much for reasons of prestige as for their intrinsic return, by a social group

---

[98] McFarlane, *T.R.H.S.*, 1957, p. 110.

[99] D. M. Turner, *An Approach to Land Values* (Berkhamsted, 1977), p. 51 et seq.

[100] *Ibid.*, pp. 38–9.

[101] McFarlane, *Nobility of Later Medieval England*, pp. 55–6; Harvey, *Westminster Abbey and its Estates*, p. 173.

unlikely to have shrunk proportionately to the peasantry, could account adequately for the rise in value of this type of estate. Equally the penury of old-established knightly families, confronted from the late twelfth century by rising prices and demands on their income, might account for the relative cheapness of knights' fees in the thirteenth century.

A further problem involved in the use of generalised figures to evaluate the cost of amortisation arises from the fact that neither fines nor purchase prices comprised the whole cost of acquisition. Legal fees surrounding both might add appreciable sums. So far as the costs of amortisation were concerned, the procedure involved in securing a licence necessitated much travelling, negotiation and bribery. The following payments made by the canons of Lincoln in pursuit of a licence granted in 1311 are probably typical enough in nature, if not always in scale:

Item to John de Beaumer clerk of the escheator so that he may be favourable and propitious to the Chapter in inquisitions taken in the course of his master's business 2s. Item to his servant 12d. Item as a gratuity to Lord Walter le Venur sub-escheator so that he may be favourable and benevolent towards the Chapter in his inquisitions in Lincolnshire 13s 4d. Item to Philip clerk to the sheriff so that he may be favourable in chapter business 6s 8d....[102]

Individually little enough, cumulatively these payments could add considerably to the total expenditure. Moreover, the whole procedure, together with the attendant cost, might be repeated if mesne lord consent was also necessary. Some lords, like Hugh le Despenser and his wife, who approved an alienation to Tewkesbury Abbey in 1326, were prepared to settle for spiritual benefits, but others preferred their rewards in this world.[103] Accounts for an alienation to the London Charterhouse at the turn of the fifteenth and sixteenth centuries show payments of £4 10s 9d to the prior of Christchurch Cathedral Priory, Canterbury, 40s to the nuns of Higham and 9s to the lord of Cobham.[104] Much might depend on the tact and persuasiveness of the alienee,

[102] Lincs. Archives Off., Bj/2/4, f45. For other examples, see Bj/2/4, passim.
[103] *Cal. Pat.*, 1324–7, pp. 318–19.
[104] P.R.O., SC 12/25/55, m35.

but it was unwise to rely on a mesne lord's piety. Indeed, in this respect, churchmen were if anything more assertive of their rights than the laity.

The extra costs possible in the normal course of land purchase were even more striking. The sum paid on the occasion of a conveyance was often only one of a number of further payments to interested parties. Open-ended commitments arising from a purchase price comprising pension or corrody agreements were a potential source of great added expense. For this reason, the canons of Bolton spent at least an extra two hundred pounds on top of the initial two hundred and fifty pounds paid for the manor of Appletreewick (N. Yorks.).[105] Even more common were payments made to the heirs of a vendor in order to keep a sale secure. Thus, in 1313, the canons of Thornton-on-Humber were obliged to pay Thomas of Lancaster sixty pounds in exchange for charters confirming the sales of Henry de Lacy at the end of the previous century. They also had to pay a further twenty pounds in addition to the purchase price of the advowson of Welton.[106] Legal challenge to title occurred all too often. The monks of Westminster paid £133 6s 8d some forty-six years after their purchase of Great Amwell in 1270 in order to terminate a plea of warranty, nearly a quarter as much again as the purchase price of £566 13s 4d.[107] As in this instance, a cash settlement was often the preferable alternative to a prolonged and costly lawsuit, but such disputes could not always be avoided or curtailed. It was a lucky purchaser who escaped with nothing more than the immediate outlay on a property, so any simple comparisons between generalised figures for fines and land prices omit an unpredictable but often large part of the equation.

Figures based solely on fines in relation to theoretical land values thus understate the cost of both purchase and amortisation to a significant extent. If the proportion were equal for each, the problem would be less intransigent, but there is no reason why this should be so. Any conclusions based on such figures must therefore be impressionistic. Yet in spite of these reservations, any

---

[105] Kershaw, *Bolton Priory*, pp. 114–15.
[106] Oxf., Bodl., Tanner 166, ff22–v.
[107] Harvey, *Westminster Abbey and its Estates*, p. 194.

framework for evaluating the cost of amortisation, however imperfect, is too useful to be totally spurned.

The picture emerging from the figures, especially from the late fourteenth century, argues strongly that the requirements of mortmain legislation weighed heavily on the church. With fines in the region of five times the annual value of a holding when land cost between fifteen and twenty years' purchase, acquisition must have been significantly more expensive for ecclesiastical buyers. How far this contention is borne out by individual experience and how evenly the burden fell on different types of churchmen can only be seen by examining as many particular transactions as possible.

Full and informative accounts survive for the common property of the dean and chapter of Lincoln. In 1305, they were licensed to receive the advowson of Bottesford-by-Messingham church (Humberside) from Thornholme Priory with a view to appropriation. The priory was given one hundred pounds, and certain lay interests were bought out at the same time for another one hundred marks. A comparatively large fine was imposed by the crown: one hundred marks for the licence itself, together with ten pounds to enter the acquisition as lay fee on 'the great roll' of the king. Even without calculating incidental expenses, therefore, the purchase price was in a ratio of approximately 2.5:1 to the fine. Fortunately, in view of the weight of royal demands, the other expenses of this transaction appear to have been modest. In all, the recorded cost of amortisation was £79 11s 8d, while the purchase and associated legal processes amounted to £168 13s 8d.[108]

At first sight the acquisition of a messuage and an acre of arable at Tansor (Northants.), together with the advowson of part of the parish church licensed in 1324, presents a less gloomy view. The vendor received £22 13s, while the crown asked a mere £2 fine; a ratio nearer to 11:1 than the 3 or 4:1 suggested by the general figures, albeit for a somewhat later period. However, Table 4 shows that, on closer inspection, the outlay on amortisation was more serious, since the incidental expenses of

[108] *Cal. Pat.*, 1301-7, p. 410; Lincs. Archives Off., Bj/2/4, ff14-v, 25; Foster, *Registrum Antiquissimum*, vol. II, p. 226 et seq.

Table 4. *Acquisition at Tansor by the dean and chapter of Lincoln*

Cost of conveyancing				Cost of amortisation			
	£	s	d		£	s	d
Travel between Lincoln and Tansor		19	9	Cost of the inquisition *ad quod damnum* at Stamford		17	3½
				Bribes for the inquisition		25	4
Purchase of dower right		13	4	Transcript of the inquisition		2	0
Livery of seisin		9	9	Travel from Lincoln to Stamford and back		2	0
				To Adam de Beauchamp for the royal licence		29	4
				To four serjeants bearing 'le maces' at court		40	0
				Fine for the licence		40	0
TOTAL	£2	2	10		£7	15	11½

One mark paid to the bailiff of the honour of Gloucester for this tenement might be charged against either account and has therefore been omitted from consideration.

obtaining the licence appear to have been heavier than either the fine itself or the routine conveyancing costs. When all recorded expenses are taken into account, the canons paid £24 15s 10d for the property itself and a further £7 15s 11½d to amortise it; a ratio closer to 3:1.[109] In this instance, therefore, providing that no expensive challenge to title later emerged, the need for a licence to alienate also accounted for a significant proportion of the total cost of the acquisition.

These Lincoln transactions are illuminating in several respects. They emphasise the variation in costs possible even within the same institution and over a relatively short space of time. In particular, they show how in one case the royal fine might constitute the most serious burden of mortmain legislation, while in another the heaviest outlay might lie in the administrative costs. The Tansor acquisition reveals starkly enough how little

[109] *Cal. Pat.*, 1321–4, p. 406; Lincs. Archives Off., Bj/2/5, ff66v, 77v, 85v, 127v, 129.

relationship the cost of obtaining a licence might bear to the value of the acquisition: most of the incidental expenses would have been the same however rich the acquisition. Houses dutifully licensing each small accession could easily find the cost of amortisation exceeding the purchase price of their gain. It was not just convenience which dictated licences covering multiple accessions, but economic self-interest unless major acquisition was involved.

The Lincoln evidence also suggests that the tentative general picture of amortisation based on fines alone may err on the conservative side and that the burden on the church was even heavier than the generalised evidence would suggest. However, in one important respect the Lincoln gains were not typical. Both involved advowsons, and although the cost of the licence to acquire Bottesford-by-Messingham church was so high, there were compensations. No layman would have been allowed to appropriate the rectory. Moreover, the full cost of the acquisition, notwithstanding the surcharge necessitated by the statute, was not great in view of the return. The inquisition *ad quod damnum* valued the alienation at twenty pounds per annum, but there are indications that a return of about sixty-five pounds was anticipated after appropriation. In practice, the yield fluctuated markedly in the years up to 1319–20 and the average income was just over fifty-four pounds per annum.[110] Even at the inquisition's valuation, the full cost of the acquisition, including amortisation, amounted to a not unreasonable twelve and a half years' purchase. When the potential for development through appropriation had been realised, the price came down to a bargain four and a half year's purchase. Thus, if churchmen were subject to certain handicaps, they were also provided with certain opportunities not open to the laity.

Unfortunately few archives are as informative as those of Lincoln, even where accounts for amortisation survive. Those left by the executors of Bishop Bitton of Exeter for the appropriation and amortisation of the church of St Melan-in-Kerrier (Cornwall), licensed in 1309, are a case in point.[111] The thirty pounds given to the prior of Mottisfont for the advowson, together

---

[110] Lincs. Archives Off., Bj/2/4, ff18, 28, 65v, 74v, 84v, 93v, 103, 111, 113v, 120, 130; Bj/2/5, ff1, 21.   [111] *Cal. Pat.*, 1307–13, p. 202.

with £6 13s 4d given to Michael le Petyt for his quitclaim, are recorded, and also the twenty-pound fine to the crown for the appropriation. Another forty shillings *pro auro Regine* was spent to the same end, and twenty-three shillings for a royal charter, presumably the licence. Sixpence more purchased the writ for the inquisition *ad quod damnum*, but details of bribes and other incidental expenses are subsumed in the general cost of carrying out the bishop's last wishes. Only the fee of three shillings to the scribe for his services on this and another appropriation is noted separately. Thus, it is not possible to estimate the full burden imposed by formal amortisation, although it was obviously heavy.[112]

An even more detailed account, though again aggravatingly incomplete, is that of the purchase of the manor and advowson of Mepal by the prior and convent of Ely in 1361. Although copious detail is preserved, it is impossible to calculate the total cost either of the property itself or of the licence to acquire it. The monks paid £241 13s 4d in cash to various parties, but also undertook a life pension of twenty marks per annum of indeterminate length, thus concealing the full purchase price. Minute account is provided of the expenses involved in journeying to and fro to get the licence, the bribes and the fees, but part payment in kind to the escheator makes it difficult to know exactly how much was spent. In addition to forty shillings in cash, he received a pipe of Ely wine. If this is assigned a rough value of four pounds, based on the cost of imported wine in that year, one arrives at a figure of £16 6s 2½d for amortisation. Assuming that the life pension would not be paid for longer than half a century, the purchase price of the property appears to have been in a ratio of somewhere between 15 to 18:1 to the cost of amortisation.[113] Many of the expenses incurred in pursuit of this licence were irreducible. Had the manor and advowson been worth half as much, the burden would have been proportionately heavier. Nevertheless, as it stands, the Mepal evidence suggests

---

[112] Ed. W. H. Hale, H. T. Ellacombe, *Account of the Executors of Richard Bishop of London 1303 and of the Executors of Thomas Bishop of Exeter 1310* (Camden Soc., N.S., 10, 1874), pp. 36–8, 44–5.
[113] C.U.L., EDC 1B/23, unnumbered; Evans, *E.H.R.*, 1936, pp. 119–20; Thorold Rogers, *History of Agriculture and Prices in England*, vol. 1, p. 639.

that mortmain requirements were not always as oppressive as they appear from Lincoln and Exeter records.

One reason why the cost of Mepal to Ely seems so reasonable is that no fine was exacted for the licence: amortisation took place under the convent's general licence to acquire property to the annual value of forty pounds.[114] The religious orders may have been under economic strain in the later medieval period, but they were still the group which had insulated itself with privileges most effectively from the full rigour of mortmain costs. For most of the fourteenth century, general licences enabled the richest church-men to make accessions without payment of fines, even if they could not escape the incidental costs of obtaining an individual licence and going through the process of an inquisition *ad quod damnum*. It is possible that this facility may have encouraged houses touched by their first financial decay to continue with small-scale accession for longer than might otherwise have been the case. More probably, the declining appetite for licences observed in the later part of the fourteenth century owed some-thing to the more stringent government policy towards acquisition under general licence. Even under the most favourable circum-stances, as at Ely in 1361 when no fine was paid and the accession was well worth the expense, the surcharge entailed by the need for a licence was hardly negligible. Under less happy conditions, when such costs might add a quarter or a third as much again to the total bill for acquisition, the additional burden could easily put the enterprise out of reach.

All too often late medieval churchmen were buying with depleted resources for defensive reasons in a market buoyant with more prosperous competitors. Chantry founders like Sir John Fastolf tried to negotiate the best possible terms for amortisation, but at worst their outlay reduced the value of what they had left to give. The position of large corporate alienees was different. In the light of evidence available, the onus of proof would now appear to lie with those who maintain that mortmain legislation was little more than a bureaucratic inconvenience to these houses. Manifestly they could not continue to absorb the extra cost and buy as they had done before.

[114] *Cal. Pat.*, 1361–4, p. 171.

CONCLUSION

The purpose of this study has been twofold: to examine the development and implementation of mortmain law and to assess how far it affected the church's ability to acquire further landed property. The nature of the sources has made it rather easier to accomplish the first of these aims. Although there are lacunae, it has been possible to trace the evolution of licensing procedure and fining practices with tolerable certainty. The thoroughness with which the law was enforced remains a matter of some doubt, but more could be discovered about this. A fuller investigation of surviving escheators' accounts and judicial records would make it possible to test the trends evident in Lincolnshire over a wider geographical area; some regional variation is to be expected and it would be useful to define its limits. Similarly, the extent of successful evasion has only been explored in relation to a few religious houses. The scope for additional work here, again on a wider geographical basis, is clear. However, while further study along these lines may modify the conclusions already reached, it is unlikely to overturn them completely. The picture which has emerged from the records examined so far conforms well enough with what might be expected from political and economic conditions in the country at large, making it improbable that the experience of eastern England was wildly aberrant.

Assessing the impact of mortmain law on ecclesiastical endowment has proved much the more difficult task. Before drawing any conclusions about mortmain controls, it was essential to establish the nature of endowment itself and this has not been easy. The availability of licences recording alienation into mortmain offers, for the first time, some country-wide data over a long period, but there have been limitations to what such licences can yield by way of general information. They lend themselves to a statistical analysis of the identity and number of recipients, but do not provide a simple answer to the question of how much land was passing into church hands. The variety of property licensed, the rents, the different sorts of land and other interests are too diverse to permit systematisation. Nor are the inquisitions *ad quod damnum* sufficiently honest to allow an alternative assessment based on valuations. The only practicable approach has been through an impressionistic survey drawn from the archives of particular institutions. Once more, it would be valuable if the conclusions based on a limited sample of houses in eastern England could be tested on a wider geographical front. Nothing, however, can be done to correct the bias inherent in the sources at our disposal. Evidence is necessarily taken from the records of the wealthiest churchmen. Little or nothing survives to provide a context for the accessions of the less affluent religious or the host of minor licensees who appeared in the late medieval period.

Notwithstanding these deficiencies of evidence, some firm conclusions about ecclesiastical acquisition after 1279 have been reached. We know that the demand for licences increased fairly steadily in the fifty years after the statute and that the bulk of them went to the religious. Illicit activities and exploitation of the opportunities to take out major leases add support to a picture of increasing religious endowments at this time. Yet it is also clear from monastic archives that this apparent hunger for property masked growing difficulty in making accessions on the old scale. By the second half of the fourteenth century, these difficulties are reflected in licence figures too. The decline in licensed accessions and the dwindling share in them taken by the religious represent a real contraction in the amount of property passing into mortmain, even if this is somewhat exaggerated in the graphs compiled from licences alone. For the rest of the Middle Ages, it was a case of generally smaller accessions passing into the hands of fewer and poorer recipients.

The rôle of mortmain restrictions in promoting this profile of accession is far from obvious. It has been easiest to isolate when it ran counter to prevailing economic and social pressures, as in the half-century after the enactment of *De viris religiosis*. Once mortmain control tended in the same direction as other signal factors, as happened in the changing society of the mid-fourteenth century, its individual significance becomes harder to determine. Nevertheless, one cannot doubt that mortmain requirements could become burdensome in an economic climate increasingly hostile to those who were once foremost among ecclesiastical purchasers. It must also remain probable, if incapable of proof, that the need for a licence at times put acquisition beyond the means of some churchmen who could otherwise have afforded it. For donors the problem was less acute. The cost of amortisation either coerced them into greater generosity or reduced the value of their gifts. It was less likely to deter them altogether. Complaints from late medieval benefactors suggest that they haggled over the price, but grudgingly paid it.

One thing is overwhelmingly certain whether one looks at mortmain legislation from the point of view of officialdom or from the point of view of the church: namely the extent of change over the two and a half centuries between 1279 and the Reformation. It is this fluidity that makes simple generalisations about mortmain legislation and its effects misleading. Indeed, it explains why historians have so often appeared to differ radically in their judgements of the subject. What was true at one period was no longer so at another. This is particularly evident with regard to the success enjoyed by the 1279 statute in controlling ecclesiastical accession and the extent to which the crown exploited licences and pardons for fiscal purposes.

In the light of subsequent events, it is all too easy to undervalue the initial achievement of *De viris religiosis* in curbing acquisition. Although there was a period of nearly two centuries when mortmain controls did little more than reinforce existing trends, for the first twenty years after the statute land purchase was called virtually to a halt. Even when legally resumed or driven underground, it never again attained its former scale. Although some large properties were acquired, most new accessions were of a modest nature and often marked recoveries of church fee. To impose a pattern of behaviour which has been shown to run contrary to economic dictates for a whole generation and to precipitate a permanent reduction in the scale of purchase was no mean feat. It is only after the introduction of fines in

1299 that one can justify Plucknett's contention that the flow of land to the church continued unhindered except for a royal levy. There then ensued a period when the advent of general licences and the widespread adoption of enfeoffment to use neutralised what little sting the statute had come to possess for many institutions until the reforms of the late fourteenth century. Thus, in the space of little more than a hundred years, the impact of the 1279 statute swung from one extreme to the other and, in a modified way, back again.

Recent historiographical tradition has encouraged us to view politics and law in terms of the unending struggles of monarchs to augment resources ill matched to ambitions and accordingly to attach fiscal significance to mortmain legislation. Unfortunately, the evidence will not bear such an interpretation with any degree of conviction. Certainly, licensing requirements were exploited in the interests of revenue; briefly at first in times of emergency and, after the mid-fourteenth century, more systematically. But the absence of fines before 1299 makes it difficult to accept that *De viris religiosis* was enacted with finance in mind. Even when the crown was at its most rapacious, it would be unduly cynical to assume that money had become its sole objective. A sincere attempt to discriminate between needy and affluent petitioners for licences is consistently evident. General licences which restricted accessions to the holder's own fee were reserved for the richly endowed. Fines were adjusted to the means of individual alienees and both fine and sealing fee were pardoned in deserving cases. It could be argued that, in its judicious levying of fines, the crown supported the poorest churchmen in improving their lot and inhibited further aggrandisement on the part of the already overblown. Only in the reign of Henry VII are there signs of ruthless exaction regardless of merit.

If the consequences of mortmain legislation changed and developed in the period after 1279, so did the legislation itself. The wide scope for interpretation found in thirteenth- and four-teenth-century legal practice allowed the statute to stretch like a glove to fit practical needs, but there were limits to what could be achieved by this means. That informal adjustment would not suffice for ever became clear with the legislative ban on collusive actions in 1285. Subsequent legislation was concerned not just with evasion of *De viris religiosis*, but also with the changing identity of alienees. The 1279 statute was called into being when concern focussed on the extensive buying of a few relatively large houses and did not prove adequate when social and economic change no longer made religious the prime recipients. Lay anxiety shifted imperceptibly towards the accessions of boroughs and gilds and even more towards proliferating chantry foundations. The additional legislation of 1391 and 1532, which brought these bodies more firmly within the law, shows how distant mortmain problems of the late Middle Ages had become from those of the thirteenth century.

Possible changes in the balance between lay and ecclesiastical landholding during the thirteenth century originally directed my attention towards mortmain legislation, and it is the fate of the thirteenth-century alienees which remains of principal concern to economic historians. Encroachments were certainly made on lay fee, but when seen in proportion, they were not as far-reaching as contemporaries feared or modern scholars suspected. The relationship of ecclesiastical acquisition to other aspects of the economy was also close, although there are problems involved in this. Relatively few institutions could individually acquire land on a scale large enough to affect lay society, but it is just those few on which we rely for most of our knowledge of the medieval economy. Without monastic archives, evidence relating to matters such as the exploitation of estates and the condition of the peasantry at this time would be very thin. Our profile of ecclesiastical acquisition after 1279 is in large measure associated with our profile of the medieval economy as a whole because each is based on records from almost identical members of the community. One would thus expect broad agreement between the two and it can be found. There is a strong correlation between the agrarian crisis of the early fourteenth century and the pause in the upward thrust of licences at the same date, although political factors are also likely to have played their part. Again, the decline in licences granted after the middle of the fourteenth century coincides remarkably with the first appearance of the Black Death. Even the plateau reached in the 1330s and 1340s suffers from the ambiguity so often observed in the evidence from the controversial decades before 1348. The dismal record of licensed alienations to the church in the fifteenth century also accords only too well with arguments put forward for a stagnant economy at this time, although once more it is not wholly attributable to economic causes. Of course evidence of this sort is not sufficiently independent to act as a check on interpretations of an economy which are drawn largely from ecclesiastical sources in the first place, but it can help to clarify points in those interpretations which remain obscure. This is particularly true for the period before the Black Death. Although licences held up well until the middle of the fourteenth century, evidence from within the houses themselves suggests that their prosperity was already faltering, thus adding weight to the view that some economic decline had set in before the onslaught of epidemic disease.

Mortmain tenure touched many nerves in medieval society. Consequently its study has offered more insights into the nature of that society than one might superficially have expected. Quite apart from mirroring the fate of the English economy, trends in late medieval acquisition have provided further proof, if that were needed, of the shift in spiritual preoccupations between the thirteenth and the fifteenth centuries. At the same time, new legislative measures and their enforcement have demonstrated the force of continuing lay concern about property passing into perpetual ownership, even if recipients were no longer capable of acting as a decisive economic force in the local community. Politics too have been reflected, whether in the crown's response to urgent demands from its subjects for restrictive action or in its increasingly exploitative attitude towards existing controls. It is hardly surprising that far-reaching ripples should be caused by interference with the accessions of a body as collectively wealthy and influential as the church. What is more surprising is the time it has taken for us to appreciate what a vein of riches lies concealed behind a well-known statute.

Appendix

THE STATUTE OF MORTMAIN
1279

Rex iustitiariis suis de banco salutem. Cum dudum provisum fuisset quod viri religiosi feoda aliquorum non ingrederentur sine licentia et voluntate capitalium dominorum de quibus feoda illa inmediate tenentur; et viri religiosi postmodum nichilominus tam feoda sua propria quam aliorum hactenus ingressi sint, ea sibi appropriando et emendo et aliquando ex dono aliorum recipiendo, per quod servitia que ex huiusmodi feodis debentur et que ad defensionem regni ab initio provisa fuerunt indebite subtrahuntur et domini capitales escaetas suas inde amittunt; nos super hoc pro utilitate regni congruum remedium providere volentes, de consilio prelatorum, comitum, et aliorum fidelium regni nostri de consilio nostro existentium providimus, statuimus, et ordinavimus quod nullus religiosus aut alius quicunque terras aut tenementa aliqua emere vel vendere, aut sub colore donationis aut termini vel alterius tituli cuiuscunque ab aliquo recipere aut alio quovis modo, arte, vel ingenio sibi appropriare presumat sub forisfactura eorundem, per quod ad manum mortuam terre et tenementa huiusmodi deveniant quoquo modo. Providimus etiam quod si quis religiosus aut alius contra presens statutum aliquo modo, arte, vel ingenio venire presumpserit, liceat nobis et aliis inmediatis capitalibus dominis feodi taliter alienati illud infra annum a tempore alienationis huiusmodi ingredi et tenere in feodo et hereditate. Et si dominus capitalis inmediatus negligens fuerit et feodum huiusmodi ingredi noluerit infra annum, tunc liceat proximo capitali domino mediato feodi illius infra dimidium annum sequentem feodum illud ingredi et tenere sicut predictum est; et sic quilibet dominus mediatus faciat si propinquior dominus in ingrediendo huiusmodi feodum negligens fuerit ut predictum est. Et si omnes huiusmodi capitales domini huiusmodi feodi qui plene fuerint etatis et infra quatuor maria et extra prisonam per unum annum negligentes vel remissi fuerint in hac parte, nos statim post annum completum a tempore quo huiusmodi emptiones, donationes, aut alias appropriationes fieri contigerit, terras et tenementa huiusmodi capiemus in manum nostram, et alios inde feoffabimus per certa servitia nobis inde ad defensionem regni nostri facienda; salvis capitalibus dominis feodorum illorum wardis, escaetis, et aliis ad ipsos pertinentibus ac servitiis inde debitis et consuetis. Et ideo vobis mandamus quod statutum predictum coram vobis legi et decetero firmiter teneri et observari faciatis. Teste rege apud Westmonasterium, xiiii⁰ᵉ die Novembris. (Taken from Powicke, Cheney, *Councils and Synods*, vol. II, pt II, pp. 864–5.)

BIBLIOGRAPHY

MANUSCRIPT SOURCES

Bodleian Library, Oxford
Ashmole 801	Ely Convent cartulary
Laud Misc. 642	Alvingham Priory cartulary
Tanner 166	Thornton Abbey annals

British Library
Add. MS 5845	Crowland Abbey register
Add. MS 35296	Spalding Priory register
Add. MS 37022	Pipewell Abbey cartulary
Egerton 3047	Ely Convent cartulary
Stowe 937	Pipewell Abbey cartulary
Harley 742	Spalding Priory register
Harley Charter 52 H 20	Bullington Priory deed
Cott. Calig. A xiii	Pipewell Abbey cartulary
Cott. Claud. D xii	Daventry Priory cartulary
Cott. Faust. B i	Barlings Abbey cartulary
Cott. Otto B xiv	Pipewell Abbey narrative
Cott. Vesp. A vi	Ely Convent cartulary

Gentlemen's Society, Spalding
Wrest Park Cartulary	Crowland Abbey cartulary

Lincolnshire Archives Office
6 Anc. 1/32–8	Crowland Abbey court rolls
Bj/2/4–5	Lincoln, dean and chapter accounts

Northamptonshire Record Office
Fitzwilliam Accs. 233, 2388	Peterborough Abbey accounts
Westmorland Coll. Box 2	Thorney Abbey deeds

Public Record Office
C47	Gild returns
C60	Fine rolls

C66	Patent rolls
C143	Inquisitions *ad quod damnum*
CP 25(1)	Feet of fines
DL 41/1/19	Duchy of Lancaster miscellanea
E136	Escheators' accounts
E159	Memoranda rolls
E368	Lord treasurer's remembrancer rolls
E371	Originalia rolls
E372	Pipe rolls
SC 12/25	London Charterhouse accounts
Ancient Deeds A 128	
B 3869	

University Library, Cambridge

Add. MSS 3020–1	Thorney Abbey cartulary
Add. MS 4401	Thorney Abbey rental
EDC 1B/3–5, 8, 15, 19, 23–4	Ely Convent deeds
QC Boxes 1–2	Crowland Abbey accounts

PRINTED SOURCES

Abstracts of Final Concords, ed. W. Boyd, W. O. Massingberd (London, 1896).

Account of the Executors of Richard Bishop of London 1303 and of the Executors of Thomas Bishop of Exeter 1310, ed. W. H. Hale, H. T. Ellacombe (Camden Soc., N.S., 10, 1874).

Annales Monastici, ed. H. R. Luard, 5 vols. (Rolls Series, London, 1864–9).

Anonimalle Chronicle, The, ed. V. H. Galbraith (Manchester, 1927, repr. 1970).

Borough Customs, ed. M. Bateson, 2 vols. (Selden Soc., 18 and 21, 1904–6).

Bracton on the Laws and Customs of England, ed. G. E. Woodbine, trans. S. E. Thorne, 4 vols. (Harvard, 1968–77).

British Borough Charters, ed. A. Ballard, J. Tait, M. Weinbaum, 3 vols. (Cambridge, 1913–43).

Calendar of Close Rolls, 1272–1509, 47 vols. (H.M.S.O., 1900–63).

Calendar of Fine Rolls, 1272–1509, 22 vols. (H.M.S.O., 1911–62).

Calendar of Inquisitions Miscellaneous, 7 vols. (H.M.S.O., 1916–68).

Calendar of Inquisitions Post Mortem, 19 vols. (H.M.S.O., 1904–55).

Calendar of Patent Rolls, 1232–1575, 68 vols. (H.M.S.O., 1906–73).

Cartularium Monasterii de Rameseia, ed. W. H. Hart, P. A. Lyons, 3 vols. (Rolls Series, London, 1884–93).

Cartulary of the Abbey of Old Wardon, ed. G. H. Fowler (Beds. Historical Rec. Soc., 13, 1930).

Cartulary of the Wakebridge Chantries at Crich, The, ed. A. Saltman (Derbyshire Archaeological Soc. Record Ser., 6, 1971).

Chronica Majora, ed. H. R. Luard, 7 vols. (Rolls Series, London, 1872–83).

Chronica Monasterii de Melsa, ed. E. A. Bond, 3 vols. (Rolls Series, London, 1866–8).

Chronicle of Walter of Guisborough, The, ed. H. Rothwell (Camden Soc., 3rd ser., 89, 1957).

Chronicon Abbatiae de Evesham, ed. W. D. Macray (Rolls Series, London, 1863).

Chronicon Abbatiae Rameseiensis, ed. W. D. Macray (Rolls Series, London, 1886).

Chronicon Petroburgense, ed. T. Stapleton (Camden Soc., 47, 1849).

Close Rolls, 1227–72, 14 vols. (H.M.S.O., 1902–38).

Corpus Juris Canonici, 2 vols. (Lipsiae, 1879–81).

Councils and Synods, ed. F. M. Powicke, C. R. Cheney, 2 vols. (Oxford, 1964).

Documents of the Baronial Movement of Reform and Rebellion: 1258–67, ed. I. J. Sanders (Oxford, 1973).

English Register of Godstow Nunnery near Oxford, The, ed. A. Clark (Early English Text Soc., London, 1911).

Fasciculi Zizaniorum, ed. W. W. Shirley (Rolls Series, London, 1858).

Final Concords of the County of Lincoln, ed. C. W. Foster (Lincoln Rec. Soc., 17, 1920).

Henry of Pytchley's Book of Fees, ed. W. T. Mellows (Northants. Rec. Soc., 2, 1927).

Historia Anglicana, ed. H. T. Riley, 2 vols. (Rolls Series, London, 1863–4).

Layettes du Trésor des Chartes, ed. M. A. Teulet, 3 vols. (Paris, 1866).

Lincoln Wills, ed. C. W. Foster (Lincoln Rec. Soc., 5, 1914).

Lincolnshire Domesday and the Lindsey Survey, The, ed. C. W. Foster, T. Longley (Lincoln Rec. Soc., 19, 1924, repr. 1976).

Ministers' Accounts of the Earldom of Cornwall (1296–7), ed. L. M. Midgley, 2 vols. (Camden Soc., 3rd ser., 66 and 68, 1942–5).

Ordonnances des Roys de France de la Troisième Race, ed. M. de Laurière et al., 21 vols. (Paris, 1723–1849, repr. 1967).

Paston Letters, The, ed. J. Gairdner, new edn, 3 vols. (London, 1896).

Bibliography

Records of Harrold Priory, ed. G. H. Fowler (Beds. Historical Rec. Soc., 17, 1935).

Registrum Antiquissimum, ed. C. W. Foster, K. Major, 10 vols. (Lincoln Rec. Soc., 1931–73).

Rerum Anglicarum Scriptorum Veterum, ed. W. Fulman (Oxford, 1684).

Rotuli Hundredorum, 2 vols. (Rec. Comm., 1812–18).

Rotuli Parliamentorum, 6 vols. (Rec. Comm., 1783).

St. Alban's Chronicle, The, ed. V. H. Galbraith (Oxford, 1937).

Select Charters, ed. W. Stubbs, 9th edn (Oxford, 1913).

Statutes of the Realm, 9 vols. (Rec. Comm., 1810–22).

Taxatio Ecclesiastica (Rec. Comm., 1802).

Treatise on the Laws and Customs of the Realm of England commonly called Glanvill, The, ed. G. D. G. Hall (London, 1965).

Valor Ecclesiasticus, 6 vols. (Rec. Comm., 1810–34).

Year Books, ed. A. J. Horwood, L. O. Pike, 20 vols. (Rolls Series, London, 1863–1911).

  ed. F. W. Maitland et al. (Selden Soc., 1903–53).

SECONDARY SOURCES

Altschul, M., *A Baronial Family in Medieval England: The Clares* (Baltimore, 1965).

Aston, M. E., 'Lollardy and Sedition 1381–1431', *Past and Present*, 17 (1960), pp. 1–44.

  Thomas Arundel (Oxford, 1967).

Barton, J. L., 'The Medieval Use', *L.Q.R.*, 81 (1965), pp. 562–77.

Bean, J. M. W., *The Decline of English Feudalism* (Manchester, 1968).

Bishop, T. A. M., 'Monastic Demesnes and the Statute of Mortmain', *E.H.R.*, 49 (1934), pp. 303–6.

Boissevain, J., *Saints and Fireworks* (London, 1965).

Bourchier-Chilcott, T., *The Law of Mortmain* (London, 1905).

Brand, P. A., 'The Control of Mortmain Alienation in England 1200–1300', in ed. J. H. Baker, *Legal Records and the Historian* (London, 1978), pp. 29–40.

Bridges, J., *The History and Antiquities of Northamptonshire*, 2 vols. (Oxford, 1791).

Brooke, R., *La Graunde Abridgement*, 3rd edn (London, 1586).

Calder-Marshall, A., *The Enthusiast* (London, 1962).

Cam, H. M., *Studies in the Hundred Rolls* (Oxford Studies in Social and Legal History, 6, 1921).

Bibliography

Carpenter, D. A., 'Was there a Crisis of the Knightly Class in the Thirteenth Century? The Oxfordshire Evidence', *E.H.R.*, 95 (1980), pp. 721–52.

Charanis, P., 'The Monastic Properties and the State in the Byzantine Empire', *Dumbarton Oaks Papers*, 4 (1948), pp. 53–118.

Chénon, E., *Histoire Générale du Droit Françtis Public et Privé*, 2 vols. (Paris, 1926–9).

Chew, H. M., 'Mortmain in Medieval London', *E.H.R.*, 60 (1945), pp. 1–15.

Coss, P. R., 'Sir Geoffrey de Langley and the Crisis of the Knightly Class in Thirteenth-Century England', *Past and Present*, 68 (1975), pp. 3–34.

Davis, G. R. C., *Medieval Cartularies of Great Britain* (London, 1958).

Denholm-Young, N., *Seignorial Administration in England*, 2nd impression (London, 1963).

Desmond, L., 'The Statute *De Viris Religiosis* and the English Monks of the Cistercian Affiliation', *Cîteaux*, 25 (1974), pp. 137–55.

Dobson, R. B., *Durham Priory 1400–1450* (Cambridge, 1973).

Douie, D. L., *Archbishop Pecham* (Oxford, 1952).

du Boulay, F. R. H., *The Lordship of Canterbury* (London, 1966).

Duncan, J., Derrett, M., 'The Reform of Hindu Religious Endowments', in ed. D. E. Smith, *South Asian Politics and Religion* (Princeton, 1966), pp. 311–36.

Esmein, A., *Cours Elémentaire d'Histoire du Droit Français*, 2nd edn (Paris, 1895).

Espinas, G., *Les Finances de la Commune de Douai* (Paris, 1902).

Evans, S. J. A., 'The Purchase and Mortification of Mepal by the Prior and Convent of Ely, 1361', *E.H.R.*, 51 (1936), pp. 113–20.

Finlason, W. F., *An Essay on the History and Effects of the Laws of Mortmain* (London, 1853).

Fryde, N., *The Tyranny and Fall of Edward II* (Cambridge, 1979).

Galbraith, V. H., 'Articles Laid before the Parliament of 1371', *E.H.R.*, 34 (1919), pp. 579–82.

Graham, R., *English Ecclesiastical Studies* (London, 1929).

Graves, C. V., 'The Economic Activities of the Cistercians in Medieval England (1128–1307)', *Analecta Sacri Ordinis Cisterciensis*, 13 (1957), pp. 3–59.

Gross, C., 'Mortmain in Medieval Boroughs', *Am.H.R.*, 12 (1907), pp. 733–42.

Habakkuk, H. J., 'English Landownership, 1680–1740', *Ec.H.R.*, 10 (1939–40), pp. 2–17.

Bibliography

'The Long-Term Rate of Interest and the Price of Land in the Seventeenth Century', *Ec.H.R.*, 2nd ser., 5 (1952), pp. 26–45.

'The Market for Monastic Property, 1539–1603', *Ec.H.R.*, 2nd ser., 10 (1958), pp. 362–80.

Hand, G. J., *English Law in Ireland 1290–1324* (Cambridge, 1967).

Harvey, B., *Westminster Abbey and its Estates in the Middle Ages* (Oxford, 1977).

Hill, B. D., *English Cistercian Monasteries and Their Patrons in the Twelfth Century* (Illinois, 1968).

Hilton, R. H., *A Medieval Society* (London, 1966).

'Peasant Movements in England before 1381', *Ec.H.R.*, 2nd ser., 2 (1949), repr. in ed. E. M. Carus-Wilson, *Essays in Economic History*, 3 vols. (London, 1954–62), vol. II, pp. 73–90.

Hockey, S. F., *Quarr Abbey and its Lands 1132–1631* (Leicester, 1970).

Holmes, G. A., *The Estates of the Higher Nobility in Fourteenth-Century England* (Cambridge, 1957).

Holt, J. C., *Magna Carta* (Cambridge, 1965).

Hyams, P. R., 'Origins of a Peasant Land Market in England', *Ec.H.R.*, 2nd ser., 23 (1970), pp. 18–31.

Jenkinson, H., 'Mary de Sancto Paulo, Foundress of Pembroke College, Cambridge', *Archaeologia*, 66 (1915), pp. 401–46.

Jennings, J. M., 'London and the Statute of Mortmain: Doubts and Anxieties among Fifteenth-Century London Testators', *Medieval Studies*, 36 (1974), pp. 174–7.

'The Distribution of Landed Wealth in the Wills of London Merchants 1400–1450', *Medieval Studies*, 39 (1977), pp. 261–80.

Jones, A., 'A Dispute Between the Abbey of Ramsey and its Tenants', *E.H.R.*, 91 (1976), pp. 341–3.

Jones, E. D., 'Some Economic Dealings of Prior John the Almoner of Spalding, 1253–74', *Lincolnshire History and Archaeology*, 12 (1977), pp. 41–7.

'The Crown, Three Benedictine Houses and the Statute of Mortmain, 1279–1348', *The Journal of British Studies*, 14 (1975), pp. 1–22.

Jones, W. R., 'English Religious Brotherhoods and Medieval Lay Piety: The Inquiry of 1388–9', *The Historian*, 36 (1974), pp. 646–59.

Kershaw, I., *Bolton Priory* (Oxford, 1973).

King, E., 'Large and Small Landowners in Thirteenth-Century England', *Past and Present*, 47 (1970), pp. 26–50.

Peterborough Abbey 1086–1310 (Cambridge, 1973).

Knowles, D., Hadcock, R. N., *Medieval Religious Houses: England and Wales*, 2nd edn (London, 1971).

Kosminsky, E. A., 'Services and Money Rents in the Thirteenth Century', *Ec.H.R.*, 5 (1935), repr. in ed. E. M. Carus-Wilson, *Essays in Economic History*, 3 vols. (London, 1954–62), vol. II, pp. 31–48.

Studies in the Agrarian History of England in the Thirteenth Century (Oxford, 1956).

Kreider, A., *English Chantries: The Road to Dissolution* (Harvard and London, 1979).

Lennard, R., *Rural England 1086–1135* (Oxford, 1959).

Little, A. G., *Franciscan Papers, Lists and Documents* (Manchester, 1943).

'The Franciscans and the Statute of Mortmain', *E.H.R.*, 49 (1934), pp. 673–6.

Luchaire, A., *Manuel des Institutions Françaises* (Paris, 1892).

McFarlane, K. B., 'The Investment of Sir John Fastolf's Profits of War', *T.R.H.S.*, 5th ser., 7 (1957), pp. 91–116.

The Nobility of Later Medieval England (Oxford, 1973).

Maddicott, J. R., 'The English Peasantry and the Demands of the Crown 1294–1341', *Past and Present*, supp. 1 (1975).

Major, K., 'The Finances of the Dean and Chapter of Lincoln from the Twelfth to the Fourteenth Century: A Preliminary Survey', *Journal of Ecclesiastical History*, 5 (1954), pp. 149–67.

Miller, E., 'The State and Landed Interests in Thirteenth-Century France and England', *T.R.H.S.*, 5th ser., 2 (1952), pp. 109–29.

'War, Taxation and the English Economy in the Late Thirteenth and Early Fourteenth Centuries', in ed. J. M. Winter, *War and Economic Development* (Cambridge, 1975).

Milsom, S. F. C., *The Legal Framework of English Feudalism* (Cambridge, 1976).

Morgan, M. M., 'The Suppression of the Alien Priories', *History*, 26 (1941), pp. 204–12.

Morris, R., 'The Powerful and the Poor in Tenth-Century Byzantium', *Past and Present*, 73 (1976), pp. 3–27.

Myres, J. N. L., 'Notes on the History of Butley Priory, Suffolk', *Oxford Essays in Medieval History Presented to H. E. Salter* (Oxford, 1934), pp. 190–206.

Naughton, K. S., *The Gentry of Bedfordshire in the Thirteenth and Fourteenth Centuries* (Leicester University, Department of English Local History, Occ. Paper, 3rd ser., 2, 1976).

Neilson, N., *Economic Conditions on the Manors of Ramsey Abbey* (Philadelphia, 1899).

Orme, N., *English Schools in the Middle Ages* (London, 1973).

Owen, D. M., *Church and Society in Medieval Lincolnshire* (Lincoln, 1971).

Pattison, M., *Memoirs* (London, 1885).

Pegues, F., 'The Clericus in the Legal Administration of Thirteenth-Century England', *E.H.R.*, 71 (1956), pp. 529–59.

Pertile, A., *Storia del Diritto Italiano*, 2nd edn, 6 vols. (Turin, 1892–1903).

Plucknett, T. F. T., *Legislation of Edward I* (Oxford, 1949, repr. 1962).

    Statutes and Their Interpretation in the First Half of the Fourteenth Century (Cambridge, 1922).

Pollock, F., Maitland, F. W., *History of English Law*, 2nd edn, 2 vols. (Cambridge, 1968).

Postan, M. M., *The Medieval Economy and Society* (London, 1972).

Ed. Powicke, F. M., Fryde, E. B., *Handbook of British Chronology*, 2nd edn (London, 1961).

Prestwich, M., *War, Politics and Finance under Edward I* (London, 1972).

P.R.O., Lists and Indexes, *List of Inquisitions ad Quod Damnum*, 2 vols. (H.M.S.O., 1892–1912, repr. 1963).

Raban, S., 'Mortmain in Medieval England', *Past and Present*, 62 (1974), pp. 3–26.

    The Estates of Thorney and Crowland (University of Cambridge, Department of Land Economy, Occ. Paper 7, 1977).

Raftis, J. A., *The Estates of Ramsey Abbey* (Toronto, 1957).

Richardson, H. G., *The English Jewry under Angevin Kings* (London, 1960).

Rosenthal, J. T., *The Purchase of Paradise* (London, 1972).

Ross, C., *Edward IV* (London, 1974).

Savine, A., *English Monasteries on the Eve of the Dissolution* (Oxford Studies in Social and Legal History, 1, 1909).

Searle, E., *Lordship and Community: Battle Abbey and its Banlieu 1066–1538* (Toronto, 1974).

    'Seigneurial Control of Women's Marriage: The Antecedents and Function of Merchet in England', *Past and Present*, 82 (1979), pp. 3–43.

Smith, L. B., 'The Gage and the Land Market in Late Medieval Wales', *Ec.H.R.*, 2nd ser., 29 (1976), pp. 537–50.

Smith, R. A. L., *Canterbury Cathedral Priory* (Cambridge, 1943, repr. 1969).

Ed. Smith, Toulmin, *English Gilds* (London, 1870).

Southern, R. W., 'The Place of Henry I in English History', *Proc. Brit. Acad.*, 48 (1962), pp. 127–69.

Strauss, G., 'Success and Failure in the German Reformation', *Past and Present*, 67 (1975), pp. 30–63.

Stubbs, W., *The Constitutional History of England*, 3rd edn, 3 vols. (Oxford, 1887).

Thompson, F. M. L., *English Landed Society in the Nineteenth Century* (London, 1963).

'The Social Distribution of Landed Property in England since the Sixteenth Century', *Ec. H.R.*, 2nd ser., 19 (1966), pp. 505–17.

Thomson, J. A. F., 'Piety and Charity in Late Medieval London', *The Journal of Ecclesiastical History*, 16 (1965), pp. 178–95.

Thorold Rogers, J. E., *A History of Agriculture and Prices in England*, 7 vols. (Oxford, 1866–1902).

Six Centuries of Work and Wages, 2 vols. (London, 1884).

Toulmin Smith, *see* Smith, Toulmin

Tout, T. F., *Chapters in the Administrative History of Medieval England*, 6 vols. (Manchester, 1920–33).

Turner, D. M., *An Approach to Land Values* (Berkhamsted, 1977).

V.C.H. Cambridgeshire, ed. L. F. Salzman et al., 6 vols. (1938–78).

V.C.H. Huntingdonshire, ed. W. Page et al., 3 vols. (1926–36).

V.C.H. Kent, ed. W. Page, 3 vols. (1908–32).

V.C.H. Northamptonshire, ed. W. R. D. Adkins et al., 4 vols. (1902–37).

V.C.H. Rutland, ed. W. Page, 2 vols. (1908–35).

Westlake, H. F., *The Parish Gilds of Medieval England* (London, 1919).

Willard, J. F., Morris, W. A., Dunham, W. H., Strayer, J. R., *The English Government at Work 1327–36*, 3 vols. (Cambridge, Mass., 1940–50).

Wood, S., *English Monasteries and Their Patrons in the Thirteenth Century* (Oxford, 1955).

Wood-Legh, K. L., *Perpetual Chantries in Britain* (Cambridge, 1965).

Studies in Church Life in England under Edward III (Cambridge, 1934).

Youings, J., *The Dissolution of the Monasteries* (London, 1971).

Bibliography

UNPUBLISHED SECONDARY SOURCES

Standen, S. A., 'The Administration of the Statute of Mortmain' (Ph.D. thesis, Washington University, 1973).

INDEX

Abel, John, escheator, 88–9
Abingdon (Oxon.): abbot of, 32;
hospital, 46
Aethelwine, ealdorman of East Anglia,
130
Aethelwold, bishop of Winchester
(963–84), 130
Alice, servant to Henry le Vavasour,
125–6
alien priories, 85, 133, 155
Almoner, John the, prior of Spalding
(1253–74), 143, 144
Alvingham (Lincs.), 76; priory, 74, 76,
97, canons of, 76
Amcotts (Humberside), 83
Amory, John, of Horncastle, 124
Anglesey (Cambs.), priory, 132
Anonimalle Chronicle, 138
Apethorpe (Northants.), 107, 108, 112
Appleby (Humberside), 72, 84
Appletreewick (N. Yorks.), 181
articuli cleri, 29–30, 31
Arundel, Richard, earl of (1330–76), 86
Arundel, Thomas, chancellor (1386–9
and 1399), archbishop of Canterbury
(1396–7 and 1399–1414), 68–9
'Assheshe' (Isle of Wight), 31
Aston (Hereford and Worcester), 114
Athy (Ireland), friars preachers of, 87
Aumale, countess of, *see* Fortibus,
Isabella de
Austin friars, 138, 140

Badlesmere, Bartholomew de, 39
Balycur (Ireland), 80
Barbur, Thomas le, 38
Bardney (Lincs.), abbot of, 84n
Barenton, Richard de, clerk, 116–17,
119

Barlings (Lincs.), abbey, 82 122, 123,
165; canons of, 140; cartulary of, 82
Barnard Castle (Durham), college, 48
Barnwell (Cambs.): priory, 95;
convent, 96
Barnwell (Northants.), 143, 146
Barons, Petition of (1258), 15, 150
Barrow (Humberside), 165
Barton (Humberside?), church of
St James, 19; chaplain at, 19, 20
Barton, J. L., 117, 118
Baston (Lincs.), 108, 120; fraternity
of St John the Baptist, 171; gild of
Nativity of St Mary, 172
Battle (E. Sussex), abbey, 148, 161,
174; monks of, 148, 178
Bayham (Sussex), abbey, 24
Bean, J. M. W., 8, 14, 158
Beauchamp, Adam de, 183
Beauchamp, Guy de, earl of Warwick
(1298–1315), 73
Beauchamp, John de, 145
Beauchamp chantry, 135
Beaulieu (Hants.), abbot of, 34
Beaumer, John de, clerk, 180
Beddington (London), parson of, 33
Bedfordshire, 10, 150
Bekingham, Elias de, royal justice,
rector of Warmington, 58, 110, 119
Belvoir (Leics.), 84; prior of, 84
Benewyk, Richard de, 79
Bereford, Simon de, escheator south of
the Trent, 37
Berking, Richard de, abbot of
Westminster (1222–46), 148
Bescaby (Lincs.), 16
Beverley (Humberside), hospital of
St Nicholas, 51
Bisham (Berks.), priory, 62

Index

Durham, priory, 174; prior of, 84n, 100n

East Deeping (Lincs.), 119
Eastoft (Humberside), 83
Easton Neston (Northants.), 145
Edenham (Lincs.), 112
Edgar, King (957–75), 130
Edmund, son of Henry III, 178
Edward I, 20, 25, 119n; abroad, 58; financial needs of, 59; as Lord Edward, 151
Edward II, 47, 61, 73; at Lincoln, 55; financial needs of, 61, 89; war with Lancaster, 154
Edward III, 47, 50, 52, 55, 103; abroad, 154; religious foundations of, 48, 86, 133
Edward IV, 47, 132
Edward V, 47
Eleanor, Queen, of Provence, wife of Henry III, 178
Ellerton (Humberside), priory, 80
Elryngton, John, treasurer of royal household, 94
Elsham (Humberside), priory, 91–2, 157; prior of, 91; prior and convent of, 17
Elteslee, Thomas de, senior, 116
Ely (Cambs.), 99, 116, 162; bishop of, 121, 162, courts of, 121; cathedral priory, 23, 95, 98, 99, 100, 107, 108, 109, 113, 120, 155, 160, 162, 166, 168, acquisition of Mepal by, 116–17, 167, 175, 185–6, cartulary of, 95, 110, 117n, convent of, 107, 109–10, 113, 116, 163, 186, monks of, 95, 109–10, 117n, 185, prior of, 95, 120, 175, prior and convent of, 87, 95, 162, 167, 185, sacrist of, 116; see also Fressingfield
Enderby, Albinus de, 92, 124
enfeoffments to use, 68, 91–2, 101, 102, 104, 117, 118, 127–8, 157–9, 172, 190
Enfield (London), 97, 146; Chamberlain's fee in, 145
Enstone (Oxon.), 79; church, 79
Epsom (Surrey), chantry, 93

Eriswell (Suffolk), 95, 98, 160
escheat, 4, 30, 33–4, 74, 90
escheators, passim; accounts of, 10, 37, 78, 79, 82, 83n, 84, 88, 103, 169, 187; office of, 32, 73–4, 77, 88; sub-escheators, 73, 77; see also Abel, John; Bereford, Simon de; Broun, Matthew; Lincolnshire; Trussel, William; Venur, Lord Walter le
Essex, 99, 150, 159, 173
Evesham (Hereford and Worcester): almonry school, 135; chronicler of, 71
Evesham, Roger of, 23
'Exagnio', abbey, 91
exchequer, royal, 60; of the Jews, see Jews
Exeter (Devon), 186
Eye, Simon, abbot of Ramsey (1316–42), 162
Eynsham (Oxon.), abbey, 79, 82; monks of, 79

Fastolf, Sir John, 69, 70, 179, 186
Fen Drayton (Cambs.), 143
feoffees, see nominees
feudal incidents, 27; see also escheat; reliefs; wardships
Fillongley, Henry, nephew of Sir John Fastolf, 69, 71, 178
fine rolls, 55, 58
fines, 23–5, 55–71, 86–7, and passim
Firsby (Lincs.), 84n
Fitzralph, Richard, archbishop of Armagh (1347–60), 62
Fleet, William, 135, 137
Folkingham (Lincs.), 112
Forde (Dorset), abbey, 24
Fortibus, Isabella de, countess of Aumale, 111, 164
Fosse (Lincs.), prioress of, 83
Fotheringhay (Northants.), college, 48
Fountains (N. Yorks.), abbey, 149
Fowler, G. H., 157
Foxton (Cambs.), 113; church, 87, 98, 160
Franciscan friars, 29, 38, 132, 140; nuns, 132
fraternities, see gilds

208

Index

Hospitallers, 21, 33

hospitals, 36, 134, 139, 156n, 169, 171; *see also under place names*

Houctton, Michael, son of Simon de Houctton, 145

Hugate, Nicholas de, 51

Humberston (Humberside), abbey, 168

Hundred Rolls, 7, 20, 108

Huntingdon (Cambs.), 52; St Mary's Priory, 123

Huntingdonshire, 10, 96, 108, 130

Husborne Crawley (Beds.), 115

Huse, William, chief justice of king's bench, 94

'Inkelmor in Marsland' (Humberside), 165

inquisitions: *ad quod damnum*, 10, 19, 24, 39–41, 50, 52, 53–4, 58, 64–5, 68, 69, 79, 81, 93, 94, 116, 183, 184, 185, 186, 188; other, 41, 62, 75, 76, 78, 79, 82, 88, 92, 99, 105, 118, 126

Irby-in-the-Marsh (Lincs.), 84n, 100n, 169, 170

Irby-upon-Humber (Humberside), 84n, 100n, 169, 170

Ireland: chancellor in, 29n, 80; chancery in, 29n; estates in, 34; justiciary of, 29n; lieutenants of, 29n; mortmain legislation in, 29, 80

Isabella, Queen, wife of Edward II, 73

Islip, Master Simon of, archbishop of Canterbury (1349–66), canon of Lincoln (1332–49), 122

Jews, 12, 149, 150; plea rolls of the Exchequer of, 150

John the hermit, 46

justices, royal, 1, 27, 29, 35, 72, 73, 81, 88, 126; *see also* Bekingham, Elias de; Hengham, Ralph de; Huse, William; Langley, Geoffrey de; Thirning, Sir William

Keal family, 75

Keal, Ketelbern of, 75

Keal, Ralph of, 75

Kent, 6

Kibworth Harcourt (Leics.), 73

King, E., 131, 144

King's Lynn (Norfolk), hospital of St John the Baptist, 77

Kingsthorpe (Northants.), 144, 145, 146, 147

Kirkby-la-Thorpe (Lincs.), 78, 82

Kirkstall (W. Yorks.), abbey, 178

Kirkstead (Lincs.), abbey, 25; abbot and convent of, 17

Kosminsky, E. A., 7

Kreider, A., 158, 159

Kyme, Philip de, 112

Lacy, Henry de, earl of Lincoln (1272–1311), 91, 150n, 164–5, 178, 181

Lancaster, Thomas, earl of (1298–1322), 154, 165n, 181

land market, 32, 95, 101, 149, 150–2, 161, 164, 166, 167, 170, 174, 175, 176, 177–82

land tenure: in burgage, 5, 49; in chief, 16–17, 20, 24, 36, 37, 49, 52, 61, 89, 91, 162, 163; in frankalmoin, 4, 5, 6; in grand serjeanty, 49; in knight's fee, 18, 49, 109, 143–52, 160, 166, 180; leasehold, 102, 107–14, 164; in socage, 49; at will, 33; *see also* leases; licences

Langley, Geoffrey de, chief justice of the forest, steward to the Lord Edward, 150–1

Langtoft (Lincs.), 79, 108, 120

Lary, Robert, 121, 157

Latimer, Thomas de, 35

Latton (Essex), priory, 141

leases, 10, 23, 33–4, 37–8, 78, 95, 97, 163, 188; *see also* land tenure

Leeds (Kent), priory, 39

Legbourne (Lincs.), nuns of, 122

Leicester, 128; earl of, 150; gild, 129

Leicestershire, 85

Lesnes (London), abbey, 51

Lewes (E. Sussex), priory, 85

licences: to acquire land held in chief, 16, 17, 176; from mesne lords, 18, 19, 20, 21, 54, 113, 142, 180–1; in mortmain, passim; *see also* land tenure

Limsey family, 149

Index

Lincoln, 52, 55, 88–9, 183, 186; bishop of, 30, 168; cathedral, 88, 122, 140, 168, 184, archives of, 12–13, canons of, 122, 180, 183, chantries in, 136, 168, chapter of, 122, 180, chapter accounts of, 88, 136, 182, dean of, 13, dean and chapter of, 62, 88, 136, 168, 175, 182, 183, provost of common of, 136; customs of, 104, 140; earl of, 44, 52; friars at, 140; parliament of, *see* parliament; St Katherine's Priory without, 50, 55; sheriff of, 83; *see also* Lacy, Henry de

Lincolnshire, 10, 84, 90, 119, 121, 123, 143, 146, 180, 187; escheators for, 157, 169, 180; escheators' accounts for, 83, 89, 91, 92, 93, 100; gilds, 171; religious houses, 149, 155–6, 164, 168, 171, 173; sheriff of, 123, 180; sub-escheator for, 180; sub-escheator's accounts for, 32n

Little Carlton (Lincs.), 84n

Llanthony (Gwent), 118

Lollards, 138

London, 23, 40, 85–6, 95, 98, 102–4, 105, 116, 141, 149; amortisation in, 85, 89, 102–4; Beddington, parson of, 33; bishop of, 41; chantries in, 103; citizens of, 6, 102–4, 133, 134; city of, 6, 102–4; common council of, 104; Enfield, 97, 146, Chamberlain's fee in, 145; freemen of, 104; hustings courts of, 103, 104; parliament of, *see* parliament; religious houses: Charterhouse, 180, Cripplegate Hermitage, 132, Lesnes Abbey, 51, St Mary Graces, 85, 86, 133, hospital of St Mary-without-Bishopgate, 38–9, Sheen Priory, 132, 133, Stratford Abbey, 54, Syon Abbey, 132, 133; St Nicholas-in-the-Shambles, 38; St Paul's Cathedral, 140, chantry in, 62, chapel of St Mary over the charnel house in, 67, dean and chapter of, 133; Smithfield, 138; Tower, *iter* at, 103; *see also* Westminster

Longthorpe (Cambs.), 167

Louis IX, king of France, 21

Louth (Ireland), Eyre of (1301), 29n

Louth (Lincs.), 122

Louth Park (Lincs.), abbey, 55, 92, 124–7; abbot of, 33, 124–6; monks of, 122, 124–6

Luddington (Northants.), 161, 163n

McFarlane, K. B., 139, 178

Maddicott, J. R., 59

Magna Carta (1215), 25; reissue of (1217), 14, 15, 40

Maidstone (Kent), 37

Malbussh, Henry, parson of Willoughby, 124

Maldon (Essex), Carmelite friars of, 62

Malmesbury (Wilts.), abbey, 23

Malton (N. Yorks.), priory, 149

Malverne, Henry de, 114

Maple Derham (Hants.), 74

Margaret, Queen, wife of Edward I, 108

Marlborough, Statute of (1267), 15, 16, 31

Marmion, John, 163n

Mars, John, son of John de Mars, 17

Martyn, Thomas, 23, 95

Maxstoke (Warws.), priory, 85, 157

Meaux (Humberside), abbey, 69, 71, 149, 175; chronicler of, 18; monks of, 65–6; *see also* Burton, Thomas

Melton Mowbray (Leics.), 85

memoranda of 1292, 19–20, 27, 39, 40, 41, 59

mendicant orders, 29, 61, 62–3, 87, 131, 134, 140, 156n, 169; enquiry into their property, 62; *see also* Austin friars; Carmelite friars; Franciscan friars

Mepal (Cambs.), 116–17, 167, 175, 185–6

Merchant, Statute, 106

Merston, John, 93

Merton, Walter de, 151

Montacute (Somerset): prior of, 17; prior and convent of, 51

Montfort, Simon de, son of Simon de Montfort, earl of Leicester, 177

211

Index

Valence, William de, 150
Valor Ecclesiasticus, 164n
Vaudey (Lincs.), abbot of, 89
Vavasour, Constance, wife of Henry le Vavasour, 124–6
Vavasour, Henry le, 124–6
Vavasour, William, 126
Venur, Lord Walter le, sub-escheator, 180
villeins, 6, 31–3

Wahull, John de, 145
Waldeschef, William, 96, 109, 112
Walkeringham (Notts.), 34
Walmesford, Master Hugh de, 122
Walsingham (Norfolk), Franciscan friars at, 132
Walsingham, Thomas, 138
Walton (Cambs.), 143
Wanborough (Wilts.), chapel of St Catherine, 38; warden of, 38, 44
Wappenham (Northants.), 145
Warcop (Cumbria), 24
Warden (Beds.), monks of, 166
wardships, 4, 27, 74, 111, 116
Wareham (Dorset), prior of, 19
Warmington (Northants.), church, 119
Warre, Thomas la, 122
Warre chantry, 123
Warsop, John de, 122
Warwick, earls of, 176; *see also* Beauchamp, Guy de
Warwickshire, 150, 151, 159
Waryn, Isabella, widow of Robert Waryn, 79
Waterbeach (Cambs.), 132
Waterford (Ireland), 5
Waverley (Surrey), abbey, 44; annals of, 76
Welbeck (Notts.), abbey, 50, 91
Wellingborough (Northants.), church, 120
Wells (Somerset), 13; hospital, 46
Welton-le-Marsh (Lincs.), 84n, 181; church, 165
West, Nicholas, 116
West Dereham (Norfolk), abbey, 85
West Haddon (Northants.), 106
West Torrington (Lincs.), 112

'Westmerl' (West Mersea (Essex)?), prior of, 83
Westminster (London), 99–100; abbey, 120, 133–4, 140–1, 148–9, abbot of, 148, chantries at, 136, 140–1, 176, monks of, 149, 181, steward of, 145; college of St Stephen, 48; Provisions of (1259), 15, 17, 142, reissues of (1263 and 1264), 15; Statute of, II (1285), 31, 36, 37, 106, 191
Weston (Lincs.), 32
Whaplode (Lincs.), 144
Wheatfield (Oxon.), 79; church, 79
Wherwell (Hants.), abbess of, 31
Whissendine (Leics.), 133
Whitewell, Richard de, canon of Lincoln, 122
Whittington, Richard, 67
Whittlesey (Cambs.), 115
Whitton (Humberside), 91
Wigtoft (Lincs.), church, 78, 163
Wilburton, Robert de, of Ely, 117n
Wilby (Suffolk), 85
Willoughby (Lincs.), 124
Willoughby (Warws.), 97
Wiltshire, 159, 173
Winchcombe (Gloucs.), abbey, 80, 149; abbot and convent of, 79; monks of, 80
Winchelsea (E. Sussex): customs of, 104; mayor and commonalty of, 104
Winchester (Hants.): bishop of, 70; cathedral priory, 45; college, 46; St Mary's Abbey, 24; St Swithun's Abbey, 74, prior of, 74
Windsor (Berks.), forest, 46
Wisbech (Cambs.), church, 87, 98, 160
Witcham (Cambs.), 99, 109–10, 113, 116, 162
Woburn (Beds.), abbey, 50, 165
Woodhurst (Cambs.), 143
Wood-Legh, K. L., 8
Woodston (Cambs.), 96, 98, 109
Woolsthorpe (Lincs.), 84
Wooton Bourne (Beds.), 157
Wootton (Northants.), 145
Worcester: cathedral priory, 149; church of St Helen, 77, chaplain of Spagard chantry in, 77

215